T0316383

CONFLICT IN SOUTH-EASTERN EUROPE AT THE END OF THE TWENTIETH CENTURY

The dissolution of Yugoslavia and the tragic wars that followed continue to engage scholars throughout the region and the world. Ever since the fall of Slobodan Miloševic, the Scholars' Initiative, an international consortium of over 250 scholars, has endeavoured to study the period 1986–2000 as critically and objectively as possible.

It believes that ongoing research, discussion, and publication of its work will help bridge the chasm that separates serious historical scholarship from those interpretations that nationalist politicians and media in the former Yugoslavia have impressed on their populations.

This collection of articles reflects new research by ten of the Initiative's scholars and offers analysis of a wide spectrum of issues. It examines the roots of the violent collapse of Yugoslavia, considers the impact of the dissolution on minority groups, tackles some of the controversies concerning Kosovo, evaluates the most recent evidence in the controversy concerning responsibility for the deadly artillery attacks against civilians during the long siege of Sarajevo, assesses the performance of the International Criminal Tribunal for the former Yugoslavia in its trial of Miloševic, and examines the very sensitive process in Serbia of facing its violent past in the aftermath of the tragedy.

This book was previously published as a special issue of *Nationalities Papers*.

Thomas A. Emmert is Professor of History at Gustavus Adolphus College in St. Peter Minnesota. Trained at St. Olaf College, Oxford, and Stanford, he is a historian of the Balkans with a special emphasis on Serbia. Since 2001 he has served as Associate Director of the Scholars' Initiative.

Charles Ingrao is Professor of History at Purdue University. A scholar of the Habsburg Empire, he is former editor of The Austrian History Yearbook, and currently general editor of Purdue's Central European Studies Series. Since 1995 he has focused his research on the former Yugoslavia's ethnic conflicts and made 25 research trips there. Since 2001 he has served as Project Director of the Scholars' Initiative.

NATIONS AND NATIONALISM OF EASTERN EUROPE AND THE FORMER USSR

The Association for the Study of Nationalities General Monograph Series

The Association for the Study of Nationalities (ASN) is the only scholarly association devoted to the study of ethnicity and nationalism from Europe to Eurasia. With hundreds of members in more than fifty countries, ASN brings together the world's leading scholars, and policy analysts interested in the politics, economics, social relations, culture, and history of central and southeast Europe, Russia, Central Asia, and adjacent regions. Its publications, annual convention, sponsored panels, and conferences provide a unique resource for understanding the ongoing processes of nation-building and state-building in these lands. ASN publishes two peer-reviewed journals: *Ethnopolitics* and *Nationalities Papers*. Its flagship publication, *Nationalities Papers*, is the premier journal in nationalities studies that concentrates upon the geographic sphere of the former Soviet Union and Eastern, Central, and South-eastern Europe. *Nationalities Papers* is a multidisciplinary journal that publishes original and innovative scholarly articles in both the humanities and social sciences and is designed to provide a serious forum for scholars, policy makers, journalists, and others working in the broadly defined field of nationalities studies. *Ethnopolitics* is an authoritative, peer-reviewed journal that provides a forum for serious debate and exchange on the topics of ethnicity and conflict-resolution. This series is the product of special issues published by the journals and represents a critical link between the journals and the broader scholarly community.

Series General Editor:
Steven Sabol, University of North Carolina-Charlotte, USA
Editor-in-Chief, *Nationalities Papers*

Series Advisory Board:
Dominique Arel, University of Ottawa, CA, President, ASN
David Crowe, Elon University, USA, Chairman, ASN Advisory Board
Lowell Barrington, Marquette University, USA
Karl Cordell, University of Plymouth, UK
Daniel E. Miller, University of West Florida, USA
Theodore Weeks, Southern Illinois University, USA
Stefan Wolff, University of Bath, UK
Christine Worobec, Northern Illinois University, USA

Titles in the Series
Gambling on Humanitarian Intervention:
Moral Hazard, Rebellion and Civil War
Edited by Alan Kuperman and Timothy Crawford

Conflict in South-eastern Europe at the End of the Twentieth Century
Edited by Thomas Emmert and Charles Ingrao

Elections and Ethnopolitics
Edited by Florian Bieber and Stefan Wolff

CONFLICT IN SOUTH-EASTERN EUROPE AT THE END OF THE TWENTIETH CENTURY

A "Scholars' Initiative" Assesses Some of the Controversies

Edited by
Thomas Emmert and Charles Ingrao

Routledge
Taylor & Francis Group

LONDON AND NEW YORK

First published 2006
by Routledge

2 Park Square, Milton Park, Abingdon, Oxon OX14 4RN
711 Third Avenue, New York, NY 10017, USA

Routledge is an imprint of the Taylor & Francis Group, an informa business

First issued in paperback 2016

Copyright © 2006 Association for the Study of Nationalities

All rights reserved. No part of this book may be reprinted or
reproduced or utilised in any form or by any electronic,
mechanical, or other means, now known or hereafter
invented, including photocopying and recording, or in any
information storage or retrieval system, without permission in
writing from the publishers.

Notice:
Product or corporate names may be trademarks or registered
trademarks, and are used only for identif ication and explanation
without intent to infringe.

Typeset in Times by Infotype Ltd, Eynsham, Oxfordshire

British Library Cataloguing in Publication Data
A catalogue record for this book is available
from the British Library

Library of Congress Cataloging in Publication Data
A catalog record for this book has been requested

ISBN13: 978-0-415-39925-8 (hbk)
ISBN13: 978-1-138-99161-3 (pbk)

CONTENTS

Contributors

Thomas Emmert is at the Department of History, Gustavus Adolphus College, St. Peter, MN, tomo@gac.edu

Sabrina P. Ramet is at the Department.of Political Science at the Norwegian University of Science & Technology (NTNU) in Trondheim, Norway, Sabrina.Ramet@svt.ntnu.no

Nebojša Vladisavljević is at the Department of Government, London School of Economics and Political Science, N.Vladisavljevic@lse.ac.uk

Besnik Pula is a Ph.D. candidate, Department of Sociology, University of Michigan, bpula@umich.edu

Benjamin Rusek is a Research Associate at the U.S. National Academy of Sciences with CISAC, The Committee on International Security and Arms Control, brusek@purdue.edu

Charles Ingrao is at the Department of History, Purdue University, ingrao@purdue.edu

Matjaz Klemenčić is at the Department of History, Universities of Ljubljana and Maribor, matjaz.klemencic@siol.net

Jernej Zupančič is at the Department of Geography, University of Ljubljana, jernej.zupancic@guest.arnes.si

James Gow is at the Department of War Studies, King's College, London, mlmajw@btinternet.com

Ivan Zveržhanovski is a Research Assistant in the Department of War Studies, King's College, London, ivan.zverzhanovski@kcl.ac.uk

Maryanne Yerkes is a Democracy Fellow with USAIF. At the time of writing this paper she was David L. Boren Fellow 2001–2002, National Security Education Program for Educational Development, maryanneyerkes@yahoo.com

Resolving the Yugoslav Controversies: A Scholars' Initiative

Thomas Emmert and Charles Ingrao[1]

> You have your facts. We have our facts. You have a complete right to choose between the two versions.
> Simo Drljača, International Criminal Tribunal for the Former Yugoslavia (ICTY) indictee

This book is dedicated to the research and analysis of a number of scholars whose work continues to illuminate issues related to the disintegration of Yugoslavia at the end of the twentieth century. All of them are participants in an international consortium of historians and social scientists which has worked diligently during the past four years to investigate 11 themes or critical controversies surrounding the tragic events in Yugoslavia. Today, the consortium, known as the "Scholars' Initiative," has grown to over 250 participants from 27 countries, with well over half coming from all eight entities of the former Yugoslavia. Working together in careful research, discussion, and critical peer review of one another's written analysis, the members of the Initiative are reaching the stage of the project where they can begin to share some of their work. This collection is the first of two commissioned volumes of individual studies. The project will conclude with the publication in 2006 of a composite volume comprising the final analyses of the Initiative's 11 research teams.

Amid all of the bitter debates about the Yugoslav conflicts, few would deny the pivotal role that history has played in shaping people's minds in the region. Understandably, but unfortunately, each national group has tended to employ its own array of facts, many of which are either distorted or blatantly untrue. These divergent recitations of history have helped sow mistrust, resentment, and hatred among peoples who coexisted with one another for long periods of time.

In the nine years since the peace negotiations in Dayton, Ohio, the international community has endeavored in various ways to help the peoples of the former Yugoslavia move beyond the tragedy. Western media platforms such as Voice of America, Radio Free Europe, and the BBC have disseminated news and information; while philanthropic NGOs like the Soros, Friedrich-Naumann, and Bertelsmann Foundations have sponsored numerous confidence-building "people-to-people" programs. The Hague Tribunal (ICTY) has painstakingly investigated and then exposed criminal acts committed by all sides in the conflict. Nevertheless, it has remained very difficult to overcome the misrepresentations of history by "patriotic" political leaders and by the great majority of the mainstream media platforms that support their views. This has certainly been the case in Serbia, whose leaders and free media continue to minimize, ignore, or even flatly deny the criminal record of the Milošević regime. But it has also been a serious problem for Bosniaks, Croats, and Kosovar Albanians whose sense of victimhood has mortgaged their ability to acknowledge legitimate Serb grievances that helped empower populist politicians like Milošević. Moreover, so long as politicians and the media retain a de facto monopoly over public memory, perception, and interpretations, they will continue to discredit and marginalize the independent voices that challenge them. Indeed, there exist many among the region's political, academic, and media elite who privately acknowledge the misrepresentations that shape their nations' various accounts of history, but who nonetheless find it difficult to assume a public position on the problem which may subject them to ridicule and question their patriotism.

Ever since the fall of Slobodan Milošević, the Scholars' Initiative has endeavored to study the period 1986–2000 as critically and objectively as possible. It believes that the ongoing research, discussion, and publication of its work will help to bridge the chasm that separates serious historical scholarship from those interpretations that nationalist politicians and media have impressed on their populations. A start-up grant from the U.S. Institute of Peace and supplementary support from several host institutions enabled the Scholars' Initiative to hold annual plenary meetings in each of the last four years,[2] while a second major grant from the National Endowment for Democracy has funded individual research by project participants from the Yugoslav successor states.

Given gaps in the historical record and the existence of sometimes contradictory evidence, we certainly recognize that we cannot expect to resolve all of the issues under examination. In some instances we may only be able to narrow the parameters within which opposing sides can still engage in reasoned debate. We do, however, aspire to take an important first step toward narrowing the cognitive gap among peoples in the region. With thorough scholarship and by sustained interaction with the media and public officials, we strive to validate evidence and discredit un-founded, proprietary myths. Indeed, such an international consortium can furnish a common and ostensibly legitimate, alternative account on which more moderate leaders can lean for support—if not now, then perhaps at some point in the future.

Admittedly, no discussion of the Yugoslav tragedy can begin without the deeper historical context, especially the record of ethnic interaction over the past two centuries. The project's research teams have, however, focused their study and analyses on 11 key issues or controversies that inform virtually every debate among the peoples of the Yugoslav successor states. These are:

1. Kosovo under Autonomy (1974–1990)
2. The Dissolution of Yugoslavia (1986–1991)
3. Independence and the Fate of Minorities (1991–1992)
4. War Crimes and Genocide (1991–1995)

5. The International Community and the Federal Republic of Yugoslavia (FRY)/
   Belligerents (1991–1995)
6. The Safe Areas (1992–1995)
7. The War in Croatia (1991–1995)
8. Milošević's Kosovo (1998–1999)
9. U.S./NATO Intervention (1998–1999)
10. The Hague Tribunal
11. Living Together or Hating Each Other

The articles in this book reflect research stemming from seven of these 11 research teams.

Nebojša Vladisavljević challenges the prevailing argument that Kosovo's Serbs were simply manipulated by Belgrade-based intellectuals and Milošević. Using newly available sources, he demonstrates that a number of grassroots groups of Kosovo Serbs played prominent roles in mobilizing their fellow Serbs in Kosovo in a series of actions that date from the early 1980s. While dissident intellectuals and Milošević eventually aided the cause of the Kosovo Serb activists, they were not responsible for "the creation and consolidation" of the local protest networks.

Sabrina P. Ramet offers two articles dedicated to the task of tracking the roots of the violent collapse of Yugoslavia. Each of them reminds us of the complexity of the question of that collapse and of the clear lack of consensus in its analysis. In her first article she considers other scholars' efforts to explain the collapse and their emphasis on particular variables in their analyses. In the end she suggests a working synthesis of approaches that attempts to answer some of the critical questions associated with Yugoslavia's dissolution. Ramet's second article draws upon the work of Anthony F. C. Wallace from almost a half century ago concerning revitalization movements. Ramet argues that understanding the Serb national awakening in the 1980s as just such a revitalization movement will help to explain how "Serb nationalists could construe their initiatives as responses to some perceived threat coming form outside the community of Serbs, the phases in the development of that movement, and its role in impelling socialist Yugoslavia toward breakup and meltdown."

Matjaž Klemenčić and Jernej Zupančić broaden our understanding of the impact of Yugoslavia's dissolution on two of its minority groups, the Hungarians and Italians, with a special emphasis on the status of minority rights for these groups in the post-Yugoslav states. While the literature concerning relations among the main national groups of the former Yugoslavia (Serbs, Croats, Slovenes, Bosniaks, *etc.*) is extensive, much less attention has been given to the fate of Yugoslavia's several minorities. The authors demonstrate here that the record of establishing clear protections for these minorities varies dramatically from one state to the other.

Benjamin Rusek and Charles Ingrao consider the most recent evidence in the continuing controversy concerning responsibility for several deadly artillery attacks against civilians during the long siege of Sarajevo. While recognizing that additional scholarship may provide the absolute proof that confirms or denies their summary conclusions, Rusek and Ingrao are confident that most evidence to date points to Bosnian Serb forces as responsible for these attacks.

Besnik Pula examines the origins of the nonviolent resistance movement in Kosovo in an effort to look more closely at the "parallel state" that Kosovo Albanians created to deal with Serbia's repressive policies there. He argues that the parallel state was a "largely unplanned-for phenomenon" and takes an approach to his subject that "purposefully breaks with conventional frameworks of ethnic conflict, as developed particularly by international relations scholars." He breaks important new ground in this analysis, which is historically rooted and gives particular attention to events between 1988 and 1992, a time in which the parallel state began to emerge.

James Gow and Ivan Zveržhanovski assess the performance of the International Criminal Tribunal for the Former Yugoslavia in its trial of former Yugoslav President Slobodan Milošević. They conclude that at the end of the prosecution case in February 2004, the results were clearly mixed. While the quest for a "judicial measure of truth" has perhaps not been fulfilled, one might argue that the quest for "historical truth" has been advanced by a body of evidence that scholars can now use to compile as an objective account as possible of those "contentious, awful events."

Finally, Maryanne Yerkes takes us well beyond the dissolution of Yugoslavia and the period of armed conflict to examine the "sensitive process of facing the violent past" in Serbia in the aftermath of the tragedy. From October 2001 until December 2002 Yerkes interviewed young people in Serbia to discern their views on the very concept of "confronting the past" and to see how these youth perceived the various initiatives (local, national, and international) undertaken in Serbia to encourage this process. Yerkes concludes that many challenges remain in this effort to face the past, but she also offers some hope. A better understanding of the factors that affect the youth in their feelings about the process may yield new and more successful initiatives.

NOTES

1. Charles Ingrao is Director of the Scholars' Initiative; Thomas Emmert is Associate Director
2. Morović, Serbia (September, 2001) Host: University of Novi Sad; Co-organizers: City of Novi Sad, Vojvodina Assembly, Ministry of Education. Sarajevo (July, 2002) Host: United Nations Mission in Bosnia-Hercegovina; Co-organizers: Citizens' Pact for South-eastern Europe, Open Society Institute, Konrad-Adenauer-Stiftung. Edmonton (September, 2003) Host: Canadian Centre for Austrian and Central European Studies. Budapest (December, 2004) Host: Andrassy University.

Explaining the Yugoslav meltdown, 1

"For a charm of pow'rful trouble, Like a hell-broth boil and bubble":[1] Theories about the Roots of the Yugoslav Troubles

Sabrina P. Ramet[2]

We all know why the Socialist Federated Republic of Yugoslavia (SFRY) disintegrated and why the War of Yugoslav Succession (1991–1995) broke out. It was all because of Milošević/Tudjman/"the Slovenes"/communists/organized crime/ Western states/the Vatican–Comintern conspiracy, who planned it all by himself/themselves in order to advance his own personal/Serbian/Slovenian/American/Vatican interests—your choice. Or again—it all happened because of local bad traditions/economic problems/structural issues/system illegitimacy/legitimate grievances/illegitimate grievances/the long shadow of the past. Or again—it really started in 1389/1463/1878/1918/1941/1986/1987/1989/1990/1991—your pick. Of course, we all know that both the breakup and the war were completely avoidable/inevitable, don't we? And best of all, we all know that the real villain(s) in this drama can only be Milošević/Tudjman/"the Serbs"/"the Slovenes"/"the Croats"/"the Muslims"/Germany/Balkan peoples generally/the Great Powers, who must be held (exclusively/jointly) responsible for most of the killing, though some of us also know that all parties were equally guilty. Well, maybe we all know what caused the Yugoslav troubles, but it seems that we "know" different things.

Part—though, of course, only part—of the reason for the lack of consensus is a tendency, on the part of some observers, to conflate three distinct questions when undertaking to analyze the roots of the Yugoslav troubles. These questions are: (1) Why did the SFRY collapse? (2) Why did armed conflict erupt between the peoples of the area in 1991? And (3) why did people who had lived together in peace for most of 45 years take up arms against each other, in some cases with former friends and neighbors becoming each other's tormentors? It is, however, an open question whether any one theory, especially a theory stressing one independent variable, can serve to answer all three questions. On the face of it, it would seem more likely that we shall need different solutions or a combination of theories to address each of the three questions. We may also identify two subsidiary questions that are related to the three central questions specified above. These are: (4) Do the Serbs, Croats, and/or Bosniaks (Muslims) have any particular predisposition to violence, and, if so, where does it come from? And (5) how far back can intense rivalries or conflicts involving these three peoples be traced?

The question of the roots of the Yugoslav troubles continues to fascinate, absorb, and even obsess many of us who care about Yugoslavia and its successor states; but it also has a broader significance, insofar as an analysis of the roots of the troubles in Yugoslavia might provide some insight into understanding the ways in which a society may slide into war. (The question of whether the War of Yugoslav Succession should be considered a civil war or an international war is a juridical question that hinges on the importance one assigns to membership in the U.N. versus a history of cohabitation in the same state; this question, therefore, is not one that shall hold any interest for us in this context.)

What I propose to do in this article is to survey the chief theories which have been offered in the endeavor to explain what made Yugoslavia "boil and bubble." These will be aggregated into the following five categories, according to the explanatory variable that receives the most stress: (1) external factors, (2) internal/remote factors, (3) internal/proximate factors, (4) emotional factors, and (5) a combination of factors. In the process, I hope to shed light on the nature of the debates within the field concerning this most vital question. In the concluding section, I shall suggest some ways in which the insights of several of these theories may be combined to produce a stronger and more subtle theory.

External Factors

There are two versions of the approach which stresses external factors in accounting for Yugoslav troubles—the first of which looks for conspiracies involving the Great Powers, and the second of which argues that the resolution of the Cold War brought an end to the situation in which a united Yugoslavia was valuable to the West. I am unable to think of any scholarly work that advocates the conspiratorial view, though one may, nonetheless, hear this view advocated in conversations with various people in the Yugoslav successor states and find it represented on websites. The typical suspects who are rounded up for such theories are Germany, Austria, and the Vatican, sometimes adding also the United States and other European powers, who are said to have collaborated in the effort to break up the SFRY.[3] One such posting proposes, for example, to show "how Germany and the Vatican use[d] the European Union and NATO to achieve their historical aims in Yugoslavia."[4] This explanation was incorporated, in the early 1990s, into a history textbook read by high school seniors in Serbia; in the textbook's account, it was the Vatican that bore primary responsibility for having "launched a battle against Orthodoxy and Serbs through the Catholic Church [in Croatia] and its allies."[5] In other Serb publications, Germany and Austria are singled out. Not only was the demonization of Germany a theme first developed in Serbian newspapers,[6] but the threat that the war in Bosnia might ignite World War III was itself a theme found in Serbian wartime propaganda. Not very surprisingly, Milošević has made use of this theory in his defense at The Hague, where he has argued that "the foreign factor was behind those demonstrations of the

9th of March"[7] and that already, in 1989, "control over the events in Yugoslavia [was] being taken over by foreign elements as well as control of the Yugoslav crisis."[8]

A particularly extreme version of the conspiratorial approach may be found in *To Kill a Nation: The Attack on Yugoslavia*, written by Michael Parenti, the chairman of the U.S. section of the International Committee for the Defense of Slobodan Milošević. As Marko Hoare puts it, "Parenti essentially argues that the destruction of Yugoslavia was orchestrated by a conspiracy of the Western imperialist powers."[9] Among scholars, Bogdan Denitch comes perhaps the closest to attributing culpability for igniting the war to outside powers, specifically blaming Germany and Austria for failing "to keep a low profile in the East European countries that had been victims of German aggression twice within the living memory of many."[10] But Denitch's indictment of Germany and Austria is vague and avoids the outright factual error committed by some diplomats and journalists who at one time, casting logic to the wind, claimed that the "premature" recognition of Croatia and Slovenia in December 1991, promoted by Germany and Austria, was the spark that had set off the fighting the previous June. Since none of those advocating this point of view urged anyone to believe in the possibility of time travel, one may safely conclude that such claims reflected either hasty and sloppy thinking, pure ignorance, or politically motivated propaganda. Daniele Conversi offers apt criticism of the conspiratorial approach, which he says has been "particularly evident in works by international diplomats, who, rather than focusing on the internal events leading up to the war, give an exaggerated importance to external factors, in which there seems to be often a desperate apology of their profession's mistakes."[11] It is striking that most observers have chosen either to condemn Germany (and Austria) for acting unilaterally (or prematurely) or to defend the German (and Austrian) approach as a reasonable position given the political context; few, if any, scholars have been content to criticize merely the timing of the German announcement of its impending exchange of ambassadors with the two republics.

More typically (and more reasonably), scholars wishing to criticize the Great Powers have blamed them, not for conspiring to break up Yugoslavia or for setting the region ablaze, but variously for adopting policies that could only prolong the fighting. Thus, for example, Beverly Crawford criticized the German government for what she characterized as a "unilateral" decision to recognize Slovenia and Croatia,[12] while Brendan Simms, in a widely discussed book, has criticized Her Majesty's Government for having "played a particularly disastrous role in the destruction of Bosnia."[13] James Gow took aim at the American Clinton administration for refusing to use force to impose the Vance–Owen Peace Plan on the rejectionist Bosnian Serbs, claiming that this refusal prolonged the war by at least two years.[14] For that matter, I gave vent to my own frustrations with what I read as disregard for the fate of the peoples of Croatia and Bosnia in an article published in early 1994, arguing in particular that the arms embargo, imposed on U.N. member states in spite of a

7

guarantee in the U.N. Charter of the right of all members to self-defense, was in fact prolonging the war.[15] Lord Owen, who worked pro bono during the war years as European Union mediator, went further, however, and not only criticized the Clinton administration for failing to give the Vance–Owen Plan its immediate and enthusiastic support but also claimed that it was Western recognition of Bosnia-Herzegovina which set off the conflict in that republic in the first place.[16] In Owen's view, as in Gow's, the imposition of the Vance–Owen Plan could have ended the fighting sooner.

But, as already noted, there has been a second tendency, in which external factors are brought to bear in accounting for the breakup of socialist Yugoslavia and the ensuing war, *viz.*, the argument that the end of the Cold War and the collapse of communism elsewhere in Eastern Europe sealed Yugoslavia's fate. In Jasna Adler's version of this theory, "[t]he disintegration of Yugoslavia should be seen as an *inevitable* consequence of the collapse of the international communist system in Europe ... That Yugoslavia would not survive the end of communist rule in Europe was obvious."[17] But Adler uses the reference to external factors only to answer the first question (why the SFRY collapsed), referring the second question (why the fighting) to "the fundamentally opposed conceptions of Serbia on the one hand and Croatia and Slovenia on the other regarding what, if any, form a post-communist Yugoslav state should assume."[18] Gow also considers the end of the Cold War relevant for understanding processes in the Yugoslav region, noting that "the end of the Cold War remove[d] the restraint which East–West conflict had imposed on a fissiparous federation ... [and] also created a particular [and unstable] environment. Yugoslavia's conventional strategic interest was lost, reducing international concern for its future."[19] Gow combines this (external) factor with attention to internal processes within Yugoslavia to account for the violent turn that developments in the collapsing Yugoslav state took.

The chief attractions of the appeal to the conspiratorial version of the external factors approach are the attraction of apparent parsimoniousness and its exculpation of local actors for the problems with which Yugoslavia and its successor states have been afflicted. The chief debility of the appeal to external factors is the risk that one ends up downplaying the importance of internal developments in accounting for the violent dissolution of Yugoslavia. But external factors can, at the very most, answer, or contribute to answering, questions (1) and (5)—Why did the SFRY break up and when did this process begin?—which is precisely why Adler and Gow, for example, do not suggest that the end of the Cold War can constitute more than a part of the puzzle.

Internal Factors—Remote

Even on the eve of the outbreak of open fighting, there continued to be scholars who denied that the country would end up in war.[20] Yet there had been warnings about the risk of breakup since 1974 at the latest, and about the risk of war for about a decade before fighting actually broke out. These warnings were issued, in the first place, by insiders who believed that developments in their country were moving in a dangerous direction. Already in 1974, Milovan Djilas predicted, in the pages of *Saturday Review*, that come 2024 Yugoslavia would have become "a confederation of four states: Slovenia, Croatia, Macedonia, and Serbia, with Serbia itself being a federative state. It is possible that those four states may later separate and become fully independent ... In any event, when these nations attain their independent statehood, the acrimony among them will diminish and cooperation will increase."[21] Long before the appearance on the political scene of Slobodan Milošević, Djilas was quite certain that Yugoslavia could not survive as a federation, only, at most, as a confederation, and believed that Bosnia would disappear—presumably through partition. But it was only in the course of 1983 that locals began to fret that Yugoslavia might develop a "Polish situation" (a reference to the breakdown of the communist system during 1980–1981) or even evolve into a "second Lebanon" (a reference to the Lebanese civil war that broke out in spring 1976).[22] About the same time, high-ranking figures in the ruling League of Communists of Yugoslavia (LCY) began declaring, on repeated occasions, that the country was in deep crisis and that drastic measures should be found to pull Yugoslavia back from the brink.[23] Combined with a 1984 warning that it might be "only a matter of time before another bloodbath occurs between Serbs and Croats,"[24] these early signals are sufficient to alert us to the presence of internal problems that, at the very minimum, seemed sufficiently serious to contemporary observers to warrant concern about the future. But these warnings leave open the question of whether the roots of Yugoslav troubles should be traced primarily to remote factors or rather, primarily, to more proximate factors.

As with theories referring Yugoslav problems to external factors, theories favoring attribution to remote factors come in two types. The older school is the "national character" school, which in turn comes in various guises; the younger school, associated above all with the name Robert D. Kaplan, seeks to trace the fighting, if not the collapse of the Yugoslav state itself, to so-called "ancient hatreds," cited by British Prime Minister John Major as constituting an obstacle to any peaceable agreement.[25] As has been noted by various observers, to the extent that one believes that the primary source of the Yugoslav breakup and war lies in a people's national character, formed over centuries, or in other factors emerging already in the remote past, even centuries or millennia earlier, at least two things follow: first, the issues over which Serbs, Croats, and Bosniaks have disputed recently come to be seen as mere triggers for the reactivation of the more fundamental animus that sets one nation against another; and, second, the entire notion of international intervention in the attempt to bring peace to the region comes to appear as the most vapid sort of self-delusion.

National Character School/Historical Determinism

The grand-daddy of the national character school of thought, at least when it comes to explaining the behavior of Yugoslavs, is Jovan Cvijić, who, in a work published in 1914, traced the Serbian state's ambitions to expand to the coast to Serbs" "love of freedom."[26] In the English-speaking world, Dinko Tomašić's 1948 book, *Personality and Culture in Eastern Europe*, takes its departure from his belief that the Balkan region has been uniquely plagued by war and strife and that this allegedly unique degree of conflict is due to the "Dinaric" character (as Tomašić calls it). Family organization and particularly father–son relations and sibling rivalry are said, by Tomašić, to underlie "the remarkable lack of emotional balance which is noticed by all students and observers of Dinaric society,"[27] and to which he traces Dinaric bellicosity. As Tomašić tells it, "The Dinarics like to see themselves as great martyrs, as well as great heroes. In their ballads and in their school textbooks they present themselves as people who have been unjustly persecuted by their enemies, and who have greatly suffered to save the world, but without being rewarded for it."[28] Emotional imbalance figures as a central explanatory variable for Tomašić, who suggests that this factor could explain why "Dinaric warriors" allegedly make better guerrilla fighters than regular army troops.[29] But the Dinaric's unbalanced temperament also leaves him prone "to be as excessive in violence as he is boundless in all other expressions of self-assertion."[30] After warning that the Dinaric warrior may be inclined to torture and mutilate his victims, Tomašić concludes that in conditions of communist dictatorship, a "lifeless state of mind, a mass paralysis of energies, or a mass religious man may easily develop."[31]

Tomašić was not the first to articulate such views, however. Some twenty years earlier, Sir Neville Henderson, the British ambassador in Belgrade, had sent a report to the Foreign Office in which he described Serbs, as a people, as tending to be warlike, disinclined to compromise, chauvinistic, despotic, corrupt, conceited, and suspicious of members of other nationalities.[32] Nor was Tomašić, two decades later, the last adherent of this school to try to identify modal traits of Serbs and other Yugoslavs. Two recent adherents of this school are Branislav Anzulović and Lenard J. Cohen. Both Anzulović and Cohen believe that the Serbs developed patterns of behavior over a period of centuries, both believe that those behavioral patterns incline Serbs toward violence, and both believe that Serbs have a particularly highly developed tendency to view their nation as a collective victim. But ultimately they locate the sources of this alleged Serbian complex in different places.

For Anzulović, it is the poets and clerics who are mostly to blame for instilling in Serbs a culture of violence. As evidence, he quotes extensively from a traditional folk song, in which Serbian Prince Marko is described as having cut off the arm and put out the eyes of the beautiful Rosanda, as well as from Prince Njegoš's *Mountain Wreath*, which he describes as "a call to genocide," Vuk Drašković's *Knife*, and other materials.[33] He also quotes from an appeal issued by a group of Paris-based

10

Orthodox theologians and intellectuals in late 1991, who reproached Serbian Orthodox bishops for having played a part in stirring up resentment over sufferings of half
a century earlier and thereby inciting Serbs to hatred.[34] Anzulović wants his readers
to conclude that, because of the influence of myths, literary products, the activity of
clerics, and the culture more generally, Serbs developed a proclivity to violence. But
he says that it "would be an error to assume that the memory of the Serbian medieval
empire necessarily led to the latest war for a Greater Serbia, but equally erroneous
to deny a connection between the two."[35] The key, says Anzulović, is the use made
of these myths by elites over the years, especially by Serbian intellectuals in the
course of the 1980s.[36] While Anzulović believes that the mythological baggage he
sums up with the phrase favored by Orthodox clerics—"Heavenly Serbia"—created
ready-made discourses of self-justification to legitimate violence on the part of Serbs
against their enemies, he also writes that "[o]ne cannot explain a nation's violent
expansionist adventure merely in terms of the psychological makeup of its members," and cautions that one must deal with the specific factors in a given case and
identify such "circumstances [as] may facilitate the eruption of a collective murder-
ous frenzy."[37] Toward the end of his book, he returns to the question of elite
manipulation of myths, warning that

> [m]yths and lies are used to justify uninformed policies and hide the ignorance and
> amorality of their makers. If the latter believe in the myths they use, as they often do,
> myths become even more dangerous than if they are used cynically. Some of the
> myths that have contributed to the brutal disintegration of the former Yugoslavia are
> still taken for truths by many people all over the world. If unchallenged, they will lead
> to new failures.[38]

Anzulović hopes that his theory will answer all three questions—explaining not only
the breakup of Yugoslavia and the eruption of violent conflict in the region, but also
the willingness of Serbs (he is not discussing Croats and Bosniaks) to engage in
violent behavior. But, unlike Tomašić, he makes a point of allowing for the
possibility of change in a national culture. In a key passage, he writes,

> is it possible suddenly to reverse one's attitude toward crucial historical events,
> personalities, and myths cherished for a very long time, and realize that false gods
> have been worshiped? Efforts to dethrone false idols and expose bitter truth as a better
> foundation for the future always encounter strong resistance. However, total victory
> over fateful myths, violent habits, and national traumas is not necessary. It is sufficient
> to weaken them by showing that unrealistic visions of the past and expectations of the
> future lead to mistakes, and that national identity can be strengthened with a
> celebration of real achievements in the nation's past. If the reexamination of deeply
> entrenched ideas and attitudes gathers sufficient vigor, the direction in which a nation
> has been moving can be changed.[39]

As already noted, Lenard Cohen traces the allegedly violent patterns of behavior
among Serbs to different sources from those identified by Anzulović. In fact, Cohen
casts his net more widely, in his *Serpent in the Bosom*, subsuming also the "fateful

myths" deplored by Anzulović. Indeed, Cohen describes Serbia quite explicitly as a society in which "collectivist nationalism has historically excited the popular imagination, and *is rooted in the mythic core passed from one generation to another.*"[40] Cohen offers fewer specifics than Anzulović, no doubt because his purpose is to recount some of the events of the Milošević era, but he does suggest that the centuries-long experience of being subordinate to the Ottomans may have had dramatic effects on the Serbian "collective political personality," emphasizing that "the illiberal facets in the Serbian political legacy were reinforced by the long period of Ottoman rule."[41] Like Anzulović, Cohen is worried about "historically shaped factors" (Cohen's phrase). Among these factors, Cohen mentions

> a strong penchant for centralized modes of political control, and particularly "heroic leaders" who can maintain political order and preserve the "unity" of the nation; a disinclination to accept rules-of-the-game which would allow Serbs to accept minority status within other multinational Balkan political units dominated by other ethnic groups; a predilection for statist collective unity in the face of a perceived external danger to the Serb nation (including identification of nonconformists as traitors or enemies, and a suspicion of democratic pluralism as a potential threat); and an exaggerated emphasis on sanguinity—"Serbian blood and origins"—territorial control, and national religious myths as defining features of collective identity. This historical experience of the Serbs—especially under the long period of Turkish domination, and the nineteenth and twentieth century struggles with Austria-Hungary's and Germany's intervention in the Balkans—also created a deep sense of victimization in the Serbian political psyche and political culture.[42]

Cohen articulated the same theory in an earlier work,[43] in which context he praised Vladimir Dvorniković, an adherent of the national character school of political analysis, for having "identified some of the fundamental divisions, bonds, and behavioral characteristics that have characterized the South Slavic peoples."[44] Dvorniković, according to Cohen, believed that the "stubbornness," "fierceness," and "passionate outbursts" allegedly associated with and characteristic of the "Yugoslav psyche" serve to explain "an intensity and inconsistency in political life that went beyond the pattern found in most countries."[45] Cohen accepted Dvorniković's conclusion about the "intensity" of feeling among Yugoslavs and argued, in *Broken Bonds*, that "The basis for such intense feeling can be traced to the transgenerational socialization of negative stereotypes regarding the history and behavior of other groups."[46] This, in turn, explains "the population's predilection for political extremism" which was shown to full view in World War II and again in the War of Yugoslav Succession (1991–1995), according to Cohen.[47] Thus, Cohen provides an answer to question (4)—whether the people of the Yugoslav region have a "particular predisposition to violence" and, if so, how it developed. For Cohen, the answer is yes, and the origin lies in the aforementioned "transgenerational socialization" and patterns of behavior developed centuries ago. In fact, the national character approach does not seem to provide the guiding principle in the narrative chapters in Cohen's books, which focus on the actions of contemporary figures and their consequences. But the national character approach raises its head once more in the closing paragraph of *Broken Bonds*, where Cohen expresses the utterly reasonable worry that the residents of the region may have been "so deeply affected, alienated, and perhaps even psychologically damaged by the appalling warfare" that those in leadership positions will have their work cut out for them, but also voices the pessimistic sentiment that "Lacking the will and wisdom to overcome their difficulties, the leaders and citizens of the Balkan region *will remain mired in the current 'frenzy of hate", or forever chained to its roots and consequences.*"[48]

One attraction of the national character school lies in its reassurance that, to the extent that "they" are not like "us," "we" shall most likely never have to deal with problems similar to "theirs." The approach is also attractive to those who believe that the remote past not only has *some* weight but actually is likely to have more weight than more proximate factors. A weakness of this approach is that, once one has established, to one's own satisfaction, that a particular nation is apt to behave in such and such a way, then other internal factors such as the character of the state, the state of the economy, and the nature of personalities holding power inevitably seem to fade into the background, even if they are explicitly mentioned. Critics of the national character approach do not deny that different societies have different cultural assumptions, customs, and ways of doing things, or that these differences may be traced back in time; what they deny is that the remote past should have some special priority over the more proximate past. Rather, critics may suggest, societies develop ways of doing things which are revised either under the influence of external factors (such as foreign influences) or under the pressure of necessity (when an existing practice is shown to be dysfunctional) or incrementally as a by-product of cultural development and creative innovation. In other words, critics of the national character school do not need to deny the importance of the past in order to find historical determinism objectionable.

Nineteenth-Century Sources

For the purposes of this article, I shall consider that factors dating from December 1918 or later are "proximate" and that factors dating from before December 1918 are "remote." What this approach suffers in terms of arbitrariness it gains in terms of clarity. Within the latter set (the pre-1918 "remote" set), I shall consider any theory to involve "ancient hatreds" if it connects the outbreak of the War of Yugoslav Succession to events taking place before the fall of Rome in 476 CE or if the observer in question specifically uses the phrase "ancient hatreds" (or some equivalent) to explain the problems at hand. But a purely nominalist approach would not suffice, by itself, to differentiate reasonable arguments from absurd speculations, because among those now categorized as advocates of including "remote" factors in the equation one finds the distinguished historians Ivo Banac and Ivo Goldstein. But neither of these scholars looks any further back than the nineteenth century in the

13

quest for the roots of more recent problems. Banac, for example, argues, in an article for *Daedalus*, that in order to comprehend the conflict of the 1990s, one should "begin with the continuity of individual South Slavic national elites and states (where they existed), with special emphasis on national and political ideologies, not with 'modernization" studies and research of social structures."[49] In his view, the "Greater Serbian" idea which developed in the nineteenth century laid the groundwork "for permanent clashes between the Serbs and their western neighbors."[50] Accordingly, only the death of the Greater Serbian project would bring an end to the threat of violence from Belgrade. But, for all that, the center of gravity in Banac's argument is the more proximate past, and, accordingly, his ideas will be discussed at greater length in the section on proximate factors.

Like Banac, Goldstein identifies a dreadful dynamic at work in the nineteenth century, due to the development of national consciousness among Serbs and Croats, the activities of religious organizations, and the role of politicians. Thus, according to Goldstein, in spite of "the fact that the ordinary people were intermarried and had many other contacts, differences among them always smoldered. The reasons for this were religious intolerance, xenophobia, and the habit of people to use national instead of economic or other reasons to explain conflicts."[51] The result was that fault lines separating national groups began to be laid down—fault lines along which groups could be mobilized for conflict in the future. For that matter, both Noel Malcolm and Mitja Velikonja, in their respectively magisterial histories of Bosnia, point to the religious rivalries that developed in Bosnia in the course of the nineteenth century—rivalries both between the Catholic and Orthodox Churches and between the Christian community as a whole and the Islamic community.[52] But Velikonja also points out, constructively, that there was *less* religious conflict in Bosnia than had been seen in many European countries ruled by Christian kings and princes, and that the history of Bosnia is therefore characterized by religious coexistence as well as by religious division.[53]

The strengths and debilities of a modest "remote factors" approach, tracing present-day problems no further back than the nineteenth century, are, I believe, the same as the strengths and debilities of the "proximate factors" approach, which will be discussed in the next section.

Theories of "Ancient Hatreds"

The theories of Banac, Goldstein, Malcolm, and Velikonja, while sensitive to developments in the nineteenth century, avoid sliding into "ancient" domains in which the past is viewed so darkly and so out of focus as to roll all the historical threads into a tangled ball. When Major and others claimed that the conflicts between Serbs and Croats could be traced back to "ancient hatreds" going back thousands of years which, in Major's words, "reappeared" with "the collapse of the Soviet Union and of the discipline [which] that exerted over ancient hatreds in the old

Yugoslavia,"[54] they unwittingly claimed that the conflicts had begun even before the Slavs had arrived in the Balkans and, most certainly, long before the ancestors of today's Serbs and Croats had converted from their pre-Christian polytheistic religion to Christianity. Robert Kaplan has recently been the best-known advocate of this approach, which inspired his book, *Balkan Ghosts.* In an earlier contribution to the *New Republic*, Kaplan offered the following short cut to understanding the violent collapse of socialist Yugoslavia:

> Tudjman, Milošević, and everyone else in Yugoslavia are victims of history. For centuries their forebears lived in a state of poverty and illiteracy, where rumor filled the vacuum created by the absence of books and documentation. Then came four-and-a-half decades of Communist totalitarianism, when many, many books were published—all containing lies. The Serb–Croat war in Yugoslavia is the upshot of a few million minds, all collectively disoriented, and all finally granted free expression.[55]

It scarcely seems worth the trouble to point out all of the errors in fact and lapses in thinking in this bit of foolishness.

A variation on the theme of "ancient hatreds" is the "civilizational" approach taken by Harvard professor Samuel P. Huntington in his much debated national bestseller, *The Clash of Civilizations.* For Huntington, the present age is characterized by an increase in conflict across what he calls "civilizational fault lines." These fault lines are defined, in the first place, by differences of religion, so that, in his view, "people who share ethnicity and language but differ in religion may slaughter each other, as happened in Lebanon, the former Yugoslavia, and the [Indian] Subcontinent."[56] In Huntington's view, the danger of fault lines has been "most notable" in post-communist states where, he writes, "culture replaced ideology as the magnet of attraction and repulsion."[57] In a 1968 work, Huntington had expressed his conviction that "Leninist" systems, as he called communist systems, had solved the problem of political institutionalization and therefore were, in his view at that time, likely to prove to be stable over the long term, in spite of their manifest failure to solve the problem of system legitimation (the importance of which Huntington downplayed).[58] But if system legitimacy or illegitimacy is not a factor worth considering in accounting for system decay, then where should one look for an answer? In 1968, Huntington thought the answer was insufficient institutionalization relative to political participation; nearly twenty years later, Huntington was looking to differences in culture to explain why political order broke down and why at least some conflicts broke out. Hence, in *Clash* he portrays the "fault line" between Muslims and non-Muslims as running especially deep, so that he concludes that "[f]ault line conflicts are particularly prevalent between Muslims and non-Muslims."[59] And hence, in his view, the Bosnian war, in which Bosnian Muslims fought Christian Serbs and Croats, was an "intercivilizational" war.[60] Huntington does not say, of course, that Muslims and non-Muslims have hated each other since "ancient" times; what he says rather is that their civilizations have evolved in such different directions, since long ago, that conflict (or hatred, if one likes) is far more natural between them than understanding.

The chief attraction of the ancient hatreds approach is that it grants its supporter license to banish all thinking, to allow oneself to slumber in comfortable contentment in the misguided certainty that all present problems can be referred back to unknown and unknowable mysterious events taking place deep in the past, covered by the vapors of time. It is not by mere coincidence that Bosnian Serb leader Karadžić was fond of urging this theory, from time to time, as proof of the irrelevance of any Western intervention; nor is it any wonder that one may find advocates of this approach among all three parties to the conflict. The chief debility of this theory is that it leads its believers away from any understanding of what makes states collapse or former neighbors go to war with each other. Of all the theories that have been applied to the Yugoslav case, it is perhaps the most misleading.

The chief attraction of Huntington's civilizational thesis is its air of sophistication and, in the post-9/11 world, the way it may be marshaled against the entire Islamic world. Its chief debility is much the same as the ancient hatreds approach, in that someone who traces conflicts to "intercivilizational fault lines" is unlikely to give much emphasis to such factors of system illegitimacy, or economic decay, or the role of human agency.

Internal Factors—Proximate

Most scholars, even if in the endeavor to explain the roots of the Yugoslav crisis they have made some room for analyzing events in the nineteenth century, have placed their emphasis on developments since 1918, since 1941, since 1945, or even since 1987. While scholars may differ on the dating of the beginning of the problems that drove the Yugoslav state over the brink, one may speak of a broad consensus among most scholars in the field that "proximate factors" are the most relevant in responding at least to questions (1) and (2). But this "consensus," such as it is, is superficial, because among those who emphasize "proximate factors" are those emphasizing economic deterioration, those who argue that the political system itself was a major factor for all that happened, those presenting an event-driven account together with those stressing human agency (in particular the role of specific political figures), those looking to decisions made during the transition from communism, and those referring causation to a multiplicity of proximate factors.

Economic Deterioration

Many scholars have noted that economic deterioration played a part in bringing socialist Yugoslavia into crisis and that the growing sense of desperation among many Yugoslavs, some of whom were, by the end of the 1980s, unable to afford to heat their homes during winter, made them receptive to political mobilization. Erika

Harris, for instance, has emphasized the importance of economic factors in pushing Yugoslavia into crisis and toward collapse, highlighting the oil price hike of 1974 as a critical watershed.[61] But Susan Woodward has endeavored, in her *Socialist Unemployment: The Political Economy of Yugoslavia 1945—1990*, to represent economic deterioration, and specifically unemployment, as the critical variable in the equation. Unemployment, Woodward argues, impaired the political establishment's "capacity to enforce policy goals," undermined "the delicate balance in constitutional jurisdictions of the federal system," negatively impacted "the system's capacity to adapt politically to the requirements of new economic and social conditions," and undermined "the country's ability to manage unemployment itself."[62] For Woodward, political cleavages in socialist Yugoslavia were

> defined not by nationality or liberal/conservative party factions, but by the package of policies on credit, domestic and foreign currency, investment, and individual employment that coalesce[d] around territorial defense and commodity trade. This line of conflict was formed before the changes of 1958—1967.[63]

Accordingly, for Woodward, nationalism is only an epiphenomenon of discontent generated by unemployment, which is the heart of the problem.[64] But Woodward does not want her analysis to be read as unicausal reductionism and specifically allows that other factors enter into the equation;[65] what sets her apart from other analysts is her decision to stress unemployment as the principal source of the decay of the socialist Yugoslav state.

Systemic Factors

Theories that trace the roots of the collapse of the Yugoslav state and the outbreak of conflict at least in part to systemic factors may highlight the fundamental illegitimacy of the system, its clumsiness and general dysfunctionality (acknowledged by Yugoslavs themselves in the "old days" in their endless jokes about collective leadership and the rotation of cadres), the erection of the federation along ethnic lines with a guarantee of a right of secession, and the juridical instability springing from the frequent constitutional changes.[66] Paul Lendvai, for example, stresses the flaws in the structural design itself, pointing to the ethnically inspired federal system as a Pandora's box.[67] It was this design, according to Lendvai, which gave the competition between elites at the federal and republic levels its specific character and endowed inter-elite rows with such "explosive force."[68] Or again, Goldstein, while noting the confluence of a number of destabilizing factors, captures the spirit of the 1980s perfectly in noting the "state of paralysis" induced in a system characterized by collective leadership, fixed rotational schemes, and terms of office so short as to prevent any important plans from being implemented.[69] The fate of the long-term plans for economic and political stabilization, associated with the names Boris Kraigher and Tihomir Vlaškalić, comes to mind.

17

Reneo Lukić, George Schöpflin, John Allcock, and I have also given non-exclusive stress to systemic factors, placing the emphasis on the failure of legitimation. For Lukić, the absence of the rule of law was the single most important weakness in socialist Yugoslavia, guaranteeing that the functioning of the state depended, up to 1980 (or more accurately, until Tito took ill in late 1979), on Tito's personal authority.[70] But Lukić does not consider that this is the entire story, and explicitly rejects the notion that, with the death of Tito, it was only a matter of time before the Yugoslav federation imploded; in other words, Lukić believes that it would have been possible to preserve a unified Yugoslav state. But if so, according to Lukić, it would have had to take the form of "an asymmetrical federation or confederation," which, he argues, "would have been, by all measures, the best outcome for the nations and national minorities of former Yugoslavia."[71] For Lukić, the failure of legitimation provides part (note, only part) of the answer to the question of why socialist Yugoslavia collapsed. The rest of the answer to that question as well as the answer to the question of why that collapse was associated with violent conflict must be sought, says Lukić, in human agency, and in particular in the actions of Serbian leader Slobodan Milošević.

Schöpflin made an earlier and important contribution to the analysis of the Yugoslav crisis in an essay published in 1985, in which he warned of processes of political decay unfolding in socialist Yugoslavia and other communist states in Eastern Europe. Schöpflin wrote that the remedy for political decay in Eastern Europe was pluralization, *i.e.*, authentic democratization and "the acceptance of autonomous sources of legitimacy for social institutions."[72] But "by reason of the [Yugoslav] party's unwillingness to accept the redistribution of power through democratization, the systemic crisis accelerates and is expressed in new, and potentially more damaging forms."[73] Allcock concurred with Schöpflin's analysis, noting the importance of the fact that the system was unable to legitimate itself over the long term and characterizing Yugoslav socialism as "anti-modern,"[74] even as Steven Burg and Paul Shoup, while including other factors in the equation, pointed to "the inadequacy of existing political arrangements [at the beginning of the 1990s] for moderating or constraining" nationalist parties.[75]

Together with Lukić and Allcock, I have stressed the failure of legitimation[76] and have noted that that failure alone was not sufficient to push the country into war; an enabler—or, in the event, a number of enablers, including not only Milošević but various others as well[77]—would be needed. Together with Schöpflin, I have argued that only authentic pluralization could have saved Yugoslavia (and that to have had time to work, it would have needed to have been set in motion by 1985 at the very latest).[78] And, for that matter, I have also included economic deterioration[79] and the ethnically based structure of the federation[80] in the equation. Yet although the economic, structural, and legitimation factors explain the collapse of the Yugoslav federation, they do not account for the outbreak of war—at least not by themselves.

Here I agree fully with Lukić (and, for that matter, Sadkovich[81]) that one must bring human agency into the story if one is going to understand why war broke out.

The strength of the emphasis on systemic factors lies in its ability to explain why illegitimate systems are less able to cope with economic crisis than more legitimate systems, while stressing the reason why politicians who do not respect the laws of the land are able to do more damage in states where rule of law is less well established. The systemic focus does suggest very strongly that one is misled to believe that the peoples of the Yugoslav region have any "particular predisposition to violence" (as per question [4]) and, by way of dating the origin of the problems (question [5]), suggests that they should be seen as arising with system malfunction. The weakness of theories stressing systemic factors is that such theories cannot, by themselves, answer questions (2) or (3). For this purpose, some additional theoretical apparatus will be needed.

Human Agency

The works of Anzulović, Cohen, Kaplan, and Woodward, however different in other respects, all tend in the direction of minimizing human agency. Cohen even criticizes British historian Noel Malcolm for having allegedly traced the problems in Kosovo to "the actions of evil leaders."[82] The scholarly consensus, however, is that human agency must be made a part of the story, though most, if not all, scholars would probably also agree with Roger Petersen's commonsensical caution that "there is no reason to assume that elites always constrain and manipulate masses rather than the other way around."[83] Among those who have stressed human agency, one might mention Ivo Banac,[84] Jasna Dragović-Soso,[85] Thomas Emmert,[86] Bariša Krekić,[87] Reneo Lukić,[88] Branka Magaš,[89] Dennison Rusinow,[90] Louis Sell,[91] and Vladimir Tismaneanu.[92] But, of course, agreeing that someone did it is not the same as reaching an agreement on exactly *who* was the responsible party. That said, all scholars with whose work I am familiar include Milošević among the chief malefactors. Disagreement arises as soon as scholars take up the question of who else should be thought to have contributed either to the collapse of the SFRY or to the stoking of war. Warren Zimmermann, the former U.S. ambassador to Belgrade, begins his memoirs with the bold assertion, "This is a story with villains,"[93] and quickly dismisses any notion that economic problems or ethnic tensions were sufficient to dismantle the country; on the contrary, according to Zimmermann, it "was destroyed from the top down."[94] And while he blames Milošević in the first place for the tragedy that befell the country, Zimmermann also reproaches Tudjman for "arrogance in declaring independence without adequate provisions for minority rights,"[95] and the Slovenes for their alleged "'Garbo' nationalism" ("they just wanted to be left alone," Zimmermann explains[96]). Indeed, Zimmermann considers the Slovenian disassociation from the SFRY irresponsible, because in building their own independent state the Slovenes, according to Zimmermann, "left the twenty-two

19

million Yugoslav citizens they had abandoned twisting in the wind of impending war."[97] The implication is that, by remaining within the Yugoslav federation, the Slovenes could have made a decisive contribution to averting the war that Milošević and Borisav Jović, whose term as president of the collective presidency was coming to an end in May 1991, had been preparing since before the election of Franjo Tudjman to the Croatian presidency.[98]

John Fine, Jr seems at first sight to offer the same list as Zimmermann. Milošević is described by Fine as "a brutal authoritarian," while Croatian President Tudjman and Slovenian President Kučan are criticized for their alleged desire for "instant gratification."[99] But Fine spends more of his time mounting accusations against Tudjman than criticizing Milošević, referring at one point to "the massive death and destruction unleashed by the chauvinism that blots Tudjman's record."[100] For Fine, the declarations of independence by Slovenia and Croatia were "hasty" and "irresponsible," and these two republics deserve "the lion's share of the responsibility for the war that followed."[101] Fine mentions the illegal importation of weaponry by the Slovenian and Croatian governments for the use of their territorial defense forces (or police, in Croatia's case), but he does not mention either the equally illegal confiscation, on Milošević's and Jović's instructions, of the weapons which had been assigned to those forces or the arming of Serb militias in Croatia, both of which pre-dated the importation and, indeed, inspired it. Fine's solution, offered in retrospect, is to suggest that a military coup, if staged prior to 25 June 1991, might have averted the disaster that ensued.[102] In fact, there were rumors of a coup in early 1991.[103]

But there are problems with assigning equal blame to Tudjman and Kučan, on the one hand, and the Belgrade regime, on the other. One problem is that many of Milošević's provocative actions *preceded* actions taken by Tudjman and Kučan, and even preceded Tudjman's election. Certainly, the organization of the famous mass "meetings" in Novi Sad, Podgorica, and Priština, which drove the locally elected governments to resign, allowing Milošević's men to take over,[104] took place before Tudjman had been elected—and, as late as March 1990, Ivica Račan, the chief of the reformed Communist Party in Croatia, still expected to be elected president of Croatia.[105] And again, the Milošević regime's use of the press to radicalize Serbs pre-dated by nearly three years any parallel process in Croatia, let alone Bosnia. In one example, recounted by *Vreme* editor Miloš Vasić, "On 15 March [1991], Milošević summoned all the mayors of Serbia to a meeting [and] outlined a strategy for provoking ethnic conflict in Croatia ... A massive media campaign convinced the Serbs in Croatia that they were in danger of a 'new genocide" ... The initiative was now in Milošević's hands, and on 1 April the first fighting began at Plitvice National Park."[106] A second problem is that Milošević's record of unconstitutional and illegal actions dwarfs whatever may be laid to Tudjman's or Kučan's account.[107] A third problem is that although Tudjman and Milošević reportedly discussed a partition of Bosnia at Karadjordjevo in March 1991, Milošević put much more time into planning the war than did Tudjman and entertained greater ambitions than Tudjman. On the other hand, both Milošević (beginning in late 1987) and Tudjman (beginning in spring 1990) used the press to stoke up resentments about what had happened during World War II or afterwards and to stoke up group hatred. As Vasić said on one occasion, "You must imagine a United States with every little TV station everywhere taking exactly the same editorial line—a line dictated by David Duke [the Louisiana Nazi]. You too would have war in five years."[108] Both Milošević and Tudjman also organized military actions to promote the ethnic cleansing of Muslims. Both of them funded and backed (and, in Tudjman's case, commanded) forces that set up detention camps in which members of other nationality groups were abused.

Adam LeBor, author of an elegantly written biography of Milošević, casts his net widely, tracing the collapse of the Yugoslav federation to that state's failure to inculcate a sense of shared community and to the weakness of the constitutional structure, which did not protect non-Serbs from Serb overrepresentation and domination. He also faults Tito for failing to overcome the various problems of the socialist federation and, more concretely, for removing the Serbian liberals from power in 1972—an event that LeBor considers a turning point in socialist Yugoslavia's history. But, for LeBor, to the extent that Milošević should be considered a war criminal, so too should Tudjman.[109] Indeed, at this point of time—largely because of the Croatian Army's involvement in fighting against the Army of the Republic of Bosnia-Herzegovina (the army loyal to the government headed by Alija Izetbegović)—Tudjman is routinely seen as co-responsible with Milošević and, for that matter, Bosnian Serb leaders Radovan Karadžić and Gen. Ratko Mladić, and others, for the loss of life in Bosnia, while Martin Špegelj's memoirs stand as an indictment of Tudjman for having unnecessarily prolonged the war and for having unnecessarily delayed the reconquest of areas of Croatia under Serb insurgent/Yugoslav Army control.[110] It is when one turns to a consideration of the years 1987–1990, the years during which Yugoslavia moved decisively toward disaster, that the role of Milošević seems decisive. Admiral Mamula records how, shortly after the 8th Session of the Serbian party, at which Milošević had staged his famous coup, the Admiral, then serving as minister of defense, and his deputy, Veljko Kadijević, held discussions with Ante Marković and Stanko Stojčević in Croatia, with France Popit and Milan Kučan in Slovenia, and with Branko Mikulić in Bosnia. Mamula and Kadijević felt that the coup was potentially dangerous for the entire country; all of the figures with whom they conducted conversations agreed with this analysis, but they were unwilling to undertake any decisive actions in response.[111] I had occasion to discuss this lack of response with Milan Kučan in 1999, hoping for some revelation; instead, the impression I obtained was that while everyone was prepared to agree that this was a "dangerous" development, none of them had any idea just how dangerous it was or what it could mean for the coming years. Nonetheless, Stane Dolanc, the veteran Slovenian politician who was at one time suspected of wanting to succeed Tito as president of Yugoslavia, approached

General Ljubičić on his own and suggested that perhaps the party presidency, of which the general had become a member, could discuss Milošević's coup; Ljubičić, a close ally of Milošević at the time, signaled his disinclination to honor Dolanc's request by asking if he should also submit a report about developments in Slovenia. Several months later, Stipe Šuvar, Croatia's representative in the party presidium, tried to use a plenary session of the Central Committee to remove both Milošević and Kučan, but Šuvar did not devote sufficient time to winning over the party leaderships of Montenegro, Macedonia, Bosnia-Herzegovina, and, for that matter, his native Croatia, and his plan failed.[112] But Milošević was building his popular support with a rapidity that astonished his party comrades. A combined party–army move against Milošević might have been successful if it had been undertaken quickly, according to Louis Sell, but by summer 1988 Milošević had grown so strong that it would have been "unthinkable for the federal authorities to order the army or police to act against him."[113]

The memoirs of Raif Dizdarević also provide convincing documentation of the incendiary role played by Milošević in these years. Dizdarević served as chair of the presidential council of Bosnia-Herzegovina 1978–1982, president of the Federal Assembly 1982–1983, foreign minister 1984–1988, and president of the SFRY state presidency 1988–1989, and shows how, during the crucial years leading up to Slovenian and Croatian secession, Milošević disregarded not only the laws and established procedures of the system, but also his colleagues in the political establishment, setting in motion actions that were generally understood to be destabilizing. On 27 September 1988, Dizdarević recalls, he and other members of the state presidency held talks with Petar Gračanin, then president of Serbia, and Milošević, in order to emphasize the dangers inherent in Serbian policies and behavior.[114] Milošević listened politely but ignored the concerns of the presidency, which were not *his* concerns. In Dizdarević's account, Milošević emerges as the mastermind behind the destabilizing "meetings" that overthrew duly elected governments in three federal units. Dizdarević understood the danger full well and told a group of Bosnian leaders in October 1988 that "if this method [of removing office holders] is accepted, the consequences will be catastrophic."[115] But although Dizdarević believes that Milošević played the most important role, during the years 1987–1989,[116] in pushing the country toward breakup and war, he too does not believe that Milošević accomplished this singlehandedly. Indeed, Dizdarević shows how the wave of Serbian nationalism which Milošević rode had emerged earlier, and provides an account of a critical session of the LCY Central Committee held in December 1981 at which leading figures in the Serbian party demanded a redefinition of Serbia, granting it special status within Yugoslavia. Draža Marković, one of the most prominent Serb communists at that time, shocked the country on that occasion with his speech, in which he said that Yugoslavia consisted of five peoples: Slovenes, Croats, Serbs, Macedonians, and Montenegrins. That list omitted the Bosniaks (called "Muslims" in the official terminology of that time)—an omission that no one considered accidental.[117] In other words, Milošević emerges in Dizdarević's account as simultaneously responding to a wave of Serbian nationalism which had emerged earlier, and catering to Serb nationalist demands and feeding Serb nationalist passions (via the Belgrade press and television) for his own purposes, and collaborating with others within the context of a vortex of nationalist passions which no one ultimately controlled, but which many exploited (not only in Serbia but in other republics as well). Massimo Nava, in his 1999 biography of Milošević, confirms Dizdarević's account, noting that Milošević did not conjure up Serb frustrations, but rather understood the sentiments of Serbs at that time and played to them.[118] Viktor Meier, Adam LeBor, and Louis Sell would also agree with these points, I am certain. And, for that matter, one may find a general corroboration of these points in the testimony of Ante Marković, who served as prime minister of the SFRY from March 1989 to December 1991, at the trial of Slobodan Milošević.[119]

Banac[120] and Dragović-Soso[121] provide the most thorough accounts of the way in which Serbian intellectuals contributed to creating a climate in which only nationalist discourse came to be seen as legitimate, in which hatred became a badge of patriotism, and in which people like Milošević and Karadžić could build power. The 1986 Memorandum issued by the Serbian Academy of Sciences and Art figures as a key moment in their accounts.[122] Their approach reminds us that theories emphasizing human agency need not focus on the role of political leaders and may, in fact, bring to light ways in which currents emerging from within society can influence the political environment, revealing in the process ways in which political leaders respond to impulses and pressures "from below."[123] But one should not forget that, some 15 years earlier, *Croatian* intellectuals had played a similar role, parading out their sundry fears and phobias and demanding constitutional changes to enhance the status of Croats qua Croats.[124] The difference is that, in 1971, the LCY had responded with repression, while, in 1986, the already moribund LCY did little except squawk. There was no effective response. (This is not to endorse the repression of 1971–1972; history would prove that it was a dysfunctional response. But the lack of response the following decade was even more short-sighted and dangerous.)

Theories emphasizing, in whole or in part, human agency are enormously attractive because, when states collapse or wars erupt, most of us want to know who is responsible. It is one of the most basic and most natural questions. And, inevitably, there are figures who can be found to have played crucial roles in such events. But was Milošević, for example, the mastermind of the war, as suggested in the indictment under which he is currently being tried, or merely, rather, "the knight-errant of Serbdom," as Rusinow has put it?[125] The chief strength of theories emphasizing human agency is that they avoid the pitfall of telling the story as if there were only impersonal forces at work—indeed, as if there were no free choice. Theories emphasizing human agency keep free choice—and thus, human responsibility—in focus. When used with sophistication, they avoid attributing all that goes wrong to a single individual. But there is no reason why theories of human agency should fail to acknowledge the enormous support that populations have sometimes given their leaders as they have happily marched off to self-destructive wars or the systemic factors that make it possible for ambitious leaders to take their societies down the road to destruction.

Democratization

It has increasingly been argued by scholars that, during the process of democratization, states are in great danger of succumbing to nationalism or sliding into war. In fact, Jack Snyder estimates that democratizing states are about 50% more likely than the "average state" to go to war.[126] The mobilization of nationalism is often the instrument that takes such states down the road to war. But why nationalism? Snyder's answer is that established elites in democratizing but still only semi-democratic (or even, not-yet-democratic) contexts may use nationalism in order to narrow the range of allowable political discourse and retain power.[127] But why was such a strategy successful in Serbia at all? Juan Linz and Alfred Stepan provide an answer. In their view, in multiethnic settings, the order of elections is critical—specifically, the choice to hold elections first at the national (or if one prefers, all-union) level or first at the regional level. In Spain, as they point out, the first elections were held at the national (all-Spanish) level, with all-union parties campaigning hard in the Catalán and Basque regions. The result was that four of the all-union parties and their local affiliates garnered 67.7% of the vote in Catalonia and 51.4% of the vote in the Basque country.[128] The upshot was that Spain held together and democratized successfully. In Yugoslavia, as in the Soviet Union, elections were held at the regional (*i.e.*, republic) level before they were held at the all-union level. The result was that politicians vying for power made their pitch at the regional level, appealing to local/regional concerns rather than to those of all the citizens of the state. But why should this result in the mobilization of nationalism? Their answer is that

> A key aspect of a totalitarian regime is that independent preexisting parties and labor, business, and religious organizations have been subject to extensive campaigns of elimination or subjugation ... The landscape of civil society is very flat. All-union independent organizations are virtually nonexistent. In all post-totalitarian polities the relative flatness of the landscape of civil society has created problems for politicians, because it is hard to represent amorphous groups. Even after liberalization, the articulation of interests based on wealth, ideology, or property relations has been strikingly less than we find in many authoritarian regimes. However, politicians are specialists in mobilizing hopes and grievances. In the context of post-totalitarianism's flattened landscape, the easiest hopes and grievances for politicians to mobilize relate to ethnicity.[129]

Erika Harris offers a somewhat different slant on the relationship between nationalism and democratization, viewing the former as "an integral part of any democratisation process," while noting that the relationship between the two is "ambiguous" at best.[130] Acknowledging the tension between the requirements of liberal democracy and the spirit of nationalism, Harris writes that "civic identity tends to lose out as soon as there is a disagreement about state-building policies. Ethnic nationalism is as much a consequence of unsuccessful state-building as it is its cause, for the disintegration of the state, the loss of its legitimacy, diminishes civic affiliation and leaves the field open to ethnic mobilisation."[131]

The theories presented by Snyder and by Linz and Stepan trace the breakup of Yugoslavia and the subsequent war to the way in which the challenge of democratization was confronted. But that, in turn, brings in elites, since it is elites who decide in what order to hold elections, and it is elites who decide how to pitch their electoral campaigns. In the Linz/Stepan theory especially, the electorate is seen as responding passively, even predictably, to the strategies of the elites, so that what people end up choosing (wanting) comes to depend on the order in which choices are presented to them. This theory is not far-fetched, since, for example, it has been widely reported that Ante Marković was the most popular political figure throughout Yugoslavia in 1989–1990, but was, all the same, unable to get his all-Yugoslav party off the ground. Whether the experience of fascism (in Spain) can be conflated with the experience of communism (in Yugoslavia and the Soviet Union) is another matter; however, this question goes far beyond the concerns of this article.

Emotional Factors and the Effects of the Past

The theories presented so far have not offered much by way of accounting for why people who had lived in peace for more than four decades should have suddenly turned on each other with such brutality (question [3]). For an answer to this question, we must turn to the writings of Marie-Janine Calic, Paolo Rumiz, and Roger D. Petersen. Since Petersen's theory is the most explicit, it will make the most sense to begin with his work, even though the most recently published of the three. Petersen's argument is that perceived individual or collective self-interest is not sufficient to explain why people commit brutal actions in wartime situations. He argues that emotion plays the crucial role here and offers narratives based on four alternative emotions—fear, hatred, rage, and resentment.[132] Explicitly rejecting a "rational choice" approach to explaining intercommunal violence,[133] he concedes that "an emotion-based account cannot explain every case" of such violence, and largely discounts rage, which often has no stable focus, "often drives the individual toward self-destructive actions," and "often produces cognitive distortions that can lead to irrelevant or counterproductive actions."[134] Among the advantages that Petersen sees in his approach are that it avoids the pitfall of treating group preferences as stable, that it can explain how, in a context of multiple cross-cutting identities, one particular identity is essentialized, and that it explains how a self-defined group comes to feel justified in committing atrocities against the members of other groups.[135]

As indicated in the subtitle to Petersen's book, his analysis focuses on: *fear*, which he sees as inspiring violence against that group which is seen as constituting the greatest threat; *hatred*, which he says is directed against a group that has been the target with similar justifications over an extended period of time; and *resentment*, which is directed toward a group seen as enjoying unjustified privilege or superior status (or as having committed atrocities against one's own group).[136] Turning to the Yugoslav case, Petersen argues that given the multiple justifications offered by Serb nationalists for fighting the Bosniaks in the 1990s,[137] hatred cannot serve as an explanation for Bosnian Serb atrocities against the Bosniaks. Instead, inspired in part by Liah Greenfeld's work,[138] he argues that the war should be understood, at least in part, as an expression of the resentment felt by Croats toward the Croatian Serbs because of the decades that the latter had dominated the upper ranks in the Croatian party and the police force, and that felt by rural Bosnian Croats and Serbs toward the urban Muslims of Sarajevo and other towns of Bosnia-Herzegovina. Moreover, both Croats and Serbs resented and feared the prospect of Muslim dominance in an independent Bosnian state, according to Petersen.[139] In turning to an analysis of the atrocities committed against Albanians in Kosovo, however, Petersen argues that hatred explains the violence there better than resentment. In his view, the history of Serb–Albanian violence, which he traces to 1912–1913, established a "schema" into which Serbs and Albanians readily slipped.[140] This analysis is implicitly Freudian, and has some resonance with other literature.

Calic, in her *Krieg und Frieden in Bosnien-Hercegovina*, provides some substantiation for Petersen's suggestion that resentment was a powerful emotion motivating violence. She cites an opinion poll from November 1991, in which nearly 60% of Muslims and 70% of Croats reported that Serbs had the greatest influence in Bosnia, with 52% of Serbs thinking the same about Croats, and 44% of Serbs thinking that Bosniaks were the dominant group in Bosnia-Herzegovina.[141] In other words, each group resented what it considered the unfair dominance of at least one of the other groups. Moreover, as she notes, nationalist politicians tried to convert resentment into the more powerful coinage of hatred, insisting, among other things, that the diverse peoples of Bosnia could not possibly coexist in the future.[142] According to Calic, the artillery bombardment of Bosnia's cities was motivated, perhaps above all, by the desire to destroy the cosmopolitanism of the cities and any possibility of the coexistence that they had embodied.[143] Finally, she provides a thorough analysis of the motivations of the combatants themselves, mentioning not only rural resentment of the cosmopolitan city but also the fact that some of the perpetrators had previous histories of pathology or law breaking, and the fact that many atrocities were perpetrated in groups, where peer pressure and conformism would be operative.[144]

What Rumiz adds to this discussion is an analysis of the relationship between *starosedioci* (old settlers) and *došljaci* (newcomers), in which, as he shows, it emerges that there was often greater sympathy between fellow "old settlers," whether they might be Serbs or Croats (as in Vukovar), than between "old settlers" and "newcomers," even if both might be members of the same national group.[145] The "old settlers" proved to be largely immune to the overtures from nationalists during 1990–1991, and, according to Rumiz, "the destruction of Vukovar and other cities of the former Yugoslavia was ... the work of 'outsiders'—of immigrants and agents of nonurban culture."[146] As if to prove the point, the Serb conquerors of Vukovar, after they had completed their conquest, spoke of rebuilding the city—not in the Habsburg style of the now-destroyed city, but rather in the Byzantine style that they identified as their own. Yet Rumiz does not want his readers to conclude that the war was a spontaneous affair. "The war was ... consciously orchestrated," he emphasizes, even if the nationalist elites made use of available fault lines between *starosedioci* and *došljaci.*

The emphasis on the role of emotion requires a differentiation between such emotions as develop in the absence of elite manipulation and those emotions which are, at least in part, the result of elite manipulation and orchestration or, perhaps, levels of intensity which are the result of elite manipulation. Both kinds are present, just as there may be syndromes widespread in a society which arise, as one might say, in the course of things as well as syndromes that are fostered by conscious elite manipulation, as I have argued in a recent work.[147] In Cohen's account, "emotions" (in the sense in which Petersen uses the term) and syndromes emerged long ago and have remained more or less stable over time. In the writings of Petersen, Calic, and Rumiz, emotions and syndromes are portrayed as much more mutable, much more subject to changing circumstances, changing relations between people (as in the arrival of *došljaci* in a region), and changing elite strategies. The emphasis on the role of emotion does not seek to explain why the SFRY collapsed, but it makes a useful contribution to answering questions (3) and (4), providing also a basis for answering the question about how far back conflicts should be traced (question [5]). Of course, if one wishes to probe the subject of individual motivation in greater depth, one should turn to the ample literature in the field of psychology. Here I am thinking, in particular, of the work of Albert Bandura,[148] Samuel Guttman,[149] Herbert Kelman,[150] Roderick Kramer and David Messick,[151] and Jo-Ann Tsang,[152] alongside others.[153]

Toward a Synthesis of Approaches

In the foregoing article, I have reviewed various approaches to explaining the Yugoslav collapse and War of Yugoslav Succession: external factors (Great Power conspiracy; end of the Cold War); remote internal factors (national character school; nineteenth-century roots; "ancient hatreds"); proximate internal factors (economic deterioration; systemic factors; human agency; democratization process); and emotional factors. I have also suggested that some combination of these will serve best to address the questions at hand. All of these approaches stress the importance of the past, though in different ways. Certainly, it is rather obvious that institutions established in, let us say, 1945, even though subsequently reformed, modified, and reorganized—such as the role of the communist party and its control of the press—may have a lingering impact for some years even after the collapse of communism. Or again, the resentments associated with memories of the interwar years (1918–1941) may have an impact on the present generation, especially to the extent that public figures allude to those years and stir up bad memories ("dysphoric rumination," as psychologists put it). Based on the foregoing, we may perhaps conclude the following.

Question (1): Why did the SFRY collapse? From the review of theories, it seems apparent that systemic and economic factors must be kept at the center of focus (while not neglecting the responsibility of those who failed to take remedial action in sufficient time or those who subverted the constitutional order). Certainly, the years of relative internal peace in socialist Yugoslavia, 1945–1985, were sufficient time in which the country could, with a more wisely developed political formula, have constructed a system capable of overcoming such economic and political storms as would come its way. Among many citizens of the SFRY there was a genuine commitment to building a common life—but the minimal demands which Yugoslavs had included the chance for a better life, fairness, respect for human rights, and a legitimate state. Had these things been achieved, collapse and war could most certainly have been avoided. This means, of course, that democratization would have had to be undertaken *before* the country's crisis of legitimation became overwhelming.

Question (2): Why did armed conflict erupt between the peoples of the area in 1991? On the basis of the brief summary presented here, I would suggest that the answer to this question must be sought not merely in the preparations taken by Milošević, beginning in early 1990 at the latest, and by Tudjman, beginning in autumn 1990 at the latest, but also in the complicity and active involvement of other actors, in the role played by Croatian intellectuals in the late 1960s (sowing resentments that would reawaken later) and by Serbian intellectuals in the 1980s, and in the resentments connected with the interwar years (1918–1941) and with World War II (1941–1945), and, for that matter, also with the massacres at Bleiburg and Kočevje immediately after World War II.

Question (3): Why did people who had lived together in peace for most of 45 years take up arms against each other? I find that I am impressed simultaneously with the capacity of the democratization school (Snyder, Linz and Stepan), the elite propaganda approach, and the emotions/syndromes approach (Petersen, Calic, Rumiz, Kramer and Messick) to contribute to explaining how and why Serbs, Croats, and Bosniaks went to war against each other. Certainly, the role of propaganda in feeding people's frenzy should not be underestimated. Where Petersen emphasized resentment and downplayed rage, I would again emphasize resentment but give some room for rage, perhaps not as a stable emotion, but as instigating certain key events, and I would also add an emotion not discussed by Petersen—*desperation*: in the context of Yugoslav economic deterioration, there were plenty of desperate people in the SFRY by the end of the 1980s, and desperate people are prepared to resort to desperate measures, especially when there are ambitious leaders egging them on with concrete demands.

Question (4): Do the Serbs, Croats, and/or Bosniaks have any particular predisposition to violence, and, if so, where does it come from? Misha Glenny's widely read *Fall of Yugoslavia,*[154] in a manner reminiscent of Tomašić's theory of "Dinaric man," promoted the theory that the people of Croatia, Bosnia, and Serbia were more prone to violence, partly—in his view—because they grew up with weapons and partly because of local traditions. In so writing, Glenny drew close to the "national character" school, one of two approaches that endeavor to answer this question. The other approach stresses emotions and psychological syndromes. These two approaches stand in opposition to each other. Where the national character school presents the behavioral patterns of one or another people as highly stable, developed over history, and predictive of likely behaviors, the emotional/psychological approach stresses that behavioral patterns are subject to certain processes and vulnerable to certain responses (resentment, hatred, fear, rage, desperation) that have certain likely behavioral expressions but which are not necessarily stable over time; quite the contrary, the emotional/psychological approach stresses that emotions may be relatively short-lived (a decade or two, under some circumstances) and scarcely constitutive of a fixed "national character."

Question (5): How far back can intense rivalries or conflicts involving these three peoples be traced? As we have already seen, the answers provided by the alternative theories examined herein are quite diverse. But what do you say to someone who insists that it "all" started in 1389? Or to someone who believes that it all started in 1987? And if these extremes do not look sensible, can one even really draw a line somewhere? Although a case can be made for asserting that the problems began in 1878 or in 1918 or in 1928 (the assassination of Stjepan Radić) or in 1941 or in 1945, or at any of a number of other points in time, almost any date selected would have something of the arbitrary to it. To my mind, the least arbitrary date—indeed, the *only* date which is not arbitrary—from which to date the beginning of problems among Bosniaks, Croats, and Serbs is 1918—the point at which these peoples entered into a common national state for the first time in history. But I prefer to think of 1918 as setting the Yugoslav peoples in a certain direction, with subsequent crises, problematic choices, atrocities, and conflicts depositing layer after layer of memories, resentments, dangers, problems, and potential for explosion. In 1921 came the Vidovdan constitution, widely viewed as unjust by non-Serbs; then came the assassination of Croatian leader Stjepan Radić by a Serb in 1928 and the assassination of King Aleksandar of the Serbian Karadjordjević dynasty by a Macedonian collaborating with the Croatian Ustaše in 1934; then came the bitter suffering of

World War II; and so on. With each new layer of suffering, the resentments grew deeper and the potential for mobilization for future conflict grew greater. Yugoslav President Tito, who ruled socialist Yugoslavia from 1945 until his death in May 1980, tried to overcome the resentments and hatreds stirred up in the course of the years 1918–1945, and made some progress. But, as the propaganda appeals of the Serbian and Croatian press at the beginning of the 1990s showed,[155] the memories of those earlier years still had the power, half a century later, to provoke anger and resentment and to contribute to ethnic mobilization. And this is an important point: it has become fashionable, at least in some circles, to deny that Milošević was a nationalist and even to deny that the War of Yugoslav Succession had an ethnic character. These well-intentioned denials are misleading, however. Milošević used the propaganda apparatus at his disposal to stir up nationalist passions, and used those nationalist passions to motivate Serbs for war. That makes him a nationalist. Whatever he may have said to his wife and pet cat in the privacy of his living room is completely beside the point. As for the claim that the war was not "ethnic," one may well ask if those making this claim believe, for example, that it was a war in which the poor were mobilized to fight against "rich exploiters" or one in which the Orthodox or the Catholics were mobilized to fight against non-Orthodox or non-Catholics? In fact, even allowing for the rural–urban resentment, propaganda endeavored to mobilize specifically *ethnic* hatreds; it was for this reason that Serbian propaganda portrayed Croats as Ustaše and Bosniaks as "Islamic fundamentalists," and that Croatian propaganda portrayed Serbs as Chetniks and communists.

At the end of most films, there is a standard disclaimer that advises viewers not to try to equate particular characters in the film with actual persons living or dead. In the title to this article, I quoted from Shakespeare's *Macbeth*. Perhaps I may add here that any resemblance between the three witches whose incantation that was and any actual persons living or dead is purely coincidental, and that any inference to that effect which some innocent but misguided reader might infer is unintended and could exist only in the mind of that misguided reader. Still, if a reader were to read the witches as representing respectively systemic factors, human agency, and emotional factors, such an interpretation would at least lead in the direction of emphasizing that only a multi-factor analysis can really handle even merely questions (1) and (2), let alone the entire complex of questions raised by the Yugoslav war.[156] Indeed, it would be a pity to try to answer all five questions, identified at the outset, with just one theory—or worse, with just one factor. Nor is there any reason to do so.

NOTES

1. William Shakespeare, *Macbeth*, IV, i.
2. I am grateful to Thomas Emmert, Jasna Dragović-Soso, Reneo Lukić, and Vjeran Pavlaković for their most helpful comments on an earlier draft of this article.

3. This approach is discussed in the context of a review of alternative explanations of the Yugoslav troubles in Davorin Rudolf, *Rat koji nismo htjeli. Hrvatska 1991* (Zagreb: Nakladni zavod Globus, 1999), pp. 19–35.

4. Rodney Atkinson, "Yugoslavia and Its Enemies, 1903–1998," <www.1335.com/Serbia.html> (accessed 28 August 2003), p. 1.

5. Gerard F. Powers, "Religion, Conflict and Prospects for Peace in Bosnia, Croatia and Yugoslavia," *Religion in Eastern Europe*, Vol. 16, No. 5, 1996, p. 1.

6. For documentation of this claim, see Sabrina Petra Ramet, "Yugoslavia and the Two Germanys," in Dirk Verheyen and Christian Søe, eds, *The Germans and Their Neighbors* (Boulder: Westview Press, 1993), p. 328.

7. Testimony of Aleksandar Vasiljević, Trial of Slobodan Milošević (TSM), International Criminal Tribunal for the former Yugoslavia (ICTY), The Hague, 17 February 2003, p. 16263, <www.un.org/icty/transe54/030217ED.htm> (accessed 22 January 2004).

8. Testimony of Aleksandar Vasiljević, TSM-ICTY, 18 February 2003, p. 16374, <www.un.org/icty/transe54/030218ED.htm> (accessed 22 January 2004).

9. Marko Attila Hoare, "Nothing Is left" [a review essay of six books], *Bosnia Report*, No. 36, 2003, p. 32.

10. Bogdan Denitch, *Ethnic Nationalism: The Tragic Death of Yugoslavia* (Minneapolis: University of Minnesota Press, 1994), p. 52.

11. Daniele Conversi, *German-Bashing and the Breakup of Yugoslavia* (Seattle: Henry M. Jackson School of International Studies of the University of Washington, 1998), p. 8.

12. Beverly Crawford, "Explaining Defection from International Cooperation: Germany"s Unilateral Recognition of Croatia," *World Politics*, Vol. 48, No. 4, 1996. For an alternative interpretation, see Sabrina P. Ramet and Letty Coffin, "German Foreign Policy toward the Yugoslav Successor States, 1991–1999," *Problems of Post-communism*, Vol. 48, No. 1, 2001, pp. 48–64.

13. Brendan Simms, *Unfinest Hour: Britain and the Destruction of Bosnia* (London: Penguin Books, 2001), p. xvii.

14. James Gow, *Triumph of the Lack of Will: International Diplomacy and the Yugoslav War* (New York: Columbia University Press, 1997).

15. Sabrina Petra Ramet, "The Yugoslav Crisis and the West: Avoiding 'Vietnam' and Blundering into 'Abyssinia,'" *East European Politics and Societies*, Vol. 8, No. 1, 1994, pp. 189–219.

16. David Owen, *Balkan Odyssey* (London: Victor Gollancz, 1995): re U.S. opposition to his plan, pp. 100–109, 170, 189, 357, 366; re. recognition, p. 46.

17. Jasna Adler, "The Disintegration of Yugoslavia: Reflections on Its Causes in a Tentative Comparison with Austria-Hungary," in Reneo Lukić, ed., *Rethinking the International Conflict in Communist and Post-communist States: Essays in Honor of Miklós Molnár* (Aldershot, England: Ashgate, 1998), p. 96, my emphasis.

18. *Ibid.*, p. 96.

19. Gow, *Triumph of the Lack of Will,* p. 12.

20. Three examples: Dennison Rusinow, "To Be or Not to Be? Yugoslavia as Hamlet," *UFSI Field Staff Reports, 1990–1991*, No. 18, 1991; V. P. Gagnon, Jr, "Yugoslavia: Prospects for Stability," *Foreign Affairs,* Vol. 70, No. 3, 1991; and Svetozar Stojanović, interview (February 1991), published as "Optimistic about Yugoslavia: Interview with Svetozar Stojanović," *East European Reporter*, Vol. 4, No. 4, 1991. See also Dennison Rusinow, "Yugoslavia: Balkan Breakup?" *Foreign Policy*, No. 83, 1991.

21. Milovan Djilas, comments, in Milovan Djilas, Emmet John Hughes, Lord Trevelyan, and Kei Wakaizumi, "A World Atlas for 2024," *Saturday Review—World*, 24 August 1974, p. 25.

22. These early warnings were reported in Pedro Ramet, "Yugoslavia and the Threat of Internal and External Discontents," *Orbis,* Vol. 28, No. 1, 1984, p. 109. For a comparison of the Yugoslav war with the war in Lebanon, see Florian Bieber, *Bosnien-Herzegowina und der Lebanon im Vergleich. Historische Entwicklung und Politisches System vor dem Bürgerkrieg* (Sinzheim, Germany: Pro Universitate Verlag, 1999).

23. See Pedro Ramet, "Apocalypse Culture and Social Change in Yugoslavia," in Pedro Ramet, ed., *Yugoslavia in the 1980s* (Boulder: Westview Press, 1985), pp. 6–11, 16–20.

24. Ramet, "Yugoslavia and the Threat," p. 114.

25. John Major, in *House of Commons Hansard Debates,* 20 October 1992, < www.publications.parliament.uk/cgi-bin > (accessed 29 January 2004), p. 1.

26. Jovan Cvijić, *Geografski i kulturni položaj Srbije* (Sarajevo, 1914), as summarized in Olivera Milosavljević, *U tradiciji nacionalizma, ili stereotipi srpskih intelektualaca XX veka o 'nama' i 'drugima'"* (Belgrade: Helsinški odbor za ljudska prava u Srbiji, 2002), p. 35.

27. Dinko Tomašić, *Personality and Culture in Eastern European Politics* (New York: George W. Stewart, 1948), pp. 27–28; see also p. 10.

28. *Ibid.*, p. 30.

29. *Ibid.*, p. 31.

30. *Ibid.*, p. 38.

31. *Ibid.*, pp. 35, 218.

32. Sir Neville Henderson's 1929 report is quoted in Arnold Suppan, "Yugoslavism versus Serbian, Croatian, and Slovene Nationalism," in Norman M. Naimark and Holly Case, eds, *Yugoslavism and Its Historians: Understanding the Balkan Wars of the 1990s* (Stanford: Stanford University Press, 2003), p. 128.

33. Branimir Anzulović, *Heavenly Serbia: From Myth to Genocide* (London: Hurst, 1999), p. 67 *et passim.*

34. *Ibid.*, pp. 122–123. On this point, see also Milorad Tomanić, *Srpska crkva u ratu i ratovi u njoj* (Belgrade: Medijska knjižara krug, 2001), pp. 40–45, 56–59.

35. Anzulović, *Heavenly Serbia*, p. 2.

36. *Ibid.*, p. 2.

37. *Ibid.*, pp. 2–3.

38. *Ibid.*, p. 180.

39. *Ibid.*, pp. 8–9.

40. Lenard J. Cohen, *Serpent in the Bosom: The Rise and Fall of Slobodan Milošević* (Boulder: Westview Press, 2001), p. 398, my emphasis.

41. *Ibid.*, p. 82.

42. *Ibid.*, p. 81. For a fuller discussion of Cohen's *Serpent*, see Sabrina P. Ramet, "In Search of the 'Real" Milošević: New Books about the Rise and Fall of Serbia's Strongman," *Journal of Human Rightsi* Vol. 2, No. 3, 2003, pp. 455–466.

43. Lenard J. Cohen, *Broken Bonds: Yugoslavia's Disintegration and Balkan Politics in Transition*, 2nd edn (Boulder: Westview Press, 1995).

44. *Ibid.*, p. 21.

45. *Ibid.*, p. 20.

46. *Ibid.*, p. 246.

47. *Ibid.*, p. 21.

48. *Ibid.*, p. 365, my emphasis.

49. Ivo Banac, "The Fearful Asymmetry of War: The Causes and Consequences of Yugoslavia's Demise," *Daedalus*, Vol. 121, No. 2, 1992, p. 143.
50. *Ibid.*, p. 144.
51. Ivo Goldstein, *Croatia: A History*, trans. Nikolina Jovanović (London: Hurst, 1999), p. 93.
52. Noel Malcolm, *Bosnia: A Short History* (New York: New York University Press, 1994).
53. Mitja Velikonja, *Religious Separation & Political Intolerance in Bosnia-Herzegovina*, trans. Rang'ichi Ng'inja (College Station, TX: Texas A&M University Press, 2003), p. 15.
54. John Major, in *House of Commons Hansard Debates*, 23 June 1993, < www.publications.parliament.uk/cgi-bin > (accessed 29 January 2004), p. 10.
55. Robert D. Kaplan, "Croatianism," *New Republic*, 25 November 1991, p. 18, as quoted in Banac, "The Fearful Asymmetry," p. 142.
56. Samuel P. Huntington, *The Clash of Civilizations and the Remaking of World Order* (New York: Simon & Schuster, 1996), p. 42.
57. *Ibid.*, p. 138.
58. Samuel P. Huntington, *Political Order in Changing Societies* (New Haven: Yale University Press, 1968).
59. Huntington, *The Clash of Civilizations*, p. 208.
60. *Ibid.*, p. 260.
61. Erika Harris, *Nationalism and Democratisation: Politics of Slovakia and Slovenia* (Aldershot, England: Ashgate, 2002), p. 146.
62. Susan L. Woodward, *Socialist Unemployment: The Political Economy of Yugoslavia, 1945–1990* (Princeton: Princeton University Press, 1995), pp. 352, 355, 359, 364.
63. Susan L. Woodward, "Reforming a Socialist State: Ideology and Public Finance in Yugoslavia," *World Politics*, Vol. 41, No. 2, 1989, p. 304.
64. Woodward, *Socialist Unemployment*, p. xv.
65. *Ibid.*, p. 339, 346–347.
66. All of these factors are mentioned by Cvijeto Job in his *Yugoslavia's Ruin: The Bloody Lessons of Nationalism* (Lanham, MD: Rowman & Littlefield, 2002), pp. 62–63.
67. Paul Lendvai, "Yugoslavia without Yugoslavs: The Roots of the Crisis," trans. Lis Parcell, *International Affairs*, Vol. 67, No. 2, 1991, p. 255.
68. Paul Lendvai, "Jugoslawien ohne Jugoslawen. Die Wurzeln der Staatskrise," in Angelika Volle and Wolfgang Wagner, eds, *Der Krieg auf dem Balkan. Die Hilflosigkeit der Staatenwelt* (Bonn: Verlag für Internationale Politik, 1994), pp. 30, 32.
69. Goldstein, *Croatia*, p. 188.
70. Reneo Lukić, *The Wars of South Slavic Succession: Yugoslavia 1991–1993* (Geneva: Graduate Institute of International Studies, Programme for Strategic & International Security Studies, 1993), p. 8. See also Job, *Yugoslavia's Ruin*, p. 61.
71. Lukić, *The Wars of South Slavic Succession,* p. 9.
72. George Schöpflin, "Political Decay in One-Party Systems in Eastern Europe: Yugoslav Patterns," in Pedro Ramet, ed., *Yugoslavia in the 1980s* (Boulder: Westview Press, 1985), p. 309.
73. *Ibid.*, p. 312.
74. John B. Allcock, *Explaining Yugoslavia* (New York: Columbia University Press, 2000), pp. 418–423, 428–429.
75. Steven L. Burg and Paul S. Shoup, *The War in Bosnia-Herzegovina: Ethnic Conflict and International Intervention* (Armonk, NY: M. E. Sharpe, 1999), p. 4.

76. See Sabrina P. Ramet, *Balkan Babel: The Disintegration of Yugoslavia from the Death of Tito to the Fall of Milošević*, 4th edn (Boulder: Westview Press, 2002), pp. 4, 375–377; and Sabrina P. Ramet, *The Three Yugoslavias: The Dual Challenge of State-Building and Legitimation among the Yugoslavs, 1918–2004* (Bloomington and Washington, DC: Indiana University Press and the Wilson Center Press, forthcoming), especially Chapter 1.

77. Those whom I have judged to have been most co-responsible with Milošević for pushing the country toward war are listed in my *Balkan Babel*, p. 71. See also pp. 7, 31.

78. Ramet, *Balkan Babel*, pp. 26–48.

79. *Ibid.*, pp. 49–51.

80. *Ibid.*, pp. 44–45.

81. James J. Sadkovich, *The U.S. Media and Yugoslavia, 1991–1995* (Westport, CT: Praeger, 1998), p. 88.

82. Cohen, *Serpent in the Bosom,* p. 385.

83. Roger D. Petersen, *Understanding Ethnic Violence: Fear, Hatred, and Resentment in Twentieth-Century Eastern Europe* (Cambridge: Cambridge University Press, 2002), p. 251.

84. Ivo Banac, ed., *Eastern Europe in Revolution* (Ithaca, NY: Cornell University Press, 1992); and Ivo Banac, "The Dissolution of Yugoslav Historiography," in Sabrina Petra Ramet and Ljubiša S. Adamovich, eds, *Beyond Yugoslavia: Politics, Economics, and Culture in a Shattered Community* (Boulder: Westview Press, 1995), pp. 39–65.

85. Jasna Dragović-Soso, *"Saviours of the Nation": Serbia's Intellectual Opposition and the Revival of Nationalism* (London: Hurst, 2002).

86. Thomas A. Emmert, "A Crisis of Identity: Serbia at the End of the Century," in Norman M. Naimark and Holly Case, eds, *Yugoslavism and Its Historians: Understanding the Balkan Wars of the 1990s* (Stanford: Stanford University Press, 2003), pp. 176–177.

87. Bariša Krekić, "An Island of Peace in a Turbulent World: Old Ragusans" Statesmanship as a Paradigm for the Modern Balkans," in Norman M. Naimark and Holly Case, eds, *Yugoslavism and Its Historians: Understanding the Balkan Wars of the 1990s* (Stanford: Stanford University Press, 2003), p. 65.

88. Lukić, *The Wars of South Slavic Succession*, pp. 8, 9. See also Reneo Lukić, "Greater Serbia: A New Reality in the Balkans," *Nationalities Papers*, Vol. 22, No. 1, 1994, pp. 49–70.

89. Branka Magaš, *The Destruction of Yugoslavia: Tracking the Break-up 1980–92* (London: Verso, 1993), pp. xiii, 241, 261.

90. Dennison Rusinow, "The Avoidable Catastrophe," in Sabrina Petra Ramet and Ljubiša S. Adamovich, eds, *Beyond Yugoslavia: Politics, Economics, and Culture in a Shattered Community* (Boulder: Westview Press, 1995), pp. 14, 18, 32.

91. Louis Sell, *Slobodan Milošević and the Destruction of Yugoslavia* (Durham, NC: Duke University Press, 2002).

92. Vladimir Tismaneanu, *Fantasies of Salvation: Democracy, Nationalism, and Myth in Post-communist Europe* (Princeton: Princeton University Press, 1998), p. 7.

93. Warren Zimmermann, *Origins of a Catastrophe: Yugoslavia and Its Destroyers*, rev. ed. (New York: Times Books, 1999), p. vii.

94. *Ibid.*, p. vii.

95. *Ibid.*, p. ix.

96. *Ibid.*, p. 71.

97. *Ibid.*, p. 146.

98. For documentation to support this claim, see Borisav Jović, *Poslednji dani SFRJ. Izvodi iz dnevnika* (Belgrade: Politika, 1995), p. 131 (entry of 26 March 1990).

99. John V. A. Fine, "Heretical Thoughts about the Postcommunist Transition in the Once and Future Yugoslavia," in Norman M. Naimark and Holly Case, eds, *Yugoslavism and Its Historians: Understanding the Balkan Wars of the 1990s* (Stanford: Stanford University Press, 2003), pp. 179, 184.

100. *Ibid.*, p. 181.

101. *Ibid.*, p. 184.

102. *Ibid.*, p. 259.

103. In early 1991, there were rumors flying around that Branko Mamula, the retired minister of defense, might seek to play the role of "Yugoslav Jaruzelski." These rumors were fueled by statements given to *Slobodna Dalmacija* (published in the issue of 11 February 1991) by Tudjman's adviser Slaven Letica and by the Croatian defense minister, Martin Špegelj, and by an article written by Viktor Meier and published in *Frankfurter Allgemeine* at the beginning of February 1991. Branko Mamula, *Slučaj Jugoslavija* (Podgorica, Montenegro: CID, 2000), p. 185.

104. Regarding the involvement of Milošević and the Serbian secret police in the planning and organization of these "meetings," see Adam LeBor, *Milošević: A Biography* (Polmont, Scotland: Bloomsbury, 2002), p. 107.

105. Mamula, *Slučaj Jugoslavija*, p. 197.

106. Quoted in Mark Thompson, *Forging War: The Media in Serbia, Croatia, Bosnia and Herzegovina*, rev. edn (Luton: University of Luton Press, 1999), p. 81.

107. For a (partial) list of Milošević's unconstitutional and illegal actions between 1989 and 1991 (never mind later), see Ramet, *Balkan Babel*, pp. 71–72. For further details, see Meier, *Yugoslavia, passim*.

108. Quoted in Sarah A. Kent, "Writing the Yugoslav Wars: English-Language Books on Bosnia (1992–1996) and the Challenges of Analyzing Contemporary History," *American Historical Review*, Vol. 102, No. 4, 1997, p. 1090.

109. LeBor, *Milošević*, pp. 9–10, 34, 254. See also p. 144.

110. Martin Špegelj, *Sjećanja vojnika*, ed. Ivo Žanić, 2nd edn (Zagreb: Znanje, 2001).

111. Mamula, *Slučaj Jugoslavija*, p. 118.

112. *Ibid.*, p. 165.

113. Sell, *Slobodan Milošević*, p. 58.

114. Raif Dizdarević, *Od smrti Tita do smrti Jugoslavije: Svjedočenja* (Sarajevo: Svjedok, 1999), p. 212.

115. *Ibid.*, p. 218, quoting himself.

116. Except for a few observations dealing with some events after that year, Dizdarević's account ends with 1989.

117. *Ibid.*, p. 90.

118. Massimo Nava, *Milosevic. La tragedia di un popolo* (Milan: Rizzoli, 1999), pp. 43–44.

119. Testimony of Ante Marković, TSM-ICTY, 23 October 2003), < www.un.org/icty/transe54/031023ED.htm > (accessed on 13 January 2004).

120. Ivo Banac, "The Dissolution of Yugoslav Historiography," in Sabrina Petra Ramet and Ljubiša S. Adamovich, eds, *Beyond Yugoslavia: Politics, Economics, and Culture in a Shattered Community* (Boulder: Westview Press, 1995), pp. 39–65.

121. Dragović-Soso, *Saviours of the Nation*, note 84.

122. See also Tim Judah, *The Serbs: History, Myth and the Destruction of Yugoslavia* (New Haven: Yale University Press, 1997), pp. 158–160.

123. See also Svetlana Slapšak, "Serbische Alternativen. Was hat den Krieg in Jugoslawien verursacht?" trans. Thomas Bremer, in Alida Bremer, ed., *Jugoslawische (Sch)erben. Probleme und Perspektiven* (Osnabrück and Münster: fibre Verlag, 1993), pp. 165–187.

124. See Sabrina P. Ramet, *Nationalism and Federalism in Yugoslavia, 1962–1991*, 2nd edn (Bloomington: Indiana University Press, 1992), pp. 109–115 *et passim*.
125. Rusinow, "The Avoidable Catastrophe," note 89, p. 21.
126. Jack Snyder, *From Voting to Violence: Democratization and Nationalist Conflict* (New York: W. W. Norton, 2000), p. 29.
127. *Ibid.*, pp. 36, 52–55, 59–60.
128. Juan J. Linz and Alfred Stepan, "Political Identities and Electoral Sequences: Spain, the Soviet Union, and Yugoslavia," *Daedalus*, Vol. 121, No. 2, 1992, p. 126.
129. *Ibid.*, p. 132.
130. Harris, *Nationalism and Democratisation*, note 60, p. 56.
131. *Ibid.*, pp. 61–62.
132. Petersen, *Understanding Ethnic Violence*, especially Chapter 1 and Introduction.
133. *Ibid.*, pp. 32–33.
134. *Ibid.*, p. 19.
135. *Ibid.*, pp. 3–4.
136. *Ibid.*, p. 25.
137. *Ibid.*, p. 83, citing Michael Sells, *The Bridge Betrayed: Religion and Genocide in Bosnia* (Berkeley and Los Angeles: University of California Press, 1998).
138. Liah Greenfeld, *Nationalism: Five Roads to Modernity* (Cambridge, MA: Harvard University Press, 1992).
139. Petersen, *Understanding Ethnic Violence*, p. 237.
140. *Ibid.*, pp. 242–248.
141. Marie-Janine Calic, *Krieg und Frieden in Bosnien-Hercegovina*, rev. edn (Frankfurt: Suhrkamp, 1996), p. 80.
142. *Ibid.*, p. 123.
143. *Ibid.*, p. 131.
144. *Ibid.*, pp. 141–146.
145. Paolo Rumiz, *Masken für ein Massaker. Der manipulierte Krieg: Spurensuche auf dem Balkan*, trans. Friederike Hausmann and Gesa Schröder, rev. edn (Munich: Verlag Antje Kunstmann, 2000), pp. 101–102.
146. *Ibid.*, p. 111.
147. See Sabrina P. Ramet, "Under the Holy Lime Tree: The Inculcation of Neurotic & Psychotic Syndromes as a Serbian Wartime Strategy, 1986–1995," *Polemos* (Zagreb), Vol. 5, Nos 1–2, 2002, pp. 83–97.
148. Albert Bandura, "Moral Disengagement in the Perpetration of Inhumanities," *Personality and Social Psychology Review*, Vol. 3, No. 3, 1999, pp. 193–209.
149. Samuel A. Guttman, "Robert Waelder and the Application of Psychoanalytic Principles to Social and Political Phenomena," *Journal of the American Psychoanalytic Association*, Vol. 34, 1986, pp. 835–862.
150. Herbert C. Kelman, "Violence without Moral Restraint: Reflections on the Dehumanization of Victims and Victimizers," *Journal of Social Issues*, Vol. 29, No. 4, 1973, pp. 25–61.
151. Roderick M. Kramer and David M. Messick, "Getting by with a Little Help from Our Enemies: Collective Paranoia and Its Role in Intergroup Relations," in Constantine Sedikides, John Schopfler, and Chester A. Insko, eds, *Intergroup Cognition and Intergroup Behavior* (Mahwah, NJ: Lawrence Erlbaum, 1998), pp. 233–255.
152. Jo-Ann Tsang, "Moral Rationalization and the Integration of Situational Factors and Psychological Processes in Immoral Behavior," *Review of General Psychology*, Vol. 6, No. 1, 2002, pp. 25–50.

153. See, inter alia, David M. Bersoff, "Why Good People Sometimes Do Bad Things: Motivated Reasoning and Unethical Behavior," *Personality and Social Psychology Bulletin*, Vol. 25, No. 1, 1999, pp. 28–39; Mikloš Biro and Slavica Selaković-Buršić, "Suicide, Aggression and War," *Archives of Suicide Research*, Vol. 2, 1996, pp. 75–79; Carolyn L. Hafer, "Why We Reject Innocent Victims," in Michael Ross and Dale T. Miller, eds, *The Justice Motive in Everyday Life* (Cambridge: Cambridge University Press, 2002), pp. 109–126; Hartmann Hinterhuber, Milan Stern, Thomas Ross, and Georg Kemmler, "The Tragedy of Wars in Former Yugoslavia Seen through the Eyes of Refugees and Emigrants," *Psychiatria Danubina*, Vol. 13, Nos 1–4, 2001, pp. 3–14; Anja Meulenbelt, "Sympathy for the Devil: Thinking about Victims and Perpetrators after Working in Serbia," *Women & Therapy*, Vol. 22, No. 1, 1999, pp. 153–160; Richard Morrock, "The Genocidal Impulse: Why Nations Kill Other Nations," *Journal of Psychohistory*, Vol. 27, No. 2, 1999, pp. 155–164; S. P. Rathee, P. K. Pardal, and T. R. John, "Diagnostic Value of SIS-II among Sub-groups of Psychotic and Neurotic Patients of Armed Forces," *SIS Journal of Projective Psychology & Mental Health*, Vol. 9, No. 1, 2002, pp. 38–48; Robert J. Shoemaker, "The Phenomenon of Dehumanization," *Pennsylvania Psychiatric Quarterly*, Vol. 8, No. 1, 1968, pp. 3–18; and Amoof R. Singh, K. R. Banerjee, and Supraksh Chaudhury, "Mental Health during War: An Experience and Lesson from the Past," *SIS Journal of Projective Psychology & Mental Health*, Vol. 8, No. 2, 2001, pp. 135–140.
154. Misha Glenny, *The Fall of Yugoslavia: The Third Balkan War* (London: Penguin Books, 1992).
155. For a comprehensive study of the Serbian, Croatian, and Bosnian press prior to and during the war, see Thompson, *Forging War*, note 105.
156. After an exhaustive review of theories emphasizing economic factors, ethnic hatreds, nationalism, cultural differences, changes in international politics, the role of individual leaders, the pre-modern character of the Yugoslav state, and structural–institutional factors, Dejan Jović has argued for the advantage of a multi-factor analysis. See D. Jović, *Jugoslavija—država koja je odumrla* (Zagreb: Prometej, 2003), pp. 23–102.

A Theory about the Causes of the Yugoslav Meltdown: The Serbian National Awakening as a "Revitalization Movement"*

Sabrina P. Ramet

The argument to be presented here is that the Yugoslav meltdown involved three factors or sets of factors: first, the various underlying problems such as economic deterioration, political illegitimacy, and structural factors which drove the system toward crisis; second, the presence and persistence of inter-ethnic resentments deriving from irreconcilable national historical narratives in which Yugoslavia's constituent peoples cast each other as "the Enemy" (usually across the Serb–non-Serb cleavage) and specifically stoked by certain ambitious political figures; and third, the emergence, in Serbia, of a national "revitalization movement" led by Slobodan Milošević, nurturing grandiose territorial fantasies. I shall also argue that understanding the Serb national awakening of the late 1980s as a "revitalization movement" helps to understand the nature of what happened in Serbia, in particular how Serb nationalists could construe their *initiatives* as *responses* to some perceived threat coming from outside the community of Serbs, the phases in the development of that movement, and its role in impelling socialist Yugoslavia toward breakup and meltdown.

Of course, the various injustices and perceived injustices perpetrated (or thought to have been perpetrated) during the years 1918–1991 did not "cause" the Yugoslav meltdown. What they did was contribute to maintaining intergroup boundaries and intergroup distrust and resentment, laying down themes on the basis of which it would be conceivable for an ambitious politician to mobilize his or her own group against others. The differences in perceptions of both more remote and more proximate history also help to account for the receptivity of the population to certain propaganda themes, indeed to *different* propaganda themes. It should perhaps be stressed that only the Serbs had a notion of national entitlement, captured in the phrase "Heavenly Serbia," and that only the Slovenes generally recalled their history without portraying themselves as victims. The difference between the behavior of self-conceived victims and those who do not think of themselves as victims is well known to psychologists.

Revitalization and Meltdown

As early as the early 1980s, leading figures in the party were warning about the dangers of "Lebanonization;" by the late 1980s, warnings about crisis and the danger of meltdown had become commonplace in Yugoslavia. Economic deterioration was a driving force in this deadly equation. During the years 1981–1988, produced national income declined every year except 1984 (when there was no growth) and 1986; gross agricultural output declined in four out of the eight years, and the growth in gross industrial output was unsteady.[1] In a word, Yugoslavia was in economic crisis—a crisis also reflected in rising foreign debt, rising unemployment, and rising inflation. People found ways to cut expenses, for example by slashing their use of electricity, and took to the streets in a series of protests. The country tottered toward apparent economic collapse, and people who had been willing to put up with the one-party system became fed up. Magazines such as *NIN, Duga, Start, Zum reporter, Mladina*, and *Svijet* filled their pages with articles and interviews that admitted the depth of the crisis and demanded change. In Slovenia and Croatia there was a considerable amount of grumbling to the effect that they were being pressed to pick up the tab for most of the bad debts accumulated by Yugoslavia. Some leading figures in the party were even admitting that the country was sinking into political crisis and even moral crisis.[2] But the translation from crisis to war was not automatic. To take a people who had been neighbors, in-laws, friends, and comrades and lead them into a fratricidal war involved a choice of strategy; it involved human agency—and money. Where the latter was concerned, Milošević diverted the U.S.$151 million raised among the Serb diaspora supposedly as a Loan for the Reconstruction of Serbia—a campaign with putatively economic purposes—into his war chest.[3]

Half a century ago, Anthony F. C. Wallace published an article outlining his concept of a revitalization movement. He provided the following definition:

> A revitalization movement is defined as a deliberate, organized, conscious effort by members of a society to construct a more satisfying culture. Revitalization is thus, from a cultural standpoint, a special kind of culture change phenomenon: the persons involved in the process of revitalization must perceive their culture, or some major areas of it, as a system (whether accurately or not); they must feel that this cultural system is unsatisfactory; and they must innovate not merely discrete terms, but a new cultural system, specifying new relationships as well as, in some cases, new traits.[4]

The rubric of revitalization movements embraces a wide array of social phenomena including political movements, reform movements of other kinds, religious cults, and utopian experiments. All of these phenomena share some common dynamics. According to Wallace, "[n]o revitalization movement can, by definition, be truly secular, but some can be relatively less religious than others."[5]

Wallace outlined a five-stage process that he considered typical for successful revitalization movements: (1) steady state; (2) period of individual stress; (3) period of cultural distortion; (4) period of revitalization; and (5) new steady state.[6] Although he alluded to the fact that some revitalization movements may fail, he did not outline the stages for failed revitalization movements. I would suggest that the stages typical in such cases would involve: (1) steady state: (2) period of individual stress; (3) period of cultural distortion; (4) period of revitalization, generating widespread euphoria; (5) resistance to the revitalization formula, with obstacles being encountered; (6) suppression or defeat of the revitalization movement; and (7) efforts to establish a new, more satisfactory steady state. I will argue that this model of failed revitalization describes what occurred in Serbia beginning in the early 1980s, and helps to explain both the Yugoslav meltdown and the way in which the Serbian and Croatian regimes mobilized their populations for war.

Steady State

According to Wallace, the first phase, steady state, is characterized by general stability, with most people finding their basic needs being met. "For the vast majority of the population," Wallace writes, "culturally recognized techniques for satisfying needs operate with such efficiency that chronic stress within the system varies within tolerable limits."[7] The point, thus, is not that everyone is happy, but that the "chronic stress" is manageable. In the Yugoslav context, the steady state drew to a close in the late 1970s, as the economy began to deteriorate, essentially reaching the point of bankruptcy by 1979 and generating very real stress among the population, stress which exceeded the capacity of "culturally [*i.e.*, socially] recognized techniques" to cope.[8]

Period of Increased Individual Stress

It is in the second phase that the stage is set for the rise of a revitalization movement. In this phase, members of the society "experience increasingly severe stress" and it becomes possible that the culture "may undergo considerable changes" during this phase.[9] While it is not possible to define exact boundaries for the start and end of this phase, in the Yugoslav case it may be associated with the early 1980s. Included in this phase were the death of Tito, the province-wide riots in Kosovo in April 1981, the rise in self-consciousness of the Serbian Orthodox Church and the Roman Catholic Church in Croatia, the appointment of the commissions headed by Boris Kraigher[10] and Tihomir Vlaškalić, tasked to study the growing dysfunctionality of the economic and political systems, and "a clear decline in the effectiveness of established decision-making institutions and procedures."[11] Discontent flared throughout the country, with Slovenes expressing resentment over the taxes they were paying to help the less developed federal units, Slovenes being especially resentful of the exit tax imposed by the Planinc government (involving a sum of 500,000 dinars to be deposited with the authorities to exit the country), Albanians bitter about their continued underdevelopment, conservative Serbs upset about the extent of federalization, and many Croats quietly nurturing ire and resentment about the quashing of the Croatian spring at the end of 1971. In Montenegro, several thousand shoppers smashed up some fifty shops in downtown Titograd in January 1983, leaving 20 people injured, when it became apparent that supplies of detergent were inadequate. About the same time, more than a thousand factory workers in

41

Zagreb went on strike for two days to demand a 40% increase in pay.[12] More significantly, opinion polls revealed a dramatic decline in the credibility of self-management and in popular confidence in the system. This in turn fueled a wide-ranging debate which splashed onto the pages of Yugoslav journals and in which even the introduction of a two-party system was broached.

Period of Cultural Distortion

Wallace used the term "the mazeway" to refer to the mental image of society and its culture which members of the society share. He believed that the continuation of familiar behavior depended upon the maintenance of a stable mazeway. When the mazeway breaks down, behaviors change. When the mazeway breaks down, people become available for recruitment into new movements, new cults, new patterns of behavior.

Wallace acknowledged that some people (whom he called "rigid") would "prefer to tolerate high levels of chronic stress rather than make systematic adaptive changes in the mazeway." Others slide into alcoholism, drug abuse, "extreme passivity and indolence," the development of "ambivalent dependency relationships," violence, breaches of sexual norms, depression, and/or any of a number of neurotic and psychosomatic syndromes.[13] Tellingly, in this phase, "culture is internally distorted; the elements are not harmoniously related but are mutually inconsistent and interfering."[14] In this pre-revitalization stage, no one is coordinating changes in the mazeway; on the contrary, pressure for change may be coming from various sectors, including literary figures, the Church, and human rights activists. As for the establishment, it is the object of much of the criticism.

In Yugoslavia, "cultural distortion" in the 1980s was most intense among the Serbs. It was the Serbs of Kosovo who mounted three shattering treks to Belgrade to confront legislators and demand protection. It was from the ranks of the Serbian Orthodox Church that a petition emerged for the protection of the Serbian people of Kosovo and their holy shrines. It was the Serbs whose Academy of Sciences and Art drafted the famous memorandum, which sent shock waves through all of Yugoslavia. It was Serbian historians who first began the process of re-examining the way in which the story about World War II had been told, rehabilitating Chetnik leader Draža Mihailović along the way. It was NIN, the leading Serbian weekly magazine, which opened up a long-overdue discussion about the concentration camps run by Tito at Lepoglava and Goli Otok and led the way in a far-ranging re-examination of the Tito era. It was Serbian television that broadcast a Kosovar Serb sobbing as she recounted what she had experienced at the hands of Albanians; the broadcast broke with the Tito-era rules of disengagement and had a mobilizing effect on Serbs. Cumulatively, these sundry breaches of the mazeway set Serbia on a path to revitalization.

Period of Revitalization

The initiation of the period of revitalization coincides with the appearance of a leader who comes to embody the hopes of the nation or group. It is at this point that the sundry, uncoordinated, and up to a point discordant themes from the preceding phase are given a focus and become the fuel for future activity. Wallace was especially interested in movements of *religious* revitalization, which he said were typically born with one or more hallucinatory visions or dreams in which the prophet-to-be believes that she or he sees a supernatural being, whether God or an angel.[15] The vision "also functions as a funeral ritual" in which "the 'dead' way of life is recognized as dead [and] interest shifts to a god, the community, and a new way."[16] As for the visionary, "he shows evidence of a radical inner change in personality soon after the vision experience: a remission of old and chronic physical complaints, a more active and purposeful way of life, greater confidence in interpersonal relations."[17]

One need only imagine Milošević as a latter-day Prince Lazar—not a great stretch of the imagination for many Serbs in the late 1980s—to see how these patterns were replicated in the Serbian case. In 1389, on the eve of his great battle with Sultan Murad's army, the Serbian prince allegedly had a dream in which an angel of God appeared to him and offered him the choice between winning the battle and establishing a great earthly kingdom, on the one hand, and losing the battle, dying a martyr for the Christian faith, and thereby winning a heavenly kingdom, on the other. According to legend, Lazar chose martyrdom and the heavenly kingdom, thereby sanctifying Serbia, celestial Serbia, for all time. For Serbs, this legend also lent their historic claim to Kosovo an air of heavenly sanction.

In April 1987, Milošević, the reincarnated Prince Lazar, was sent to Kosovo to meet with about 300 party delegates in Priština. Most of these delegates were Albanians and the meeting was supposed to be closed to the public; but about 15,000 local Serbs and Montenegrins came to the meeting hall and tried to force their way in. Police stopped them and began to beat them. Then, Milošević raised his hand and ordered the police to stop and to allow the Serbs and Montenegrins to come into the hall. Then, turning to the crowd, he said, "Nobody, either now or in the future, has the right to beat you."[18] Milošević then stayed in the hall through the night, listening to hundreds of Serbs tell their stories blaming Albanian leaders for their suffering. It was an electrifying moment for Milošević, the night that he became a prophet-king. A Serbian journalist noted, "After that night, suddenly there was a psychological change in him. All at once, he discovered he had this power over people."[19] His mentor, Ivan Stambolić, also saw the change in his long-time colleague: "Milošević was transformed, set afire by Kosovo."[20] His declaration that no one should ever beat Serbs again was rebroadcast repeatedly on Serbian television, to the point that it became a kind of mantra, establishing his extra-legal authority.

Serbs began to stage rallies holding portraits of Prince Lazar, Saint Sava, and Slobodan Milošević, and singing songs such as

> The people have a great question:
> Who will replace Tito for us?
> Now we know who the new Tito is,
> Slobodan is his proud name.
> Who[ever] touches, who[ever] touches
> Our Slobodan
> His head will fly, his head will fly
> From his shoulders.[21]

After this transformation, the prophet or prophet-king typically promotes a new cultural system or ideology, according to Wallace, and urges confidence that the community of converts will enjoy supernatural favor.[22] Revitalization movements often renounce the world, rejecting other cultures as evil and corrupt, and build up a "psychology of persecution" in which group members feel that they are facing a hostile world full of people who do not understand them.[23] Focusing on religious cults, a specific type of revitalization movement, Rodney Stark and William Sims Bainbridge concluded that "cults can emerge without authoritative leaders," though, of course, authoritative leaders may also be instrumental in their development, and added that they may develop a radically new framework incrementally, one step at a time.[24] Some religious cults also manifest what might be called "doctrinal escalation," a process in which the doctrines of the cult begin with rather moderate demands and notions and gradually become steadily more radical and more extreme. In this connection, one may recall the Transcendental Meditation movement, which, at its peak around 1975, had about 6,000 members in the U.S. and was telling its adherents that they could aspire to become "Siddhis," defined as "persons who could develop supernormal levels of consciousness, becoming invisible, flying through the sky, and knowing the future."[25]

All of these features were found in the Serb revitalization movement which gathered steam in the mid-1980s. There was, of course, the renunciation of the "wicked West" and the claim to be defending the Orthodox soul from the impure West and the infidel Muslims.[26] Milošević also began making repeated allusions to threats and dangers from outside Serbia. In May 1990, for example, he claimed that the pressures on Serbia "could only be compared to the situation of 1914,"[27] while a statue was erected to Chetnik leader Draža Mihailović, and General Milan Nedić, Serbia's own quisling during World War II, was now declared to be the "architect" of Serbian national unity.[28] Even doctrinal escalation was characteristic of the Serbian revitalization movement. Thus, Milošević began by championing the principle of "one man, one vote" (which, if operationalized according to his formula, would have weakened Slovenia and Croatia, relative to Serbia) and by calling for an "anti-bureaucratic revolution." Since people all over the world are inclined to distrust bureaucracies, this message found a ready audience and, on the face of it, scarcely seemed radical. Milošević even gave speeches in the early days emphasizing that Serbia had no interest in revising its borders with any of the neighboring republics.[29]

But processes of doctrinal escalation typically work quickly. Soon Milošević was demanding and effecting the abolition of the two autonomous provinces, demanding the passage of a fifth post-war constitution (to replace the 1974 constitution), and when the latter objective proved unattainable, pushing for the revision of Serbia's borders after all. Milošević, Ćosić, and other prominent Serbs executed a dramatic escalation when they began to insist that all Serbs were entitled to live in one state, in an expanded Serbia that would embrace all contiguous lands inhabited by Serbs. In due course, Milošević became the organizer and pay-master for processes of ethnic cleansing, diverting about 20% of the Federal Republic of Yugoslavia's (FRY's) gross national product to Serb insurgents in Croatia and Bosnia (according to official figures of the Belgrade government),[30] setting up paramilitary training centers, for example in the Tara valley in Montenegro,[31] and taking the Serbs into a war for which many had no enthusiasm. This is not to suggest that the "prophet-king" was able to anticipate the destructive force of the processes that were unfolding. Quite the contrary, Miloš Vasić has suggested that Milošević "himself was surprised by the fact that the war of ethnic extermination gained such a momentum as to make it a self-supporting suicidal machine."[32] The Serbian revitalization movement even had its scriptures—in the form of the legend of Prince Lazar, the poetry of Njegoš (especially *The Mountain Wreath*), the Srpska Akademija Nauka i Umetnosti (Serbian Academy of Sciences and Art, SANU) memorandum, and the nationalist novels *Vreme smrti* (*A Time of Death*, by Dobrica Ćosić), *The Knife* (by Vuk Drašković), and *Dictionary of the Khazars* (by Milorad Pavić). Be that as it may, these considerations do not in any way mitigate the Belgrade government's primary responsibility for the bloodshed that ensued.

The popular response to Milošević's rhetoric in Serbia was one of euphoria. He was attuned to the Serb historical narrative and touted it *against* the Yugoslav narrative forged by the Communist Party, and he seemed to offer real solutions to problems, rather than merely the continuation of the process of the "harmonization of viewpoints," as per communist practice. But euphoria is a dangerous, even pathological condition, much like infatuation, in which one's sense of reality is severely impacted, one's capacity for rational judgment is dulled, and even one's sense of self is damaged. Moreover, this was a euphoria based on the *Serb* historical narrative, which, unlike the *Yugoslav* historical narrative, could not integrate non-Serbs into a common historical project.

Resistance to Revitalization

Wallace anticipated that there would be resistance. As he noted, a revitalization movement is revolutionary in nature "and almost inevitably will encounter some resistance." The movement may choose some form of adaptation, for example by some form of "doctrinal modification" whether this might involve "adding to, emphasizing, playing down, [or] eliminating selected elements" of the original program.[33] Resistance may also create rifts within the revitalization movement,

45

involving differences over doctrine or strategy or tactics. The rift that developed between Milošević and Karadžić by spring 1993 may be taken as an instance of this.

More particularly, the Serb revitalization movement encountered resistance both internally and externally. Internal resistance came in the form of the consistent liberal critique, articulated by such people as Žarana Papić, Sonja Licht, Vesna Pešić, and Sonja Biserko, and, in some cases, associated with feminism, and the form of an inconsistent anti-war critique, associated with such opposition figures as Vuk Drašković and Zoran Djindjić. It was also manifested in the flight of draft-age men from Serbia, in the well-publicized brain drain from Serbia, in the anti-war rock concerts staged in Belgrade and elsewhere in 1991–1992, and in recurrent but inconsistent criticism from the Serbian Orthodox Church, whose prelates also lent their explicit endorsement to the Serb expansionist project.[34] In May 1992, for example, Patriarch Pavle conducted a mass for peace—this at a time when Serbian forces were making territorial gains in Bosnia—and, that same month, the Holy Synod of the Church issued a statement calling on Milošević to step down from power.[35] Then, on 14 June, the Patriarch led a procession of several thousand angry Serbs through downtown Belgrade, demanding that Milošević resign.

> After reaching the Saborna Church, Patriarch Pavle gave a 10-minute sermon, in which he criticized Milošević obliquely for having spread hatred and conflict in ways "that would shame the devil." After bemoaning recent criticism by "individual people" that the Church was "meddling in politics," the patriarch avowed that "these people ... do not have eyes or do not wish to see what is actually happening with the Serbian nation today, and in what danger the Serbian nation is from outside and inside.[36]

External resistance was demonstrated on the battlefields of Croatia and Bosnia and in the nonviolent resistance of the Albanian people of Kosovo. While the Bosnian government tried, with mixed success, to counter nationalism with a cosmopolitan secularism and the Albanians endeavored, above all, to avoid giving provocation to the better-armed Serbian state, the Croats reacted with a defensive but no less strident or intolerant nationalism (which could not be said to have been purely defensive in Bosnia-Herzegovina). There were, indeed, huge differences between the Croatian national movement, which was not embedded in a revitalization movement, and the Serbian national movement, which derived its sense of entitlement in part from its character as a revitalization movement. Moreover, although reports of repeated appearances by the Blessed Virgin Mary at the Herzegovinan village of Medjugorje, beginning in 1981,[37] were exploited by Croatian nationalists up to a point, the Medjugorje phenomenon remained above all a religious phenomenon and was, in any event, marginal to the Croatian national revival. For all that, however, Tudjman would, in due course, invoke the alleged miracle at Medjugorje in support of the Croatian national program. "The Madonna's appearance," he told a peace conference in May 1993, announced "the re-awakening of the Croatian nation," and suggested that this signified the Virgin's partiality for the Croatian side.[38] David

Bruce MacDonald has argued for a more political reading of Medjugorje than I am suggesting here. In his view, Medjugorje *was* a political phenomenon, which "elevated Croatian Catholicism to a chosen and superior religion."[39] But this is a stretch: although Tudjman, like Milošević, did his best to ingratiate himself with the Church and to instrumentalize the Church for his own purposes, Medjugorje remained, as already stated, a religious phenomenon and for most people it was viewed as such.

The twin themes of victimization and persecution also emerged in the Croatian movement, with the Serbs cast as the historic villains. Branko Miletić, a Croatian historian, asked rhetorically, "What drives the docile Serb peasant to rape, butcher and incinerate his peaceful Muslim or Croat neighbor?"[40] In Miletić's calculation, "Greater Serbianism has cost the lives of some 600,000 Croatians, 400,000 Muslims, 100,000 Albanians, and countless others this century."[41] Croatian writers seemed to put more emphasis,[42] if that is possible, than Serbian writers on the *Načertanije* penned by the Serbian Minister of Internal Affairs Ilija Garašanin in 1844, in which a Serb expansionist project was spelled out. And where the Serbian movement saw the rehabilitation of the Chetniks of World War II, its Croatian counterpart saw the rehabilitation of the Ustaše. Croatian nationalism, at least as instrumentalized by Tudjman and Šušak, had another feature in common with its Serbian counterpart, *viz.*, a program of territorial expansionism. This program was so central to the Croatian project that it was even stated, matter-of-factly, in a textbook said to have been used at the Faculty of Political Science of the University of Zagreb. This textbook asked baldly,

> Does Croatia have the right to assume such a geographical shape as will enable her survival? Of course she does. For Croatia with cancer in her womb—or even without a womb, for the Serbs and the Muslims have taken it—cannot exist long-term, never mind forever. Therefore she has a right to Bosnia-Herzegovina, regardless of who may have lived in Bosnia-Herzegovina, Croats and whoever else.[43]

On the other hand, there was little by way of doctrinal escalation in the Croatian movement, and such euphoria as there was in Tudjman's Croatia was largely limited to the months preceding the outbreak of war.

Instead of euphoria, the hallmark of the Croatian war effort was fear of Serbia and more general anxiety, even, for those fleeing from the front lines, frenzy, but for purposes of building power, fear and frenzy were as useful as euphoria. Moreover, given the commitment of Tudjman and Gojko Šušak, his eventual defense minister, to a program of territorial expansion at Bosnia's expense, not to mention their common desire to build a national state as rapidly and as irreversibly as possible, war was an essential part of their strategy. This is why Šušak, who was already a high-ranking adviser to President Tudjman, went to Borovo Selo in April 1991, accompanied by some Croatian recruits, to fire three shoulder-launched Ambrust missiles into the Serb-populated village.[44] For that matter, Martin Špegelj has argued that Tudjman did not want to see the war end in 1991, but specifically wanted it to continue for some years, in order to maintain conditions in which portions of Bosnia-Herzegovina might be annexed to the Croatian state.[45] Of course, one may well wonder how the international community, which had extended diplomatic recognition to Croatia only grudgingly, would have reacted had Croatia managed to mount a serious operation in early 1992.[46] But, as in Serbia, there were liberal pacifists who stood up to the Tudjman regime and opposed the nationalist tide. Among these people one may mention Ivo Banac, Josip Reihl-Kir, and the editorial board of *Feral Tribune.*

Does the use of Wallace's theory suggest that all sides were equally guilty? Frankly, I cannot imagine how this inference could be drawn, since Wallace's theory provides a means for explaining how and why the problem began in Serbia and provides a way to highlight Milošević's culpability as the "cult leader" of the movement. Does Wallace's theory let the international community off the hook, by suggesting that the situation was completely hopeless from the start? Again, anyone drawing this conclusion is likely to be merely dragging his or her own intellectual baggage into the discussion. Quite the contrary, insofar as Western diplomats might have been expected to have some understanding of political processes which were out of the ordinary and, for that matter, involving repeated breaches of the national constitution and laws of the land, one could have expected that some remedial action could have been taken before more than 200,000 persons lost their lives.[47]

Summary

The Serbian revitalization movement of which Dobrica Ćosić and Slobodan Milošević became champions was ultimately defeated by a combination of two lost wars, a failed economy, the growing despair and disenchantment of Serbs, and a finally successful effort on the part of the anti-Milošević opposition to mount a coordinated electoral challenge to his rule. But the effort to establish a more satisfactory steady state in the wake of the overthrow of Milošević has hit a reef—the reef of Serbian nationalism. The ideas associated with the Serbian revitalization movement are still in circulation in Serbia, as evinced in the recent electoral success of the Serbian Radical Party. The same judgment cannot be passed on the Hrvatska Demokratska Zajednica (Croatien Democratic Community, HDZ), which is increasingly assuming a moderate cast; certainly, unlike Šešelj or Koštunica, for that matter, Sanader has not made well-publicized statements suggesting a continued interest in annexing parts of Bosnia-Herzegovina.

But the sixth and seventh stages in the life of the Serbian revitalization movement—defeat and efforts to build a new steady state—do not occupy us here. What does concern us is the character of the Serb nationalist movement as a revitalization movement. It is also important to stress that there was no comparable movement in either Croatia or Bosnia, let alone Slovenia or Kosovo. But what does it matter if the nationalist mobilization in Serbia may be understood as a revitalization movement? First, this may help us to understand the appeal of nationalist movements as stress-reducing mechanisms. Second, it provides a clue as to the way in which nationalist mobilization effects radical changes in perception and behavior. Third, it highlights the relationship between the "extreme emotional excitement"[48] generated by nationalist mobilization and the aforementioned changes. Fourth, understanding nationalist mobilization in this way clarifies the role of the nationalist leader, who figures thus as a cult leader, thereby explaining his or her striking ability to act outside the law. And fifth, this understanding suggests that "de-programming" may be required, in order to return a mobilized society to something approximating its premobilized state.[49] In the absence of such "de-programming, as Robert George has suggested,[50] bad "moral ecology" can have consequences that may carry over to influence successive generations directly or indirectly.

Conclusion

The typical questions raised about the Yugoslav meltdown include: Was it "inevitable"? What role was played by specific persons or to what extent was the meltdown the result of "historical forces"? Whose fault was it? And, among less informed members of the general public, why do these people hate each other so much? The foregoing analysis suggests, however, that these questions are missing the bigger picture or, in the case of the last question, totally misguided. One may, of course, isolate individual factors such as the economic downturn, the problem of legitimacy, the fissure lines provided by the federal system, the presence of rival historical narratives, and the rise of ambitious nationalist leaders, in the persons of Milošević and Tudjman. Such an analysis certainly establishes the basic factors at play, but not necessarily *why* they produced *this particular result*, rather than some other result. The descent to internecine conflict involved a syndrome in which these sundry factors came into play, were assigned values, and operationalized. Economic deterioration, for example, was factored into discourses of resentment and blame, so that one could find someone (some other nation) to blame for one's own nation's economic difficulties: if one was a Serb, one could blame the Slovenes or the Croats or the Bosniaks; if one was an Albanian, one could blame the Serbs; if one was a Slovene, one could blame the Serbs or the underdeveloped areas or the inefficient managers of the federal fund. As Ljubomir Madžar has put it, "each one of the eight Yugoslav republics and provinces emphasized its alleged exploitation, and 'proved' that the system was set specifically against its interests."[51] The problem of legitimacy was also filtered through the lenses of the historical narrative, so that the system bequeathed by Tito was not just "the communist system," but (for Serbs) "the anti-Serb federal system, created by the Croat, Tito" or (for Croats) "the anti-Croat communist system, dominated by Serbs at the expense of Croats" or (for Albanians) "the land of the South Slavs, in which non-Slavs are second class citizens and in which the legitimate rights of the Albanians are quashed." This account already reveals the way in which the federal system itself was disparaged and demonized, even by those republic elites who owed their power to the federal principle. The Serbian party was, after 1974, arguably the most frustrated with the constitutional order, but discontent extended to Kosovo, Croatia, Slovenia, and elsewhere in the system. But discussions of the federal system were typically figured into the context set by the given historical narrative so that this factor too was filtered, interpreted, and comprehended through national lenses. And finally, Milošević as the "prophet-king" of the Serbs and Tudjman as the "all-knowing Father" of the Croats were viewed differently from one republic to the next, and framed within the perspective of each nation's historical narrative.

Revitalization movements appear because there is widespread discontent. In both the Serbian and Croatian cases, protests and memoranda emerging from the national-ist opposition in the course of the 1970s and 1980s (in the Croatian case, one may think of people such as Marko Veselica, Dobroslav Paraga, and for that matter Tudjman himself) established a template for potential nationalist mobilization, a template invoking elements of the historical narrative, a template that could be appropriated by an ambitious politician at the right moment. But revitalization movements have other features which are by no means irrelevant to this analysis. First of all, they often function as mechanisms for pecuniary accumulation, drawing funds from the members of the movement and concentrating them in the coffers of the movement leaders: the Unification Church of the Rev. Moon has operated in this way as did the Transcendental Meditation movement; so too did the Milošević and Tudjman regimes, which enriched their inner circles at the expense of their soci-eties—though politicians closer to the United States of America have shown that the use of public office for private enrichment is not limited to "revitalization" move-ments. Second, the radical break with the pre-existing society which revitalization movements effect is so rapid that their ultimate course cannot be controlled; this is why violence, even self-destructive violence, is commonly associated with revitaliza-tion movements, or at least with failed revitalization movements. Third, given the speed with which revitalization movements seek to refashion the culture, it is essentially inevitable that a large portion of their members (in this case, members of the societies) will be affected psychologically by the strife that such movements may engender. Those who escape with mere remorse or depression are the lucky ones; those who suffer post-traumatic stress disorder or other psychiatric disorders are less fortunate.[52] And fourth, the phenomenon of collective euphoria that is associated with revitalization movements in their crucial early phases provides at least part of the explanation of why people who had lived side by side as neighbors and friends could be mobilized to kill each other.[53]

NOTES

* I am deeply grateful to Mark Biondich, Audrey Budding, Cathie Carmichael, Eric D. Gordy, Danica Fink-Hafner, Matjaž Klemenčič, Dunja Melčić, Jim Sadkovich, Džemal Sokolović, Ludwig Steindorff, and Frances Trix for their most helpful comments on an earlier draft of this article. I also wish to thank Mark Biondich, Audrey Budding, Danica Fink-Hafner, Matjaž Klemenčič, and Dunja Melčić for sending me helpful materials.

1. See the detailed figures in Sabrina P. Ramet, *Social Currents in Eastern Europe: The Sources and Consequences of the Great Transformation*, 2nd edn (Durham, NC: Duke University Press, 1995), pp. 33–35.

2. See the discussion in Pedro Ramet, "Yugoslavia and the Threat of Internal and External Discontents," *Orbis,* Vol. 28, No. 1, 1984, pp. 103–121.

3. Paul Hockenos, *Homeland Calling: Exile Patriotism & the Balkan Wars* (Ithaca, NY: Cornell University Press, 2003), pp. 126–127.

4. Anthony F. C. Wallace, "Revitalization Movements," *American Anthropologist*, Vol. 58, No. 2, 1956, p. 265.

5. *Ibid.*, p. 277.

6. *Ibid.*, p. 268.

7. *Ibid.*, p. 268.

8. Michael Palairet, "The inter-regional struggle for resources and the fall of Yugoslavia," in Lenard J. Cohen and Jasna Dragović-Soso, eds, *The Dissolution of Yugoslavia* (forthcoming), pp. 4–5.

9. Wallace, "Revitalization Movements," p. 269.

10. This is the correct Slovenian spelling of his name. In Serbian sources, his name has conventionally been written "Krajger."

11. Steven L. Burg, "Elite Conflict in Post-Tito Yugoslavia," *Soviet Studies*, Vol. 38, No. 2, 1986, p. 170.

12. Ramet, "Yugoslavia and the Threat," p. 108.

13. Wallace, "Revitalization Movements," p. 269.

14. *Ibid.*, p. 269.

15. Anthony F. C. Wallace, "The Dekanawideh Myth Analyzed as the Record of a Revitalization Movement," *Ethnohistory*, Vol. 5, No. 2, 1958, pp. 119–120. Wallace's point is that political programs may *sometimes* be associated with revitalization movements and that *some* revitalization movements are religious in character. There is not a single line in his classic article devoted to the relationship between religion and nationalism.

16. Wallace, "Revitalization Movements," p. 270.

17. *Ibid.*, p. 271.

18. As quoted in the *Chicago Tribune*, 17 October 1988.

19. As quoted in the *Washington Post*, 4 February 1990.

20. As quoted in Laura Silber and Allan Little, *The Death of Yugoslavia* (London: Penguin Books and BBC Books, 1995), p. 37.

21. As quoted in Nebojša Popov, "Serbian Populism and the Fall of Yugoslavia," *Uncaptive Minds*, Vol. 8, Nos 3–4, 1995/1996, p. 99. Popov's article was originally published in Serbian in *Vreme* (Belgrade), 24 May 1993.

22. Wallace, "Revitalization Movements," p. 273.

23. John J. Collins, *The Cult Experience: An Overview of Cults, Their Traditions and Why People Join Them* (Springfield, IL: Charles C. Thomas, 1991), pp. 6, 54, citing the work of Willa Appel, and Luther A. Gerlach and Virginia Hine.

24. Rodney Stark and William Sims Bainbridge, *The Future of Religion: Secularization, Revival, and Cult Formation* (Berkeley and Los Angeles: University of California Press, 1985), p. 183.
25. Collins, *The Cult Experience*, pp. 55–56.
26. On this point, see Ivan Čolović, *The Politics of Symbol in Serbia: Essays in Political Anthropology*, trans. Celia Hawkesworth (London: C. Hurst, 2002).
27. As quoted in Popov, "Serbian Populism," p. 100.
28. *Ibid.*, p. 104.
29. See Slobodan Milošević, *Godine Raspleta*, 2nd edn (Belgrade: Beogradski izdavačko-grafički zavod, 1989), p. 264.
30. As cited in Marie-Janine Calic, *Krieg und Frieden in Bosnien-Hercegovina*, rev. edn (Frankfurt: Suhrkamp, 1996), p. 171.
31. Paolo Rumiz, *Masken füur ein Massaker. Der manipulierte Krieg: Spurensuche auf dem Balkan*, trans. Friederike Hausmann and Gesa Schrüoder (Munich: Verlag Antje Kunstmann, 2000), p. 143.
32. Miloš Vasić, "The Yugoslav Army and the Post-Yugoslav Armies," in David A. Dyker and Ivan Vejvoda, eds, *Yugoslavia and After: A Study in Fragmentation, Despair and Rebirth* (Harlow, England: Longman, 1996), p. 132, as quoted in Tom Gallagher, *The Balkans after the Cold War: From Tyranny to Tragedy* (London and New York: Routledge, 2003), p. 116.
33. Wallace, "Revitalization Movements," pp. 274–275.
34. Milorad Tomanić, *Srpska crkva u ratu i ratovi u njoj* (Belgrade: Medijska knjižara, 2001), especially pp. 39–40, 43–44, 56, 58–59.
35. Memorandum of the Holy Synod of Bishops of the Serbian Orthodox Church, *Politika*, 29 May 1992, p. 10, translated in Foreign Broadcast Information Service (FBIS), *Daily Report* (Eastern Europe), 11 June 1992, p. 56.
36. Sabrina Petra Ramet, "The Serbian Church and the Serbian Nation," in Sabrina Petra Ramet and Ljubiša S. Adamovich, eds, *Beyond Yugoslavia: Politics, Economics, and Culture in a Shattered Community* (Boulder: Westview Press, 1995), p. 117.
37. For a provocative reading of the alleged apparition, see Mart Bax, "Mass Graves, Stagnating Identification, and Violence: A Case Study in the Local Sources of 'the War' in Bosnia Hercegovina," *Anthropological Quarterly*, Vol. 70, No. 1, 1997, pp. 11–19.
38. As quoted in David Bruce MacDonald, *Balkan Holocausts? Serbian and Croatian Victim-Centred Propaganda and the War in Yugoslavia* (Manchester: Manchester University Press, 2002), p. 120.
39. *Ibid.*, pp. 121–122.
40. As quoted in *ibid.*, p. 210.
41. As quoted in *ibid.*, p. 210.
42. See, for example, Dušan Bilandžić *et al.*, *Croatia between War and Independence* (Zagreb: University of Zagreb and OKC, 1991), pp. 22–23.
43. Petar Vučić, *Politička sudbina Hrvatske. Geopolitičke i geostrateške karakterike Hrvatske* (Zagreb, 1995), p. 300, as quoted in Rusmir Mahmutćehajić, *The Denial of Bosnia*, trans. Francis R. Jones and Marina Bowder (University Park, PA: Pennsylvania State University Press, 2000), p. 74.
44. Gallagher, *The Balkans after the Cold War*, pp. 60–61. See also Ludwig Steindorff, *Kroatien. Vom Mittelalter bis zur Gegenwart* (Regensburg and Munich: Verlag Friedrich Pustet & Süudosteuropa-Gesellschaft, 2001), p. 220.
45. Martin Špegelj, *Sjećanja vojnika*, ed. Ivo Žanić (Zagreb: Znanje, 2001), pp. 218–219, 292, *et* passim.

46. Špegelj's argument is that the Croatian Army could have retaken all the lands occupied by Serbian paramilitaries and the Jugosloverska Narodna Armija (Yugoslav People's Army, JNA) by sometime in spring at the latest. For his evidence, see Špegelj, *Sjećanja vojnika,* passim.

47. For a clear expostulation of the culpability of the international community, see James Gow, *The Triumph of the Lack of Will: International Diplomacy and the Yugoslav War* (London: Hurst, 1997); also Sabrina P. Ramet, "The Yugoslav Crisis and the West: Avoiding 'Vietnam' and Blundering into 'Abyssinia,'" East European Politics and Societies, Vol. 8, No. 1, 1994, pp. 189–219.

48. Collins, *The Cult Experience*, p. 8, citing Robert S. Ellwood, Jr.

49. The concerted Allied effort after World War II to "de-program" and "re-program" the people of Germany, Austria, and Italy through carefully tailored restructuring of the educational and media systems and by engaging the churches in a dialogue of toleration stands as an important historical example of such "de-programming." The absence of any even remotely comparable international effort in post-Dayton Serbia is surely not unrelated to the persistence of support for Vojislav Šešelj's Serbian Radical Party. Regarding the Allied effort, see book by John H. Herz (ed.), *From Dictatorship to Democracy: Coping with the Legacies of Authoritarianism and Totalitarianism* (Westport, CN: Greenwood Press, 1982).

50. See Robert P. George, *Making Men Moral: Civil Liberties and Public Morality* (Oxford and New York: Oxford University Press, 1993), introduction and Chapter 1.

51. Ljubomir Madžar, "Who Exploited Whom?" in Nebojša Popov, ed., *The Road to War in Serbia: Trauma and Catharsis*, ed. Drinka Gojković (Budapest: Central European University Press, 2000), p. 173.

52. Interview research conducted among 534 adults from families living in the Varaždin Bosnian refugee camp in Croatia in 1996 and 1999 found that those interviewed suffered from "high levels of chronic psychiatric disorders and disability." Parallel research among 206 Bosnian refugees in Sweden found that their "symptoms included sleeping problems, nightmares, depression, startle reactions, a tendency toward isolation, irritability, emotional difficulty, bodily tension, and fear of places or situations resembling the traumatic event." Richard F. Mollica, Narcisa Sarajlić, Miriam Chernoff, James Lavelle, Iris Sarajlić Vuković, and Michael P. Massagli, "Longitudinal Study of Psychiatric Symptoms, Disability, Mortality, and Emigration Among Bosnian Refugees," *Journal of the American Medical Association*, Vol. 286, No. 5, 2001, p. 553; and "Civil War Stress," *Journal of the American Medical Association*, Vol. 281, No. 6, 1999, p. 503.

53. For further discussion of this point, see Calic, *Krieg und Frieden*, pp. 141–146.

Grassroots Groups, Milošević or Dissident Intellectuals? A Controversy over the Origins and Dynamics of the Mobilisation of Kosovo Serbs in the 1980s

Nebojša Vladisavljević

The mobilisation of Kosovo Serbs, barely noticeable from the capital initially but highly visible at the centre political stage between 1986 and 1988, played an important part in the political struggles of the late socialist Yugoslavia. The prevailing view in the literature is that Kosovo Serbs were little more then passive recipients of the attitudes and actions of high officials and dissident intellectuals. The elite thesis says that Belgrade-based dissident intellectuals initiated and guided the mobilisation of Kosovo Serbs, aiming to undermine the party's approach to Yugoslavia's national question and to initiate reassessment of the official policy on Kosovo and Serb–Albanian relations. According to the thesis, Milošević then took over and orchestrated the action of various groups of Kosovo Serbs in order to make the case for the removal of Kosovo's autonomy.[1] The intellectuals and Milošević have generally supported this interpretation, claiming their role in the events leading to the constitutional change to the disadvantage of Kosovo Albanians in 1989–1990.

The prevailing view on the mobilisation of Kosovo Serbs in the 1980s requires attention partly because it reflects broader debates among specialists on the former Yugoslavia and socialist and non-democratic regimes in general. Firstly, the elite thesis originates from the focus on elites, high politics and personalities, especially Milošević, as well as on the discourse rather than behaviour of political actors in research on the disintegration of Yugoslavia. Secondly, the thesis provides an implicit theory about the emergence and timing of mobilisation in socialist party-states. It is based on two, seemingly assumptions. One assumption is that the increase in grievances, originating from the deterioration of the relative position of a group, leads to the protest of its members. Since the mobilisation occurred at a time when the position of Serbs in relation to Albanians in Kosovo was not deteriorating and both the scale of their mobilisation and the inter-ethnic incidents that triggered protests were repeatedly exaggerated, many concluded that elites had a decisive role in the events. Another assumption is that the prospect of a sustained autonomous mobilisation of non-elite actors in a socialist party-state was hardly realistic and that only high officials and, to a smaller extent, dissident intellectuals possessed the resources required to make this happen.

The prevailing view on the mobilisation of Kosovo Serbs is based largely on the testimonies of Milošević's opponents in Serbia's leadership, which few bothered to reassess in the context of Serbia's repressive policies towards Kosovo Albanians in the 1990s. Ivan Stambolić, for example, claimed that protests, though rooted in legitimate concerns of Kosovo Serbs, were orchestrated by a Belgrade-based "nationalist directorate," meaning dissident intellectuals and Dobrica Ćosić, a well-known dissident novelist who had been purged from the higher party ranks for his disapproval of the party's policy on Kosovo in 1968, and amplified by Milošević.[2] However, the elite thesis is not supported by evidence. It merely reflects the lack of information about the collective action of Kosovo Serbs before 1988, since Serb–Albanian relations were then still a taboo topic outside official organisations. This problem is associated with the study of popular protest in general and in non-democratic states in particular. Since it is not easy to study groups that do not produce and store documents and are on the margins of political life, scholars often focus on documents produced by intellectuals supporting a social movement.

Drawing on previously unavailable sources, I have found that various grassroots groups of Kosovo Serbs played a decisive role in the mobilisation, originating from the post-1966 twist in the politics of inequality and their rapid demographic decline in Kosovo. I show that the mobilisation of Kosovo Serbs was autonomous through a close look into their protest networks, demands and protest strategies as well as their links with the dissident intellectuals, other confidants and high officials of Yugoslavia, Serbia and Kosovo. The high officials tolerated the mobilisation partly because of the political changes that occurred in the first half of the 1980s, partly because of the small scale of mobilisation and partly due to the moderate strategies of the protest groups. Having in mind the episodes of mobilisation in socialist Yugoslavia, such as the 1968 and 1981 protests of Kosovo Albanians, it is hardly surprising that changes in political context favourable to a group, rather than a deterioration of its relative position, often lead to the protest of its members. The argument in this article only partly touches upon the role of institutional factors in the rise of the movement of Kosovo Serbs, since I have discussed this relationship elsewhere.[3]

The Politics of Inequality and the Demographic Decline of Kosovo Serbs

The mobilisation of Kosovo Serbs in the 1980s originated from consequences of the post-1966 shift in the politics of inequality and the rapid demographic decline of Kosovo Serbs in relation to Kosovo Albanians. The policy of the League of Yugoslav Communists on Kosovo, a part of its approach to Yugoslavia's national question, proved unable to prevent the continuation of the pre-1945 politics of inequality, which was to the disadvantage of one or the other ethnonational group. Aware of the hostility of Kosovo Albanians towards the state and regime after the war, the Communist leadership sought their cooperation. The new government designated Kosovo as an autonomous region in Serbia, banned post-1918 Serb settlers from returning to the region after they had been expelled during the Second World War, opened Albanian-language schools, encouraged the cultural emancipation of Kosovo Albanians and increasingly financed development of this peripheral region. However, a range of administrative restrictions of the rights of Kosovo Albanians remained in place for security reasons, since Albania backed Stalin in the 1948 break with Yugoslavia. There was no adequate representation of Kosovo Albanians in government due to the party's policy of staffing the state apparatus with its long-serving members, most of whom during and after the war were Serbs.

A major political change in Kosovo occurred after the 1966 fall of Aleksandar Ranković, a vice-president of Yugoslavia long in charge of the security apparatus. Since most excesses of the police state had occurred in Kosovo, and some thought this to be associated with disproportionate representation of Serbs, a policy of positive discrimination was introduced to change the ethnonational make-up of the party-state and public sector. The party developed a range of policies to meet the growing demands of the Kosovo Albanians and granted more autonomy to the province in the process of the radical federalisation of Yugoslavia between 1967 and 1974. Kosovo and Vojvodina, earlier little more than administrative regions of Serbia, were granted status similar to that of republics while Serbia effectively lost jurisdiction in these parts of its territory. The new ethnonational configuration of the party-state organs and public sector and the lack of control by the central organs resulted in the shift from the policy of national emancipation of Kosovo Albanians to domination over non-Albanian population. While open discriminatory policies were largely avoided, in real life there were inequalities in the use of language, access to jobs in the huge state-controlled sector of the economy, allocation of public housing and, most importantly, inadequate protection for the rights and property of Kosovo Serbs by the courts and law enforcement agencies. Cases in which Serbs were targets of nationalist violence or their property was damaged tended to be disregarded in a variety of ways. The police officers repeatedly avoided bringing charges against Albanians, especially in areas where Serbs were a small minority, or the cases remained unresolved in the courts of law for years. Alternatively, law enforcement agencies failed to implement court decisions. Local authorities frequently turned down requests by Serbs for various licences and permits.[4]

From the 1960s Kosovo Serbs faced a rapid demographic decline, which generated an acute sense of insecurity in this community. While the proportion of Albanians and Serbs in Kosovo's population remained relatively stable in the period between 1948 and 1961 (68.5–67.1% and 27.5%, respectively), in the following two decades the proportion of the former increased from 67.1% to 77.4% and that of the latter decreased from 27.5% to 14.9%,[5] and continued to decline in the 1980s. Critical to the demographic decline of the Kosovo Serbs was the much higher rate of population growth of Kosovo Albanians, which largely resulted from a higher birth rate than the Kosovo Serbs'. The higher birth rate in turn originated from underdevelopment and traditional characteristics of this community, especially the subordinate position of women. A steady migration of Kosovo Serbs out of the province contributed to the demographic decline, in terms of their decreasing absolute numbers and shrinking territorial dispersion, and intensified their feelings of insecurity. The 1981 Yugoslav census listed around 110,000 Serbs from Kosovo living in other parts of Yugoslavia, of whom 85,000 had left the province between 1961 and 1981.[6] In the 1980s, outmigration continued. In other words, nearly a third of Kosovo Serbs had moved out of the autonomous province since 1961.

The findings of the survey conducted in 1985–1986 among Serbs who had left Kosovo indicate that more than three-quarters of the emigration originated from non-economic factors, mainly verbal pressure, damage to property or seizure of crops and land, violence (assaults, fights, stoning, attacks on children and women, serious injury, attempted and committed rape), trouble at work and inequalities in the public sector. What also emerged from the survey was that there was a clear territorial pattern of emigration largely resulting from the level of pressure and inequalities. The latter was inversely related to the proportion of Serbs in a settlement, and the critical point for a major increase in the pressure was if their numbers dropped below 20–30%. This finding was compatible with evidence from the official census that there was a strong trend towards emigration of Serbs from settlements where they accounted for less than 30% of the population.[7] Therefore, the decreasing proportion of Serbs in a settlement led to a sharp increase in pressure and inequalities, which in turn resulted in emigration. While open discriminatory policies were generally, though not always, avoided, most cases of discrimination occurred because of the lack of protection for Kosovo Serbs by the courts and law enforcement agencies.

The mix of the politics of ethnonational inequality, demographic decline and steady migration out of Kosovo resulted in mounting grievances among Kosovo Serbs. In the early 1970s a number of Kosovo Serb officials raised in Kosovo's party organs the issue of the growing Albanisation of the province and the problems this brought to the non-Albanian population. Miloš Sekulović and Jovo Šotra pointed to growing pressure on Serbs, especially those living in the countryside, to emigrate from the province as well as their inadequate protection by the law enforcement agencies, their problems in education and the obstacles to their finding employment. Kadri Reufi, an ethnic Turk, demanded that the leadership investigate the causes of the deteriorating position of this minority and claimed that the number of Turks in Kosovo was significantly reduced in the 1971 census because they were labelled Albanians. All three were removed from the Provincial Committee and public life, the effect of which was to silence other non-Albanian politicians.[8] The appeals of Serb party members and ordinary Serbs to local authorities and the provincial leadership were either ignored or rejected and the appellants harassed.

Emerging Protest Networks and Their Allies

The grievances of Kosovo Serbs could not translate into collective action in a political context hostile to any reference to their concerns, but accumulated over time and eventually resulted in the high level of politicisation of Kosovo Serbs. As a local observer put it, "in the southern socialist autonomous province each and every head of a Serb household who takes himself seriously keeps a library of petitions, appeals, pamphlets and newspaper clips."[9] The political change ultimately opened space for the collective action of various groups of Kosovo Serbs. In 1981 protests of Kosovo Albanians swept through the autonomous province. A student protest over socioeconomic issues turned into large-scale demonstrations with a demand for a republic of Kosovo. The government declared a state of emergency, deployed tanks and security forces, closed schools and factories and suppressed demonstrations. The scale of protests apparently surprised the federal leadership and raised fears of the rise of a major separatist movement. High officials now increasingly acknowledged inequalities facing the non-Albanian population, in terms of the use of language, access to jobs in the state-controlled part of the economy, allocation of public housing and inadequate protection of their rights and property by the courts and law enforcement agencies. Kosovo's high officials came under much closer scrutiny of the federal leadership and Albanian–Serb relations in Kosovo ceased to be under their exclusive control. The prevention of outmigration of Serbs and the tackling of their other concerns now became part of the party's policy.

The political change raised the expectations of Kosovo Serbs that the authorities would fully address their grievances. Soon, however, many from this community felt that the new policy had only partly been put into practice and the emigration continued. Some believed that the high officials of Yugoslavia and Serbia were not aware of the full scale of the problem, and thus arranged a number of private meetings, at times involving large delegations, with the officials and other people they thought to be influential. They met Nikola Ljubičić, president of Serbia's state presidency (1982–1984), high party officials in Montenegro, Svetozar Vukmanović-Tempo, a retired member of Tito's old guard, and Branko Pešić, a Belgrade mayor, among others.[10] In most cases the delegations were given a sympathetic hearing and assurances that the new party's course, including the policies aimed at halting the emigration of Serbs, would be implemented.

Simultaneously, a growing number of ordinary people, mainly in predominantly Serb settlements, attended local meetings of the official political organisations, mostly those of the Socialist Alliance of the Working People (SAWP, formerly the People's Front), to raise their concerns. In Kosovo Polje, a suburb of Priština with a dominant Serb population, roughly thirty political outsiders regularly debated various issues and forwarded the meetings' minutes to high officials at all levels, from Priština and Kosovo to Serbia and the federation. Although remaining within the boundaries of officially permitted dissent, they increasingly laid blame for the inequalities on Kosovo's officials, both Albanians and Serbs. Early on the core of this group, namely Kosta Bulatović, Boško Budimirović and Miroslav Šolević, jointly prepared the meetings and gradually shifted the agenda from local problems to the issues of broader political significance.[11] Parallel developments unfolded in other predominantly Serb settlements.

Despite some successes, such as that Priština's and Kosovo's officials periodically attended the meetings in Kosovo Polje, the debaters felt that the authorities would not take their problems seriously unless they gained broader support among Kosovo Serbs. Bulatović, Budimirović and Šolević therefore extended their activities beyond the official organisations and started mobilising support at the grassroots. In 1985 they extended the core group to include as informal advisors Zoran Grujić, a university professor, and Dušan Ristić, a former Kosovo high official. They agreed that the post-1981 party line on Kosovo was adequate and that they should only press the authorities to implement that policy.[12] In late October 1985 the Kosovo Polje group sent a petition to high officials of Yugoslavia and Serbia. They protested against discrimination aimed at Kosovo Serbs, and asked for the protection of their rights and the establishment of law and order. They pointed out that Kosovo was getting increasingly "ethnically clean" of Serbs, accused Kosovo's officials of the tacit approval of forced migration of Serbs out of the region and demanded that Yugoslavia's and Serbia's authorities bring that trend to a halt.[13] About 2,000 people signed the petition within ten days and by April 1986 the number of signatories had multiplied several times.

In 1986 prominent activists initiated several highly visible protests and a series of small-scale local protest events. They sent three large delegations to the capital to meet high officials of Yugoslavia and Serbia, namely in late February, early April and early November. The protest events also included a highly visible protest march of several hundred people, which unfolded under the label of collective emigration just before the party congress in May, and a number of large public meetings in Kosovo Polje, including one before Serbia's party leader Ivan Stambolić.[14] There was also a series of small-scale protests across the autonomous province, mostly in the form of public meetings or outdoor public gatherings, organised in response to specific cases of nationalist-related violence. As people became aware of the advantages of non-institutional action, they started petitioning local authorities, and sometimes managers of large state enterprises, to protest against discrimination at work.[15]

The main consequence of various post-1981 initiatives were the incipient and unconnected networks of activists and supporters in towns and villages inhabited by Serbs. Throughout 1986 the Kosovo Polje group, including the new arrival Bogdan Kecman, worked to link up the emerging local networks into a more powerful political force. Each of them took responsibility for a specific area of Kosovo and worked to strengthen links between the existing activists in the area, recruit new ones and inform potential supporters about their initiatives. Before long the Kosovo Polje group could mobilise groups of activists for protest events in and outside Kosovo within a day or two.[16] The activists' demands, initially focused on the lack of protection by the law enforcement agencies and courts and inequalities in the public sector, gradually evolved towards constitutional issues. The protesters asserted that if the provincial officials were unable to guarantee protection of the rights and property of Serbs then Kosovo should be brought back under the jurisdiction of Serbia's authorities.[17]

High officials tolerated the mobilisation for several reasons. Firstly, the highly decentralised political structure of socialist Yugoslavia, based largely on national rights and identities, encouraged groups to mobilise along national lines. After 1981 high officials had already acknowledged the grievances of the Kosovo Serbs and put emphasis on prevention of their outmigration. Unlike the Kosovo Albanian protesters in 1981 who aimed at important institutional change, the Kosovo Serbs demanded little more than implementation of the existing party policy, which was much less likely to trigger repression. Serbs, though a minority group in Kosovo, constituted a majority in Serbia as a whole and a plurality in Yugoslavia, which rendered their concerns more urgent for Yugoslavia's political class. Other political changes also mattered. The change of political generations in the first half of the 1980s brought younger politicians into the highest regional offices and many of them felt that repression against ordinary people would go against the values of their generation. Growing elite disunity, rooted in the decentralised political structure and intensified during the leadership succession, had already resulted in the deadlock at the federal level and now thwarted attempts to reach a common position on the grassroots protest.

Secondly, the small scale of mobilisation and its limited potential for expansion, which sharply distinguished it from the 1981 mobilisation of Kosovo Albanians, were also important. The movement of a minority group in a peripheral region hardly posed a threat to the regime. High officials were mainly concerned about the potential implications for political stability at the centre, since the protesters' demands were potentially highly resonant with Serbs outside Kosovo. Attempts of Kosovo Serb activists to stage dramatic protests in the capital, as in the case of the May 1986 march, were therefore prevented. High officials were hardly lenient towards prominent activists, especially after the October 1985 petition. They often conducted campaigns of abuse against the activists in the local press, and Bulatović was briefly jailed in early April 1986. Thirdly, activists opted for moderate protest strategies and repeatedly stressed that their protest was not anti-systemic. The protests often unfolded under the auspices of the SAWP partly because high officials rarely tolerated openly non-institutional initiatives and partly because the minority constituency of the movement ruled out large-scale discontent. The highly decentralised political structure of socialist Yugoslavia, including complex relationships between organs of Yugoslavia, Serbia and Kosovo, a high level of local autonomy and a large number of official organisations, provided space for the activists to organise, recruit new supporters and appeal for support.

From the early 1980s various groups of Kosovo Serbs sought contacts with influential people. Activists kept in touch with some earlier Kosovo Serb migrants, such as the managers of state enterprises and middle-rank officials in the capital and reporters of Belgrade media based in the province. The confidants helped by identifying targets for appeal outside Kosovo, since the activists knew little about institutional structure and informal political alliances, and commented on protest strategies. Activists also established contact with dissident intellectuals, including Dobrica Ćosić. Ćosić supported their cause and suggested that they make use of all legal options of appeal. Others contacts from Belgrade-based dissident circles urged radical action early on and claimed that protests of Kosovo Serbs in the capital would trigger demonstrations of hundreds of thousands.[18] Ćosić claims to have initiated the October 1985 petition at the meeting with a number of Kosovo Serbs, but that a Belgrade journalist, an earlier Serb migrant from Kosovo, actually wrote the first draft.[19] This is probably true. Although Kosta Bulatović claimed that he initiated and drafted the petition, other prominent activists suspected that this journalist, a friend of Bulatović, wrote the text.[20]

In January 1986 around 200 Belgrade-based intellectuals signed a petition supporting the cause of the Kosovo Serbs, while the writers union subsequently held a number of protest meetings. A number of dissident intellectuals had already initiated a debate on Kosovo a year before, partly from the perspective of the revisionist history of Serb–Albanian relations and partly focusing on the current grievances of Kosovo Serbs.[21] Without doubt dissident intellectuals' action alerted the general public in central Serbia to the concerns of Kosovo Serbs and made a strong impression on high officials of Yugoslavia and Serbia. However, this was only a part of the intellectuals' sweeping critique of the Communist regime and had little to do with either the creation or consolidation of the local protest networks. There was little difference between a few meetings of activists with Ćosić and their contacts with other potential allies, as the activists initiated nearly all of them. The significance of the October 1985 petition, drafted by the intellectuals, did not lie in its content, since the same demands had featured prominently in the activists' discussions in the official organisations. The Kosovo Polje group had even drafted a similar petition two years before but collected only around seventy signatures.[22] The 1985 petition became important because around 2,000 Kosovo Serbs signed the text within ten days and thus demonstrated strong commitment to their cause despite a widespread fear of job loss or imprisonment.

Nor were the dissident intellectuals the only group that helped publicise the cause of the emerging movement, since Kosovo Serb war veterans occasionally supported some activists' demands and demanded resignations of various Kosovo officials, both Albanians and Serbs. Before initiating any major protest event, prominent activists tested their ideas before at least some of the above confidants to find out whether the chosen targets and timing were appropriate. While seeking contact with, and advice from, various quarters, the protest organisers made decisions on protest strategies on their own. They firmly believed that people at the grassroots understood their problems best and could make appropriate decisions. More importantly, they were painfully aware that they, not their confidants, would have to suffer the consequences of any wrong moves.[23]

The Spread of Mobilisation and Slobodan Milošević

Before 1988 political alliances in Kosovo's leadership had rarely followed ethnona-tional cleavage and the views of most Albanian and Serb high officials shifted over time with changes in the party line. This was reflected in the demands of Kosovo Serb activists for the resignation of some Albanian and Serb officials and their occasional support for other officials, both Serbs and Albanians. The activists had generally been cautious about Serbs in Kosovo's political establishment, feeling that their loyalty lay with the party policy of the day.[24] After 1981 a number of Serb high officials originally from Kosovo, who had occupied posts in federal organs, were sent back to influential positions in Kosovo's leadership. The so-called weekend or travelling politicians, whose families stayed in Belgrade, had little connection with Kosovo Serb realities and were generally despised by ordinary people. The activists therefore continually sought allies among the leadership of Serbia, but with little success.

This changed after the visit of Slobodan Milošević, Serbia's new party leader, to Kosovo Polje in April 1987. Arriving at a previously announced meeting with the representatives of Kosovo Serbs, Milošević and Azem Vllasi, a leading Kosovo Albanian politician, witnessed a short but violent encounter of the crowd of several thousand protesters with the police. At the meeting, Milošević delivered a speech, in most part a typical speech of a high official, but his stance stood out, namely his public disapproval of the use of force by the police.[25] After the Kosovo Polje visit Milošević pulled all strings to call a session of the Central Committee of Yugoslavia and demanded that specific targets be set for the performance of party and state organs in relation to the Kosovo problem. As his intervention related only to the implementation of previously jointly approved policies and remained firmly on the Titoist course, Milošević gained support from high officials from other republics without difficulty. However, the developments initiated a conflict in the leadership of Serbia. Minor disagreements over policy details on Kosovo were exaggerated in the heat of the power struggle between factions based on the personal networks of Milošević and his former protector Ivan Stambolić, which unfolded according to the rules of the game in socialist party-states, with little influence from society.[26]

Since the 1967–1974 constitutional reforms, the main concern of high officials from Serbia was the fragmented political structure of Serbia.[27] In the aftermath of the 1981 protests of Kosovo Albanians, Draža Marković and Petar Stambolić claimed that the eruption of protests resulted from the unconstitutional extension of the autonomy of Serbia's provinces, but had little success in persuading high officials from other republics to help strengthen Serbia's central organs. Following the change of political generations, Ivan Stambolić reaffirmed the need for greater coordination between the central government of Serbia and its autonomous provinces and put emphasis on economic issues and the concerns of Kosovo Serbs. The rise of Milošević in 1987 changed little in this respect and he reiterated the demands cast by his predecessors. The change in the leadership, however, turned the fortunes of the growing social movement. While Stambolić had kept pressure on Kosovo's officials to address the problems of Kosovo Serbs and had ignored protest networks, Milošević aimed to establish control over the mobilisation by coopting prominent activists. The change partly originated from the spread of mobilisation so that it now had to be dealt with through either suppression or cooptation. Also, Milošević exploited the mobilisation for his own ends and often provoked activists to publicly denounce his opponents. The activists did not object, since they now felt a degree of protection from the federal and Kosovo officials and their protests achieved greater visibility. Prominent activists were in turn under strong pressure to channel their initiatives towards the official organisations and employ their influence over the local networks to halt non-institutional action.[28]

The growing influence of Milošević on prominent activists often failed to transform into action on the ground partly because they intended to proceed with protests until their demands had been fully addressed and partly because of the highly decentralised character of their protest networks. Although influential, the Kosovo Polje group by no means presided over the networks, and other activists at times ignored its advice. Around thirty to forty prominent activists from various parts of Kosovo, who gathered occasionally, commanded sufficient influence to prevent any initiatives they disapproved of or to start new ones. In the summer of 1988 the activists formed a protest committee, which quickly became another important decision-making centre. Neither of the three main circles of power within the social movement, however, could control a group of radical activists, who at times would not listen to anybody's advice and proceeded with action, often getting support from one or two hundred supporters. The local networks therefore proceeded with protests across Kosovo. To placate Milošević they now wrapped up all protests, even large outdoor gatherings, in the form of meetings of the official organisations. There was a growing number of cases in which local and Kosovo's officials who attended the meetings were booed at or prevented from speaking or the audience left the meeting altogether.

In the spring of 1988 prominent activists became increasingly sceptical about the claims of Milošević that a constitutional change, aimed at empowering the central government of Serbia, would occur in the near future. Convinced that the pressure from the grassroots was essential to political change, they launched a petition in May 1988, before the federal party conference, the so-called small party congress, and soon presented it to high officials of Yugoslavia and Serbia with nearly 50,600 signatures. The reason that nearly a quarter of the Kosovo Serbs found themselves signatories of the petition was that many activists signed up their whole families. Despite this wild exaggeration, the petition did have elements of a plebiscite of Kosovo Serbs. The petitioners now demanded that the federal organs temporarily establish direct rule in the province in order to establish security for the Serbs or, alternatively, recognise their right to self-defence. They also threatened that they might collectively emigrate from the province in the last resort.[29] Aware of the limits to the protest groups' organisational resources, the high officials of Yugoslavia and Serbia were nonetheless concerned that any activities under the label of collective emigration might trigger public unrest on a large scale and Milošević resolutely demanded a halt to such activities.[30]

Having to drop an important protest strategy and fearing a decline in participation by dispirited supporters, prominent Kosovo Serb activists found an alternative target, a protest in Novi Sad, the largest city in Vojvodina. After the unexpected success of the protest, the activists and their non-elite allies outside Kosovo launched a series of protests in Vojvodina and Montenegro during the summer.[31] The protests coincided with a spiralling conflict between elites of the republics and provinces over amendments to the constitutions of Yugoslavia and Serbia, partly regarding the relations between Serbia's central government and its autonomous provinces. In September the protests of Kosovo Serbs unfolded all over the province. The activists now engaged in cooperation with the Kosovo Serb intellectuals, since they needed well-educated people to deliver speeches at a growing number of protests.[32] While the local Serb intellectuals had timidly signalled their discontent with the position of Serbs in Kosovo, few of them took part in protest activities prior to the late summer of 1988.

The consolidation of support for the social movement among Kosovo Serbs and the efforts of Milošević to break the resistance of Kosovo's officials to constitutional reform gradually affected political alliances in the provincial leadership, which had rarely followed the ethnonational cleavage. The first signs of rising tensions occurred in early 1988 when several Serb officials from the Priština Committee openly supported prominent activists. The September protest campaign coincided with the break between Kosovo Albanian and Serb members of the Provincial Committee. Serbs now supported the demand of Milošević for the resignation of Kosovo's high officials for their alleged obstruction of party policy; Albanians defended their leaders and objected to the significant constitutional changes. In the aftermath of the purges of Kosovo Albanian officials and the reduction of the autonomy of Kosovo in 1989, Milošević filled key political and public sector positions with low-ranking Kosovo Serb officials, mainly ones who had little connection with the grassroots mobilisation. As the constitutional changes and greater involvement of the government of Serbia in the affairs of Kosovo met important demands of the Kosovo Serbs, the movement swiftly disintegrated.

The Protest of Kosovo Serbs and Patterns of Mobilisation in Socialist Yugoslavia

The rise and dynamics of mobilisation of the Kosovo Serbs in the 1980s reveal that shifts in political context favourable to a group, rather than a deterioration of a group's relative position, often lead to mobilisation of its members. The mobilisation of Kosovo Serbs reflected the pattern behind other important episodes of mobilisation in socialist Yugoslavia. In June 1968 Belgrade University students initiated protests against growing unemployment and increasing economic inequality and materialism. They objected to a system that set obstacles to the career advancement of well-educated young people and favoured middle-aged and often poorly qualified cadres of the revolution. Although the protest was hardly anti-systemic, high officials swiftly ended the mobilisation by a mixture of appeasing and repressive measures. In the autumn of 1968, large-scale demonstrations of Albanians broke out across Kosovo and northwest Macedonia, with demands for a republic of Kosovo, and ended with a similar response from the authorities. In 1981 another, larger wave of protests of Kosovo Albanians swept the province. The protests repeatedly erupted all over the autonomous province from March to May and involved serious clashes with the police.

These episodes of mobilisation of non-state actors erupted after the rise in political expectations of respective groups. The 1966 removal of Ranković, a symbol of the post-war police state, raised expectations in society that political and economic reforms would follow. University students were among the groups that were most interested in reforms and apparently took the political change seriously. The fall of Ranković also initiated a change in the party's policy on Kosovo, since many saw him as responsible for the excesses of the police state in Kosovo. The change in turn raised the expectations of Kosovo Albanians. In both cases the rise of political expectations was followed by a partial relaxation of repression and the two factors combined to trigger protest by the respective groups. Likewise, in 1981 the leadership succession and the increase in political instability in Yugoslavia triggered expectations among groups of Kosovo Albanians that in the newly emerging balance of power in Yugoslavia Kosovo might get republic status. The failure to transform the wave of protests into sustained mobilisations, that is, social movements, was partly due to political conditions unfavourable to sustained mobilisation and partly due to their large scale and potential for further expansion.

The mobilisation of Kosovo Serbs also resembled somewhat the pattern of collective action of Yugoslavia's working class in the 1980s. The growing discontent of the workers with the consequences of economic crisis initially appeared in the form of a sharp increase in absenteeism and sick leave rather than open protest.[33] The sudden rise in the number of strikes, a more visible and dramatic form of protest, occurred between 1985 and 1987,[34] roughly at the same time as the emergence and spread of protest networks of Kosovo Serbs. This suggests that the timing of both instances of mobilisation was due to the relaxation of the grip of the party-state on society, just like in the case of the strikes in the 1960s.[35] Moreover, the expansion of the protests of Kosovo Serbs in mid-1988 occurred simultaneously with the shift of the strategy of the miners and metalworkers from strikes to protest marches and demonstrations, largely directed at high federal officials in Belgrade. The argument that the relationship between grievances and popular protest is more complex than the elite thesis suggests holds at the local level as well. There were many more protests in the predominantly Serb settlements than in those in which they constituted a small minority. I have shown that Serbs in the latter settlements held stronger grievances, but it was much more difficult to organise protest in such an environment. Popular protest, however, may arise not only after the relaxation of repression or in a relatively permissive context, but also in response to an immediate and direct threat to the interests of a group, as the protests of Kosovo Albanians in November 1988 and February–March 1989 suggest.

Frequent exaggeration of nationalist-related incidents, which the elite thesis considers as an example of elite manipulation about Albanian–Serb relations in Kosovo, was often little more than the consequence of the recruitment and protest strategies of Kosovo Serb activists. Lacking the advantages of formal organisation and stable membership, activists often exaggerated the scale of these incidents to trigger stronger reaction among Kosovo Serbs and to attract the attention of high officials and the local press. Sometimes they framed indecent attacks of Kosovo Albanian men on Serb women as rape.[36] Partly as the consequence of these protest strategies, a level of mobilisation increased despite the fact that the rate of national-ist-related violence declined. The activists also spread rumours that vastly exagger-ated their strength among Kosovo Serbs and their support outside the province. The rumour was that tens of thousands signed the 1985 petition and that thousands participated in the May 1986 march. Repeatedly activists and their allies outside Kosovo stressed that thousands, even tens of thousands, of Kosovo Serbs were ready for collective emigration and that they would leave if the federal organs failed to swiftly address their demands. The rumour campaigns owed success to the very nature of Yugoslavia's party-state. The protest of Kosovo Serbs was politically sensitive and could not be freely reported on and debated in the local press, although the boundaries became increasingly flexible in 1987 and 1988. The mix of the information shortage about an important political issue and the lack of experience of activists, their supporters, high officials and the population at large about the real limits to collective action of ordinary people became a hotbed for wild guesses, wishful thinking and deliberate rumour campaigns. This is a common outcome in repressive social and political settings[37] and had little to do with elite manipulation before 1988.

Conclusion

Without doubt, the support of dissident intellectuals and Milošević boosted the Kosovo Serb activists' prospects of success, in terms of publicising their cause and bringing urgency to their demands for high officials. The support nonetheless mattered little in the creation and consolidation of the local protest networks. While activists engaged in contacts with a range of influential people and opted for specific protest strategies with an eye on the broader political context, they remained an autonomous political factor and largely took decisions on their own. The mobilisation originated from their discontent with the post-1966 twist in the politics of inequality and the demographic decline of Kosovo Serbs, partly resulting from their steady migration out of Kosovo, which strongly intensified this group's feelings of insecurity. The changing political context strongly shaped the timing, forms and dynamics of the mobilisation. The changes in the party line on Kosovo after 1981 resulted in a softer approach of high officials of Yugoslavia and Serbia towards Kosovo Serbs and their informal exclusion from the authority of Kosovo's leadership. These developments opened space for various groups to lobby high officials outside the province and to initiate debates about their concerns in the official organisations at the local level.

The slow response of the authorities to growing complaints shifted the efforts of some of the debaters to non-institutional action and building up the local protest networks. The relatively small-scale and grassroots character of protest and the moderate protest strategies, including mobilisation partly within the official organisations, shielded the activists from repression. Despite cooperation with Milošević, who put their demands firmly on the party's agenda, Kosovo Serb activists proceeded with non-institutional action. The reduction of Kosovo's autonomy, which met an important demand of the Kosovo Serbs, and the purge of Kosovo's leadership by Milošević and its replacement by Kosovo Serb party apparatchiks effectively closed the space for the autonomous political efforts of Kosovo Serbs. The timing and dynamics of the mobilisation of Kosovo Serbs differed little from the patterns of mobilisation of other groups in socialist Yugoslavia, especially the protests of Kosovo Albanians in 1968 and 1981, since all unfolded in the aftermath of growing expectations and the relaxation of repression centred on those groups. The case of the mobilisation of Kosovo Serbs in the 1980s reveals that a prevailing focus on elites and high politics as well as on the discourse rather than behaviour of political actors in the literature on conflicts surrounding the disintegration of Yugoslavia is misleading. Due to the gradual relaxation of repressive policies and practices, non-elite actors played an important political role even in the unlikely context of a socialist party-state.

NOTES

1. See for example Laura Silber and Allan Little, *The Death of Yugoslavia* (London: Penguin and BBC, 1996), pp. 34–47, 58–59; Tim Judah, *Kosovo: War and Revenge* (New Haven: Yale University Press, 2000), pp. 47–55; Noel Malcolm, *Kosovo: A Short History* (New York: New York University Press, 1998), pp. 339–343; and Julie A. Mertus, *Kosovo: How Myths and Truths Started a War* (Berkeley: University of California Press, 1999), Chapter 2.

2. Ivan Stambolić, *Put u bespuće: odgovori Ivana Stambolića na pitanja Slobodana Inića* (Belgrade: Radio B92, 1995), pp. 165–180.

3. Nebojša Vladisavljević, "Nationalism, Social Movement Theory and the Grass Roots Movement of Kosovo Serbs, 1985–1988," *Europe–Asia Studies*, Vol. 54, No. 5, 2002, pp. 771–190.

4. It is hard to establish the scale of inequalities between 1966 and 1981, since this was an official taboo. After 1981, however, credible evidence from official reports provided insight into the forms and pervasiveness of the inequalities. See, for example, excerpts from the report of the working group of the Federal Assembly in "Tačno i netačno: nijesu Albanci, no nepravda," *Intervju*, 11 April 1986, pp. 38–45, and "Ispitano i provereno," *NIN*, 13 April 1986. The evidence should not be confused with Milošević's propaganda in the following years. For the latter see Srdja Popović, Ivan Janković, Vesna Pešić, Nataša Kandić and Svetlana Slapšak, *Kosovski čvor: drešiti ili seći?* (Belgrade: Hronos, 1990).

5. Calculated from the figures for Serbs and Montenegrins from *Jugoslavija 1918–1988: statistički godišnjak* (Belgrade: Savezni zavod za statistiku, 1989), p. 48. Montenegrins, who comprised less than 15% of this section of Kosovo's population, saw the Serb identity as more inclusive, shared with all Serbs.

6. See Srdjan Bogosavljević, "A Statistical Picture of Serbian–Albanian Relations", in Dušan Janjić and Shkelzen Maliqi, eds, *Conflict or Dialogue: Serbian–Albanian Relations and Integration of the Balkans* (Subotica, Yugoslavia: Open University & European Civil Centre for Conflict Resolution, 1994), p. 23, and Ruža Petrović and Marina Blagojević, *The Migrations of Serbs and Montenegrins from Kosovo and Metohija: Results of the Survey Conducted in 1985–1986* (Belgrade: SANU, 1992), pp. 82–85.

7. Petrović and Blagojević, *The Migrations of Serbs and Montenegrins*, pp. 85–92, 100–104, 111–173.

8. Miloš Sekulović, interview with the author, Belgrade, 18 August 2000. For details see Zejnel Zejneli, *Ko je izdao revoluciju* (Priština: Jedinstvo, 1988), pp. 74–105, p. 12.

9. Aleksandar Tijanić, *Šta će biti s nama* (Zagreb: Globus, 1988), pp. 130–131, p. 2.

10. For an account of one of the meetings see excerpts from the diary of Draža Marković in Mirko Djekić, *Upotreba Srbije: optužbe i priznanja Draže Markovića* (Belgrade: Besede, 1990), pp. 209–210.

11. Boško Budimirović and Miroslav Šolević, interviews with the author, Belgrade, 15 and 17 July 2001, respectively.

12. Boško Budimirović and Miroslav Šolević, interviews with the author, and Dušan Ristić in Miloš Antić, "Srbija nema rešenje za Kosovo," *Borba*, 11 February 1993, p. 13.

13. "Zahtevi 2016 stanovnika Kosova," *Književne novine*, 15 December 1985, p. 2. The expression "ethnically clean" comes from the petition.

14. For details see Vladisavljević, "Nationalism, Social Movement Theory and the Grass Roots Movement of Kosovo Serbs", pp. 772–773.

15. See, for example, "Šta je ko rekao u Kosovu Polju: stenografske beleške razgovora u noći 24. i 25. IV 1987," *Borba*, 8, 9–10 and 11 May 1987, p. 17.

16. Boško Budimirović, Miroslav Šolević and Bogdan Kecman, interviews with the author, Belgrade, 15 and 17 July 2001 and 29 August 2000 respectively.

17. See "Šta su Kosovci rekli u Skupštini," *NIN*, 23 and 30 March and 6 and 13 April 1986; and "Šta je ko rekao u Kosovu Polju", pp. 1–18.

18. Miroslav Šolević and Boško Budimirović, interviews with the author. See also Dobrica Ćosić, *Piščevi zapisi, 1981–1991* (Belgrade: Filip Višnjić, 2002), pp. 169–170, 186–188.

19. Ćosić, *Piščevi zapisi*, pp. 169–170.

20. Boško Budimirović and Miroslav Šolević, interviews with the author.

21. For details on the views and action of the intellectuals in relation to Kosovo see Jasna Dragović-Soso, *"Saviours of the Nation": Serbia's Intellectual Opposition and the Revival of Nationalism* (London: Hurst, 2002), Chapter 3. For the text of the intellectuals' petition see "Zahtev za pravnim poretkom na Kosovu," in Aleksa Djilas, ed., *Srpsko pitanje* (Belgrade: Politika, 1991), pp. 260–261.

22. Miroslav Šolević, interview with the author.

23. *Ibid.*

24. Boško Budimirović, interview with the author.

25. Vladisavljević, "Nationalism, Social Movement Theory and the Grass Roots Movement of Kosovo Serbs," p. 774.

26. Nebojša Vladisavljević, "Institutional Power and the Rise of Milošević," *Nationalities Papers*, Vol. 32, No. 1, 2004, pp. 183–205.

27. Draža Marković, interview with the author, Belgrade, 16 August 2000.

28. Boško Budimirović, Miroslav Šolević and Bogdan Kecman, interviews with the author, and Dušan Ristić in Antić, "Srbija nema rešenje za Kosovo."

29. The author's copy of the petition. See excerpts in "Iz peticije 50.000 potpisnika," *Danas*, 5 July 1988, p. 23.

30. Boško Budimirović and Miroslav Šolević, interviews with the author, and Mićo Šparavalo, a prominent activist, in Sava Kerčov, Jovo Radoš and Aleksandar Raič, *Mitinzi u Vojvodini 1988. godine: radjanje političkog pluralizma* (Novi Sad: Dnevnik, 1990), pp. 243–244.

31. See Darko Hudelist, *Kosovo: bitka bez iluzija* (Zagreb: Centar za informacije i publicitet, 1989), pp. 153–221.

32. Stevan Marinković and Migo Samardžić, prominent activists, in Kerčov *et al.*, *Mitinzi u Vojvodini*, pp. 229–220, 241.

33. Marjan Korošić, *Jugoslavenska kriza* (Zagreb: Naprijed, 1988), p. 63.

34. See the table showing the numbers of strikes and participants in strikes in Yugoslavia between 1978 and 1988 in Salih Fočo, *Štrajk izmedju iluzije i zbilje* (Belgrade: Radnička štampa, 1989), p. 62.

35. Neca Jovanov, *Radnički štrajkovi u SFRJ od 1958. do 1969. godine* (Belgrade: Zapis, 1979), p. 75.

36. For details see Tijanić, *Šta će biti s nama*, p. 128.

37. James Scott, *Domination and the Arts of Resistance: Hidden Transcripts* (New Haven: Yale University Press, 1990).

The Emergence of the Kosovo "Parallel State," 1988–1992[1]

Besnik Pula

Introduction

This article examines the origins of the nonviolent resistance movement in Kosovo in the early 1990s, with the purpose of explaining the dynamics that led to the emergence of the so-called "parallel state" of Kosovo Albanians.

Though current public images of Kosovo have largely been shaped by the events surrounding the violent conflict of 1999 and NATO intervention, as well as postwar ethnic violence and questions over Kosovo's unresolved status, a critical but largely understudied phase of the ethnic conflict in Kosovo is the emergence of the Albanian "parallel state" during the early 1990s. Analysts largely agree that the ethnic conflict of the 1990s, rather than being a continuation of historical "ethnic hatreds" from past centuries, is part and parcel of the political dynamics that led to the disintegration of the multinational Yugoslav federation.[2] Kosovo being an autonomous province of Serbia and a constituent unit of the Yugoslav federation, the social and institutional contours of the Kosovo conflict were directly shaped by the institutional structures and cultural identities existing in the Yugoslav system. The purpose of this article is to trace the political dynamics that initiated conflict and explicate both the institutional and political reasons why the Albanian response to Serbia's forceful abolition of Kosovo's self-governing status in 1989 led to a nonviolent response, in the form of the parallel state. I argue that the parallel state was a result of constitutional histories, the institutional context, local political dynamics, the nature of Serbia's policy in Kosovo, as well as drastic changes taking place internationally during the period of 1988–1992. I make this point by demonstrating how the "parallel state" was a largely unplanned-for phenomenon, emerging as a result of autonomous acts of various institutional segments, and—at least in its earliest phase—not a conscious political project of the ascending Albanian political leadership.

The Kosovar "parallel state" (sometimes also called the "shadow state" or "parallel society") throughout most of the 1990s consisted of a loose conglomeration of educational and cultural institutions, health services, social assistance networks, political parties, local financial councils, and a government-in-exile, all nominally coordinated by a political center led by the Democratic League of Kosovo (LDK) and its leader, Ibrahim Rugova. Not a state in the traditional, Weberian sense, it is here conceptualized as a national movement that sought to preserve the basic framework of a state inherited from the period of autonomy, defy the Serbian state's

authority by demonstrating a collective political will to protest through civil dis-
obedience, and elicit international support for the goal of secession. This description
of the parallel state, however, is based on the political structure that was the outcome
of institutional developments between 1989 and 1992; here it is the dynamics that led
to this outcome that are analyzed. The other term, "Albanian movement," refers to
the nationally defined social movement for secession that emerged in Kosovo in the
period 1988–1992. It refers not to a single organization, but rather to the mass-based
movement, which included virtually all of Kosovo's Albanian community, which
organized collectively under a common political platform through shared collective
goals, experiences, and cultural repertoires of contention.

The approach here purposefully breaks with conventional frameworks of ethnic
conflict, as developed particularly by international relations scholars. First, the
approach taken here breaks with the assumption that ethnic collectivities innately
function as social and political units. National identity and the sense of national
belonging, or what Rogers Brubaker calls "nationness," is here treated as a contingent historical phenomenon and a property of the political field, constituted institu-
tionally and discursively, and not as a primordial or naturally given property of the
ethnic collectivity.[3] Second, the approach taken here situates the Kosovo conflict
within the particular historical context of the Yugoslav break-up and the general
hopes and uncertainties that emerged in post-Cold-War Europe. The historical
approach taken here breaks with models that theorize ethnic conflict within frameworks of strategic action and that carry with them unexamined ontological assumptions and understandings about social reality.[4]

The approach taken here draws heavily from the "process-oriented" approach to
social movements, as articulated by scholars such as Doug McAdam, Sidney Tarrow,
Charles Tilly, Mayer Zald, and others. Broadly speaking, this school of thought has
developed three key factors in explaining the emergence of social movements,
defined as sustained collective challenges to elites, opponents, or authorities, based
on social solidarities and common goals.[5] Such contentious collective action is a
result of the interaction among *political opportunities*, *mobilizing structures*, and
framing processes.

Borrowing from structuralist approaches to the study of social movements and
revolutions, *political opportunities* represent the changes in political opportunities
and constraints that produce incentives and disincentives for groups to engage in
contentious collective action. These factors are not consistently present in each case
of contention, but rather represent a "set of clues," such as the opening of institutional access to groups who have previously been excluded, the emergence of rifts
or new alignments within ruling elites, the availability of allies, and decline in the
state's will or capacity for repression. Most importantly, these are factors that are
external to the contending group, and appear to the group in the form of incentives,
constraints, and resources.[6] *Mobilizing structures* are defined as "those collective
vehicles, both formal and informal, through which people come together and engage

in collective action."[7] While political opportunities may offer incentives for contentious collective action, mobilizing structures are central in bringing individuals together to organize for collective action. Finally, opportunities and mobilizing structures are translated into sustained collective action through *framing processes*, the shared ideas, meanings, symbols, and identities that join individuals together into social movements. In turn, during the course of contention, social movements transform these ideas, meanings, symbols, and identities, or create entirely new ones.[8]

The object of the article, however, is not to intervene in theoretical debates in issues of ethnic conflict, social movements, or the break-up of states. As such, the explication and analysis of causal mechanisms is not its primary purpose. These, however, are implicitly embedded in the narrative; the choice of events, the sequential ordering of objects of analysis, the use of concepts, and the narrative structure itself conceal implicit understandings of causal mechanisms and their primacy over other possible ones. The preceding theoretical discussion was an effort to provide a conceptual framework and make those understandings explicit.

The article proceeds largely in the form of a historical discussion. It begins by briefly discussing the historical origins of the political problems of sovereignty in Kosovo, and why the issue of sovereignty resurfaced as a contentious issue in the late 1980s. Second, it discusses the structural bases of ethnic polarization, as well as the dynamics that led to polarization during the 1980s. It then proceeds to examine the Albanian response to Belgrade's efforts to abolish Kosovo's self-governing status. It analyzes the dynamics of protest, and examines the contingencies that led to the emergence of an Albanian counter-elite that was able to dominate a rising movement and gain control of a newly emerged institutional structure. The historical reconstruction is based on historical sources, newspaper articles, interviews with particular actors, as well as materials drawn from existing sources. As indicated above, the article particularly dissects the events in the period between 1988 and 1992, which is the critical period when the parallel state emerged.[9]

Kosovo and Questions of Sovereignty

In retrospect, it was the institution by Yugoslav communists of a federal system based on the Soviet model in 1945 that gave saliency to questions of Kosovo's constitutional status.[10] The Communist Party of Yugoslavia (CPY) had, both in the interwar period and during its wartime resistance, given support to various Albanian movements in Kosovo for national recognition. For instance, in 1923, the CPY issued a programmatic statement in which it resolved that the party's duty was to "help the movements of oppressed nations in their goals of creating independent states, Croatia, Slovenia, Macedonia, Montenegro, as well as the liberation of the Albanians."[11] In 1939 it recognized its cell in Kosovo as a separate branch of the party organization.[12] In 1942, in the midst of war, the Yugoslav communist leader Tito stated that the CPY "will never depart from the principle stated by our great teachers and leaders, Lenin and Stalin, which is the right of every nation to self-determination, including secession."[13] For Tito, this included the Albanians of Yugoslavia.[14] At the end of 1943, the founding conference of the National Liberation Committee of Kosovo—regional political authorities that the CPY had established in all parts of Yugoslavia, which included communists and non-communists alike—adopted a resolution endorsing the union of Kosovo with Albania. The Bujan Resolution, so named because the meeting was held in the small village of Bujan in northern Albania, was strongly reprimanded by the leadership of the CPY. At the end of the war, in 1945, a newly constituted Assembly of the People's District Council, which included Albanian communists but was dominated by Serbs, adopted a new resolution expressing "the wish of the entire population of the district to join a federated Serbia as its constituent part." In the following month the resolution was accepted by the Anti-Fascist Liberation Council of Yugoslavia (AVNOJ), serving as the country's postwar government, and in September the National Assembly of Serbia passed a law regulating the status of the autonomous district (*oblast*) of Kosovo, and setting its boundaries.[15] These critical events during World War II would establish Kosovo as an autonomous province of Serbia, whose constitutional status would undergo several changes up until Yugoslavia's eventual break-up.

The origin of the "Kosovo question" as a direct *constitutional* question within the framework of Yugoslav federalism is thus to be found in the CPY's wartime policies, its nominal commitment to the Leninist principle of self-determination, and its decision to imitate the Soviet model of nationally based territorial divisions in the postwar political organization of Yugoslavia. In the process, the question of Kosovo's status became intricately linked with Yugoslavia's nationalities policy. Although Yugoslavia's six republics were largely conceived as national homelands for the country's major national groups Albanians, already forming the majority of Kosovo's inhabitants, were recognized as a national minority and not as a constituent national group. Throughout the 1950s Kosovo would enjoy a symbolic territorial autonomy, and the Yugoslav secret police, the UDBa, was particularly active in the province in search of "subversive elements" among the Kosovo Albanians.[16]

The UDBa's repressive policies in Kosovo were publicly exposed in 1966, when Tito dismissed his security chief and former right-hand man, Serb communist Aleksandar Ranković, from all official and party posts. The marginalization of the unitarist wing in the CPY, whose main proponent had been Ranković, opened the way for a series of major political and economic reforms, including greater devolution of power and the augmentation of the self-governing powers of the provinces.

Already in 1963 Kosovo's constitutional status within the Serb republic was made symmetrical to that of Serbia's northern province, Vojvodina. In 1968, in a major concession to demands of regional party leaders, the Executive Committee of the

League of Communists of Serbia (LCS) agreed to drop Metohija from the province's name, legalize the use of the Albanian flag, end the use of the Serbian name *Šiptari* to refer to Yugoslav Albanians in favor of *Albanci*, and made the Kosovo party independent.[17] Constitutional amendments passed in 1969 and 1971 revised the constitutional status of the provinces, recognizing them as territorial units at the federal level. Furthermore, federal authorities set up a special federal fund for underdeveloped regions, in which Kosovo got top priority. The most significant constitutional reforms in Yugoslavia, those of 1974, further decentralized the federation and assigned autonomous provinces virtually equal powers to those of republics. The provinces became republics in virtually all but name.[18]

Economic Transformation and Social Crisis: The Riots of 1981 and Their Aftermath

The year 1981 was a watershed both for Kosovo and for Yugoslav politics. At the height of Yugoslavia's economic crisis, massive riots in Kosovo shook Yugoslav politics to its foundations and brought attention to the scale of social and economic problems that had engulfed the province. Intensive, federally funded investments throughout the 1960s and 1970s transformed Kosovo's economic base—from a largely agricultural economy, Kosovo became heavily industrialized, particularly in extractive industries built on Kosovo's mineral wealth. In spite of these measures, however, Kosovo remained poor even by Yugoslav standards. In 1979, per capita income was 30% of the national average, and approximately one-seventh of that of Slovenia, the wealthiest republic.[19] The growth rate of Kosovo's "social product," the measuring standard of economic output in Yugoslavia, was over 50% below the Yugoslav average.

The economic changes did, nonetheless, rapidly transform Kosovo's social structure. The growth of state administration and industrial employment was drawing a large part of the populace away from agricultural work and forming an educated, well-paid stratum of blue- and white-collar employees. However, economic stagnation beginning in the late 1970s meant that job creation could not keep up with the number of new entrants in the labor market. In particular, the swelling of university students meant that many of the nearly 10,000 annual graduates of the University of Prishtina could not find adequate employment after graduation. Besides the growing ranks of the unemployed, which by the early 1980s reached a rate of around 60% and particularly affected those under 25,[20] many Kosovars turned to emigration. During the 1970s around 100,000 Kosovars left to find employment in other parts of Yugoslavia or outside of the country.[21] For those who remained, public administration became a place to find work; employment growth in the administrative sector was faster than that of the industrial sector and it was where a disproportionately high share of central government funds were allocated. By the beginning of 1980, one in every four employed Kosovars was a well-paid civil servant.[22]

Furthermore, demographic changes transformed Kosovo's national structure. While a state census conducted in 1948 showed that Albanians constituted a majority of Kosovo's postwar population, by 1981 the proportion of Albanians grew from around 68% to 77% of the province's rapidly growing population.[23] Demographic growth and measures of positive discrimination to correct for the underemployment of Albanians in the state sector for many Serbs and Montenegrins meant a growing fear of the "Albanianization" of Kosovo. This induced a growing outmigration of Serbs from Kosovo, though in the 1970s Serbs still constituted a disproportionate number of managerial and white-collar workers and a smaller number of the unemployed. They also had on average higher incomes and were disproportionately represented in the party leadership.[24]

Demographic pressures, social dislocation, and the failure of the socialist employment system to secure employment for many of the new entrants in the labor market led to the growing illegitimacy of the system. It could be argued that the riots of 1981 were a manifestation of the burgeoning challenge to the Yugoslav political and economic system; however, this challenge was largely channeled through the frames of nationality policies and the language of constitutional reform. Yugoslav authorities seized on one of the slogans chanted during the protests, "Kosovo Republic," to characterize the riots as motivated by nationalism and "counter-revolutionary" to the ideals of Yugoslav socialism. Though the idea of republic status for Kosovo, or even the secession of Kosovo and other Albanian-inhabited parts of Yugoslavia, was harbored by a variety of clandestine political groups that emerged with every new generation of young educated Albanians, it was, at the time, regarded by the provincial party leadership as politically implausible.[25] At any rate, the riots unleashed a wave of hysteria in the party circles of post-Tito Yugoslavia, and brought about a level of systematic repression unseen in postwar Yugoslavia.[26]

While the Serbian party had raised the issue of what was deemed to be the excessive autonomy of the provinces on several occasions,[27] Serb unitarists in the federal and Serbian parties seized on the 1981 riots and the growing grievances of the Serb minority in Kosovo to push for the recentralization of Serbia.[28] It was in the figure of Slobodan Milošević that these two moments joined together, who used the grievances of Kosovo Serbs to push through a series of constitutional amendments in 1987 that recentralized some of the provincial powers to the Serbian republic. These moves by Serbia were also supported at the federal level, which increasingly began seeing the constitutional overhaul of the country as a cure for the institutional and economic crisis Yugoslavia experienced in the 1980s.[29] For Serbia, the only Yugoslav republic territorially divided into provinces, the reintegration of the provinces was central to this reform platform, and the Serbian party under Milošević made recentralization its main goal. In spite of growing protests, particularly in Kosovo, Milošević pushed through a series of new constitutional reforms intended to reduce the autonomy of the provinces even further. The campaign for reform—accompanied by truculent media attacks against dissenters, populist rallies, and threats

76

and intimidation against the Kosovo provincial leadership—provoked growing unrest among the Kosovo Albanians, as evidenced by strikes and the growing number of street protests throughout Kosovo.

The events of 1987 and 1988 drove an increasingly divisive wedge between Kosovo's Albanians and Serbs. As Kosovo's Serbs were mobilized by Milošević's radical reform agenda—facilitated in no small part by its nationalist overtones —Albanians became increasingly restive. The decisive moment in Albanian political mobilization came in November 1988, when the miners of Trepça staged a march to protest the constitutional changes and the attacks against the provincial leadership. This protest event was in effect a *defense* of the constitutional principles of 1974 and the provincial leadership in Kosovo under attack by Milošević. As such it subverted the meaning protest events had gained after 1981—as irredentist "counter-revolution- ary" activity. This appealed to a whole different stratum of Kosovo's Albanians—not the radical youth and students who had been at the forefront of the 1981 protests, but the working and professional classes of Albanians who were well-integrated into the Yugoslav socioeconomic system and *directly* affected by the political changes threatened by Milošević. The Trepça protest was, after all, a protest of the working class—the class upon which Yugoslav socialism was ideologically premised—and as such more deeply challenged the authorities than the student movements of 1981. The miners' revolt also instilled a deep rift within the provincial party.[30] The transformative moment came in February 1989, when the miners staged a dramatic eight-day hunger strike to demand the resignation of the party leadership, which had, in the preceding months, been replaced by a group of Milošević loyalists hand- picked by Belgrade. In November 1988 the miners' protest incited a massive march by 100,000 Albanians from throughout Kosovo to the capital to protest constitutional changes. The hunger strike of 1989 and the violent response of the regime fundamen- tally discredited the leadership and the legitimacy of the state; following that event, intellectuals, industrial workers, professionals, and others began more openly to air their opposition to the constitutional changes being pursued by Milošević. The miners' strike opened up possibilities of resistance and dissent which could not be easily suppressed by the traditional repressive measures at the regime's disposal. Peace activist Howard Clark, having interviewed an Albanian writer, observes:

> Until the miners' action, [the writer] suggests, most people felt it was impossible to find a means of struggle that would not lead to war or else they were deterred by possible condemnation within the [Yugoslav League of Communists] or investigation by the police. "After this strike, that was over, people said OK, me too."[31]

1989 and the Emergence of Ethnically Divided Pluralism

Thus far I have discussed the historical reasons why Kosovo's constitutional status was a salient issue in Yugoslav politics, raised periodically as a question within the general problem of federalism in Yugoslavia, and how it became politically

77

explosive in the 1980s. Following that I have sketched an outline of the major social and economic transformations that took place in Kosovo from the 1960s to the 1980s, and the major events that created the social bases for national mobilization and polarization. I will now more closely discuss the developments after 1989, when the Serbian party led by Milošević undertook a policy of abolishing Kosovo's autonomous powers and effectively shutting out Albanians from official institutional life. In what follows I describe how this policy and the dynamics it generated led to the emergence of the parallel state as a form of a nonviolent resistance against Serbia's takeover.

In 1989 Serbia adopted its first constitutional reforms that began rolling back the autonomous powers that Kosovo had gained from the Yugoslav constitution of 1974. Kosovo was fraught with protests throughout 1988–1989, and dissatisfaction was already high at the time the constitutional reforms were passed. As Kosovo's largely submissive and unpopular provincial leadership remained marginal to the developments, it was other elements of Kosovo's society which came to the fore to speak out against the reforms undertaken by Serbia. Intellectuals and other professionals, housed in Kosovo's state-sponsored cultural institutions and in the state bureaucracy, became increasingly vocal in expressing their opposition to the constitutional reforms, as well as the repressive measures that the authorities had taken against Kosovo's Albanian population. One of the first acts of dissent was the Apeli 215 ("Appeal 215"), an appeal to end repression and Belgrade's political assault against Kosovo's self-government, signed by 215 Albanian intellectuals in February 1989.[32] During 1989 critical views began appearing in state-owned media too, as traditional party censorship began to disintegrate. The open dissent emerging in the ranks of state institutions had been unthinkable in the past; however, the unraveling of socialist regimes in Eastern Europe generated hopes in Kosovo for a "democratic spring" there as well and opened the way for an emerging pluralism that Kosovo had not experienced during five decades of communist rule.

While the pro-democracy Yugoslav Democratic Initiative (UJDI) had established a branch in Kosovo as early as 1989, the year 1990 marked the emergence of a number of independent political organizations. Kosovo's first human rights groups emerged at the time, as well as an independent trade union resulting from the disintegration of the state-sponsored union organization. However, the most remarkable event was the establishment of the Democratic League of Kosovo (LDK) in December 1989. Although its initial role in the framework of the rapidly transforming political system was unclear even to its founders[33]—largely a group of politically inexperienced writers and intellectuals—the LDK rapidly became Kosovo's most massive political organization and, after political pluralism was formally introduced throughout Yugoslavia, its first non-communist political party. The LDK's founding meeting elected literary critic Ibrahim Rugova as its leader, and its membership exploded in the initial months, claimed at the time to number more than half a million.

How did the LDK manage to mobilize such an enormous number of individuals in the span of a few months? The fact is that while the leadership of the LDK came largely from a group of writers gathered around Kosovo's official Writers' Association, what became the rank and file of the organization was largely the result of the transformation of the Socialist Alliance for Working People (SAWP), the regime's official front organization. It was this organizational network that became the LDK's central mobilizing structure.[34]

Sociologists Jim Seroka and Radoš Smiljković, in their 1986 study of the SAWP, call it "an association of associations."[35] It included virtually all citizens and, unlike the Communist League, did not require formal commitment to the principles of Marxism-Leninism and Yugoslav self-management. The SAWP included under its wing virtually all formal and non-formal groups and associations, and its organizational network stretched widely, from professional associations to neighborhood organizations at the village level. In the 1980s, the organization at its various federal, republican, and provincial levels, included around 80% of the country's population over the age 15. It was also one of the central forums where, in accordance with legally established procedures, all proposals for constitutional amendments were open to public discussion. Its mobilizing potency in Kosovo is thus evident, given the contentiousness of these issues in the prevailing political environment.[36] It is largely the result of segments of the SAWP collectively switching their loyalty to the LDK that partly explains the immediate growth of the LDK, as well as the fact that it was the first group to espouse a largely Albanian-centered political outlook fully opposed to Serbia's policies in Kosovo.

While pluralism was taking root in Kosovo, it became, however, extremely polarized on ethnic bases. The new local political organizations were exclusively Albanian, while Serbs and Montenegrins remained tied to the state apparatus, now coming under the direct control of Belgrade. Serbian parties that emerged after single-party rule crumbled in Serbia were primarily branches of Belgrade-based parties, and few expressed opposition to Milošević's policies in Kosovo. Detentions, persecutions, and terror against Kosovo's Albanian population by a now exclusively Serbian police force drove a strong wedge between the populations which short-circuited the possibility of genuine liberalization, as the question of Kosovo's status became the fundamental political issue around which all contention revolved.[37]

Creating the Basis for the Parallel State: The Rebellious Assembly

While during 1990 Kosovar parties remained hopeful that free elections might create opportunities for political change, Milošević would make sure that no such possibility came about. In December 1990 Serbia held its first free elections, while that same year all provincial governing institutions in Kosovo were forcefully suspended or dissolved, making regular elections in Kosovo impossible. Repression and human rights abuse intensified; now Albanians were targeted collectively. This was done with the introduction of special legal authorizations that permitted the regime to massively lay off Albanian employees from jobs (the majority of which were in state-owned institutions and enterprises), threaten the education system in the Albanian language by forcing Albanian teachers to adopt Belgrade-approved curricula, shut down Albanian-language media, including the only Albanian-language daily, and violently suppress any open manifestation of discontent. This further homogenized Albanians of all socioeconomic backgrounds into a single political block, and indicated that in Milošević's Serbia Albanians represented a politically and socially undesirable lot. The collective stigmatization of Albanians in the 1980s had now become a policy of collective repression and persecution.

With the exception of a few small groups, the main political demand voiced by Albanian parties in 1990 was the reversal of Serbia's constitutional reforms and recognition of the right of Kosovo to become a republic within Yugoslavia. Officially, the desire for sovereignty was proclaimed on 2 July 1990, by the Albanian delegates of Kosovo's provincial Assembly—who had no formal connection with the LDK or any other opposition group. The proclamation was in fact conceived by several activists behind the scene; the LDK leadership was completely unaware of the Assembly's intentions.[38] The move came as a surprise to Belgrade as well, since it believed that it had secured the loyalty of the provincial leadership in toeing its line. However, this rebellious act by the Assembly forged the link between Kosovo's formal institutions and the Albanian opposition groups led by the LDK, turning the formal leadership and the opposition groups into a unified block. Faced by this threat, Serbia responded by suspending the Assembly and all of Kosovo's provincial governing organs altogether, thus establishing direct rule in the province, and reinforced its security presence with more police troops from Serbia. This, however, did not stop the Assembly from carrying out work clandestinely, in a series of acts that ultimately formed the basis for the parallel claims to sovereignty that defined Kosovo politics throughout the 1990s. In a secret meeting in September 1990, the Assembly met in the town of Kaçanik in southeastern Kosovo and adopted the "Constitution of the Republic of Kosovo," thereby sealing the political will of Kosovo's Albanians.[39] These acts by the Assembly, considered by the majority of Albanians to be fully legitimate and in compliance with the legal and constitutional order of Yugoslavia, laid the groundwork for the claim to legitimate sovereignty that formed the basis of the parallel state of the 1990s. The clandestine institutions retained the allegiance of Kosovo's Albanians as Kosovo's only legitimate government; Serbia, on the other hand, saw the moves as threatening acts of a secessionist minority that needed to be suppressed by any and all means.

As late as May 1991, at its first congress, the LDK's position was that Kosovo should become a republic within a Yugoslav confederation—a new loose federal order advocated at the time by Slovenia and Croatia. However, the demand for republican status became untenable only a month later, when Yugoslavia entered its first phase of disintegration with Slovenia and Croatia's departure. The LDK, which had virtually turned into a coalition of a variety of political currents among Kosovo's Albanians, was facing two difficult challenges. First, more radical currents within the party called for radical demands—the unification of all Yugoslav Albanians into a single republic, and their unification with Albania as the rectification of a historical injustice. Kosovar analyst Shkëlzen Maliqi calls this a conflict between "legalists" and "anti-legalists" (a more appropriate term would be "historisists"), the former maintaining that the demand for independence should adhere to some legal basis in the former Yugoslav constitutional order, and the latter viewing the conflict in stark historic terms that demanded radical solutions.[40] Second, the LDK had to strategize its actions based on the rapidly unfolding developments that followed Yugoslavia's disintegration, including the outbreak of fighting in Slovenia and Croatia and the diplomatic intervention of the European Community (EC) and the United States. During the summer of 1991, the LDK partly resolved its dilemmas by making Kosovo's independence its main political objective.[41] Additionally, working with other Albanian parties in the Coordinating Council of Political Parties (CCPP) and the clandestine Assembly, the LDK coordinated the organization of a referendum on Kosovo's independence in September 1991. Throughout 1991, referendums became a prevalent practice among minorities and majorities throughout Yugoslavia to claim the right to self-determination, and Kosovar Albanians organized their own.[42] The referendum, which overwhelmingly displayed the Albanians' popular will for independence, not only gave popular legitimacy to the LDK's goals, but presented Yugoslavia and the West with an unquestionable desire for independence.

The referendum indicated the overwhelming support of the Albanian population for independence. From little over one million registered voters, 99% were in favor of independence. Eighty-nine percent of those registered to vote participated in the secretly organized poll. The referendum was held between 26 and 30 September 1991, four days after the Assembly had adopted a "Resolution on Independence and Sovereignty of Kosovo." The Assembly met on October 19, proclaimed the independence of Kosovo and duly amended the Kaçanik constitution to reflect the popular vote for independence.[43] From this point on, the common goal of the Albanian movement—affirmed by "popular will"—became independence. After the referendum, any alternative platform or support for compromises over this issue became tantamount to national treason.

By 1992, Kosovo had developed two irreconcilable political blocs, the regime that introduced a Serbian nationalizing project and was bent on breaking the political will of Albanians by force if necessary, and a popular Albanian secessionist movement that maintained its position that Kosovo was "occupied" and viewed the Serbian takeover as completely illegitimate and the Serbian regime as a colonial authority engaged in brutal repression. These antagonisms reflected not only at the institutional level of politics, but pervaded all social life, thus forming the basis for the segregated, parallel political and social frameworks that Albanians and Serbs maintained in Kosovo during most of the 1990s.

Creating Control: Limiting Counter-Violence

The end of the Cold War and the rapid diminution of Yugoslavia's strategic importance to the West made the country vulnerable to greater pressure to respect international human rights norms. Concerned with the instability in Kosovo, in April 1989 the European Parliament adopted a resolution that condemned Serbia's policies in Kosovo and implored the authorities to abide by international human rights norms. In February 1990, the European Parliament passed another resolution condemning Yugoslavia's human rights violations and urging compromise between the Serbian authorities and Albanian leaders.

During the same period, the U.S. Congress also adopted a series of resolutions that condemned Serbia's policy in Kosovo. The House of Representatives, through a resolution adopted in June 1989, expressed its concern over human rights violations in Kosovo. A similar resolution was passed by the Senate in the following month. In November 1990, the Senate passed its harshest measure to date, blocking U.S. economic aid to Yugoslavia unless the country took measures to respect human rights in Kosovo. In addition, Western media became increasingly interested in the developments in Kosovo, and reports containing horrific tales of police violence were becoming available to Western policymakers and publics through organizations such as Amnesty International and Helsinki Watch (later Human Rights Watch).

The LDK quickly caught on—it was Serbia's violent repression that was bringing Western attention to the Albanians' plight. The LDK, and especially the Council for the Defense of Human Rights and Freedoms (CDHRF), in 1990 began intensifying their human rights monitoring efforts throughout Kosovo, producing daily and monthly reports accounting cases of police violence, brutal treatment of Albanians while in custody, and other cases of ethnically driven maltreatment and violence perpetrated by the authorities.

Human rights monitoring and reporting became a key activity of LDK and CDHRF branches, and in this respect there was an overlap in the interest and activity of the two organizations. The presence of LDK branches and CDHRF activists in virtually all towns and villages throughout Kosovo created a dense network of monitors that could quickly react to any instance of violence in their locality. These individuals were usually prominent members of the local community, and in severe incidents they would be accompanied by delegations from the capital. The monitoring network they were part of had dual purposes. Besides recording cases of police violence, it concurrently served another function, which was to monitor and control the behavior of the local populace so as, first, to ensure that the local community was acting in accordance with the policy set in Prishtina, and, second, to prevent any acts of counter-violence against police action that would fulfill Rugova's worst nightmare of giving Serbia "a pretext to initiate a massive campaign of murder and expulsion."[44]

In larger urban areas, after street demonstrations were discontinued in 1990, police repression eased up and took place in a largely predictable manner. Albanian residents and police learned to coexist and by 1993 achieved a modus vivendi based on the principle that Albanians would be permitted to conduct private economic activity and take part in activities organized by parallel institutions, but they would defer to police authority. However, the situation in rural areas was less tenable. After the removal of autonomy, forces of the Serbian Ministry of Interior (MUP) began a campaign of random house raids throughout villages in Kosovo allegedly to search for hidden weapons. The raids, usually conducted as night, were intended to humiliate as much as to actually confiscate weapons, and were accompanied by arrests, beatings, and even the death of family members.[45] Few villagers resisted the raids, but the events constituted the greatest threat of provoking violent reactions by villagers trying to defend themselves. Peace activist Howard Clark describes one such incident, which occurred in December 1991 in the village of Prekaz in the traditionally unruly Drenica region, when villagers fired shots at a police battalion marching into the village. The day after the incident, the village was immediately visited by LDK and CDHRF activists.[46] The activists went to the village with two purposes: first, to report the incident, and, second, to urge restraint among the population.[47] Having been previously proselytized into the movement by activists of the blood reconciliation campaign, villagers were now being monitored by local activists who were overseen by political leaders in the capital. Thus, the LDK established a highly effective system of control that for several years enabled it to maintain the fragile peace and the mantle of nonviolent resistance.[48] As an LDK activist told Clark,

> When the police make incursions into the villages and terrorize them, we—the people of the LDK—try to be the first ones to speak with the police so they can see we are there. For example, we went to Gllogovc when we had been warned. Not to calm the people—that was impossible, the police had already done their work—but to make an act of solidarity, to witness. That's very important. Otherwise, the police or army can take advantage of some piece of stupidity.[49]

Why Nonviolence?

In his work on social movements, Sidney Tarrow writes that protesting groups organize collective action based on "repertoires of contention," a concept he borrows from Charles Tilly.[50] Repertoires of contention represent a set of models for organizing collective action which groups and individuals can draw from and know how to use and implement. Thus, in laying their claims, contending groups can resort to a variety of collective actions, including nonviolent manifestations such as public demonstrations, strikes, and sit-ins, or violent acts such as damage of objects, violence against representatives of authority, and terrorism.[51] Drawing from a variety of scholarly research, Tarrow argues that social movements and the forms of protest they employ are intricately linked with the development of the modern state. Furthermore, forms of protest are "modular," in the sense that, once developed, they spread and are used by a variety of groups with different goals, operating in different geographic localities and under different regimes and national contexts.[52] In addition, movements are not limited to a single form of protest but often employ a multitude of different forms, depending on opportunities, resources, and strategic goals.[53] However, a repertoire that a movement can draw from is usually rather fixed— changes in existing forms are usually only marginal and innovations of new forms are rare.[54]

In the early 1990s, the "repertoire of contention" found in Kosovo consisted of three major forms of protest: public demonstrations, strikes, and guerilla attacks against law enforcement agents. By 1992, nearly all of these types of public protest ended, were stifled, or, as in the case of guerilla attacks, became marginal. By 1992, the parallel state had taken its institutional shape and gained a popularly supported leadership, and the LDK claimed ultimate authority in all political matters within the Albanian movement. The Albanian movement came to be known both locally and internationally as a nonviolent resistance movement—with Rugova gaining the mantle of an "Albanian Ghandi"—which defied Serb authority by maintaining a set of parallel institutions.

Why did all forms of public protest subside and the maintenance of parallel institutions become the only form of defiance? Or, to put it another way, why was armed resistance never seriously considered as an option in 1990–1992? The answer to these questions is key to explaining the Albanian movement's strategic commitment to nonviolence.

As indicated above, in the 1990s three forms of public protest were typically practiced in Kosovo. With the exception of guerilla attacks, the other forms of protest were conventional, nonviolent types of protest.[55] Consequently, the marginalization of guerilla attacks meant that the chances of armed conflict being provoked by the Albanian side were greatly reduced.

Although small guerilla groups existed in Kosovo in the early 1980s, these disintegrated through either weak organization, the lack of weapons, or the murder or imprisonment of militants.[56] During 1987, for instance, organizations such as the Popular Movement for the Republic of Kosovo (LPRK) staged guerilla attacks and various acts of sabotage against the authorities.[57] However, clandestine groups such as the LPRK were on the fringes of Kosovar politics. Repressive measures taken after 1981 took a toll on many underground activists, weakening their organizations. In addition, many former underground activists had joined mainstream parties such as the LDK (although these were not necessarily individuals who had been involved in or supportive of violence), causing tensions between the latter and those who continued operating in clandestine groups. In 1989 and the early 1990s, clandestine groups were in no position to gain popular support. Their influence among the youth—the segment of the population most likely to be involved in violent acts—was also curbed by public groups such as the Youth Parliament, which was active in the organization of nonviolent protest events.[58]

Disagreements arose between the LDK, on one hand, and the Youth Parliament and other groups, on the other, concerning the organization of nonviolent protest events. Borrowing from symbolic protest events that became prevalent in Eastern Europe in the late 1980s and early 1990s, the Youth Parliament organized a series of nonviolent protest events such as the petition "For Democracy, Against Violence," symbolic demonstrations where protestors carried an empty casket to symbolically "bury the violence," and protests against curfews by knocking on pots and pans and shaking keys during curfew hours. The LDK's objections to such events resulted in the stifling of initiatives such as these, and, soon after, public demonstrations subsided.

The Youth Parliament and other groups that were organizing peaceful protest events were the first to introduce forms of action that are by most standards considered genuine acts of nonviolent protest and resistance. Strikes were another form of nonviolent protest that took place. The protest march of Trepça miners in November 1988 and the miners' hunger strike in January 1989 triggered a series of solidarity strikes in enterprises throughout Kosovo. From November 1988 to September 1989, strikes or other work halts occurred in 230 enterprises in the province, with a loss of nearly two million labor hours.[59] Strikes became the chief weapon of the Independent Trade Unions of Kosovo (BSPK). In September 1990, the BSPK called for a one-day general strike to protest the firing of 15,000 Albanian workers. The general strike halted work throughout Kosovo and demonstrated a powerful show of solidarity. However, the strike failed to achieve its aims; rather, Serbia responded by firing an additional 5,000 workers.[60] By 1991, Serbia had dismissed nearly 150,000 Albanian workers, representing 90% of the employed workforce.[61] By instituting such drastic measures, Serbia pulled the plug on strikes and arrested the political power of the BSPK.

Serbia's repressive policies and the LDK's stifling of initiatives resulted in the cessation of public protest events. The main reason why the LDK wanted people off the streets was its fear of massive reprisals, which was Rugova's consistent personal fear.[62] In addition, the fledgling Albanian movement was beginning to gain sympathy among the publics in the northern Yugoslav republics and Western policymakers precisely due to its nonviolent nature, which would have been jeopardized by any endorsement of violence. Furthermore, the LDK was able to control counter-violence through the institutional mechanisms of control it had developed, as discussed above.

Moreover, the option of full-blown armed resistance became largely impracticable due to the inability of former provincial defense forces to organize into a resistance movement. In 1989, Serbia disbanded Kosovo's Territorial Defense force and in 1990 it removed most Albanians (around 3,500) from the provincial police force. In 1991, a group of former defense employees attempted to form a secret defense force, but the effort failed.[63] During the same period, a group of former police working under the cover of their trade union operated as a shadow police force. However, their efforts also ended in 1994, when around 200 of them were arrested and tried for attempting to set up a parallel ministry of the interior.[64] While there is speculation concerning whether any of these groups could have been successfully transformed into an armed force if they had been managed properly and provided with sufficient financial and political support, Rugova's lack of political will to organize a defense force and preference for a passive policy were important factors that thwarted its realization.[65]

Hence, with virtually all opportunities for armed resistance removed and Rugova's firm position in maintaining a policy of passive resistance, there appeared little opportunity for an armed uprising. As Maliqi writes, "the strategy of nonviolence was somehow self-imposed as the best, most pragmatic and most efficient response to [Serbia's] aggressive plans."[66] It was also self-imposed because, realistically, the means to respond to Serbia's takeover with an orchestrated campaign of violence were extremely limited, and because Rugova's fear of reprisals muffled any serious initiatives to prepare for armed struggle. In addition, the strong solidarities and the LDK's elaborate network of activists ensured that no violent incident would get out of hand.

Resilient Institutions

As indicated previously, the Assembly and other provincial governing institutions were part of a larger framework of political, economic, and cultural institutions operating in the province. Besides its government and administrative apparatus, each republic and province in Yugoslavia had its own set of intricately linked and state-supported economic, social, and cultural institutions.[67] While this fact alone illustrates why the abolition of Kosovo's autonomy concerned not only its government and administration but the entire institutional structure of the province, it also presented Milošević with an additional challenge of reintegrating the province into Serbia's political and administrative system after Kosovo's self-governing powers had been removed. As these institutions were staffed and led mostly by Albanians who were against the abolition of Kosovo's self-governing powers, Belgrade faced the problem of bringing these institutions in line with its policy of reintegration. Belgrade's solution was odiously simple: by using an obscure republican law, it instituted so-called "emergency measures" in all organizations, and then demoted or fired all those who did not or potentially would not abide by Belgrade's policies. In the economic sector, if one discounts economic losses, this policy proved successful as Serbia took control over most Kosovar enterprises. In other sectors, especially education, Belgrade's policy would have an unexpected consequence. Namely, Belgrade's expulsion of Albanian personnel en masse resulted in their regrouping and the reconstruction of the institutions from which they had been removed. The resilience of institutions in the face of suppression is therefore the key factor that led to the creation of Kosovo's parallel social organization.

As argued by the Kosovar legal scholar Esat Stavileci, the expulsion of Albanians from their jobs was chiefly a political act without a sound legal basis. In examining official dismissal warrants, he finds political beliefs or activities to be the main grounds for dismissal.[68] As such, more than the loss of a job itself, revulsion was provoked by the fact that workers were dismissed on the basis of their nationality, which resulted in the strengthening of solidarity and the commitment to collectively resist Serbia's takeover.[69] Resistance was chiefly organized through the establishment of parallel institutions (or, in the view of those organizing them, the *legitimate* institutions of Kosovo). While such resistance was practically impossible in the case of enterprises, it was possible in institutions where public services were the main activity (see Table 1 for a list of affected institutions).[70] There were mainly two sectors that successfully organized sustainable parallel structures: education and health care. Given the purposes of this paper, here I only trace the emergence (rather than the evolution) of parallel organizations and the factors that enabled their sustainability in the short term.

Parallel Education: Teachers against the State

The first conflict between Serbian authorities and schools in Kosovo began in 1990, when the Albanian teachers refused to abide by a new curriculum adopted by the Serbian Ministry of Education and continued to use the old curriculum set by the dissolved provincial authorities.[71] In 1990, Serb authorities paid Serb teachers double the salary they paid Albanian teachers, then in February 1991 they completely stopped paying salaries to Albanian teachers. Furthermore, according to the Ministry's plans for the 1991/1992 school year, less than 30% of Albanian students finishing primary school would have the opportunity to enroll in secondary schools, while there were 700 *more* slots available for Serb students than there were primary school graduates.[72] The first closure of an education facility also occurred in 1990, when the Serbian Assembly passed a law that resulted in the closure of the Medical Faculty of the University of Prishtina. In August 1991, 6,000 secondary school teachers and 115 principals were dismissed, and at the start of the 1991/1992 school year the authorities used police to prevent Albanian students from entering school premises.[73]

The key actors behind the organization of parallel schools were the Alliance of Albanian Teachers (LASH) and the Independent Teachers Union (SBASHK). Barred from entering school buildings, students went to classes set up in makeshift classrooms in private houses, basements, and garages, among other locations. While initially seen as only a temporary measure, the parallel school system was the only alternative remaining after the authorities prevented Albanian teachers and students

TABLE 1 Institutions closed down or taken over by Serbian authorities

Municipality	Institutions					
	Economic	Educational	Health care	Cultural	Media	Total
1. Prishtina	62	16	22	4	4	108
2. Mitrovica	26	5	3	—	1	35
3. Peja	25	—	7	—	1	33
4. Ferizaj	19	—	2	—	1	23
5. Gjilan	18	—	4	—	1	23
6. Prizren	10	1	1	—	—	12
7. Lipjan	11	1	—	—	—	12
8. Kamenica	7	2	1	—	—	10
9. Gjakova	10	—	—	—	—	10
10. Vushtrri	8	1	—	1	—	10
11. Deçan	9	—	1	—	—	10
12. Rahovec	5	1	1	—	—	7
13. Klina	6	1	2	—	—	9
14. Podujeva	3	—	2	—	—	5
15. Dragash	5	—	—	—	—	5
16. Kaçanik	4	—	1	—	—	5
17. Skënderaj	4	—	1	—	—	5
18. Viti	4	—	1	—	—	5
19. Istog	2	—	—	—	—	3
20. Suhareka	3	—	—	—	—	3
21. Gllogoc	1	—	—	—	—	1
22. Malisheva	2	—	—	—	—	2
23. Shtime	1	—	1	—	—	2
Total	245	28	49	6	8	338

Source: Pajazit Nushi, "Krimet kundër njerëzisë dhe gjenocidi kundër shqiptarëve," in Esat Stavileci and Nushi, *Të vërteta për Kosovën* (Prishtina: Lidhja Shqiptare në Botë, 2000), p. 109.

from entering school buildings in 1992.[74] Primary education was less targeted than secondary education. Out of 441 primary schools, 41 functioned in alternative premises, while 60 out of 66 secondary schools operated outside of their original facilities.[75]

The University of Prishtina also became a target of the Serbian authorities. After closing the Medical Faculty, Serbia instituted a series of measures in 1991 to purge the university's 13 faculties, removing all Albanian teaching staff and promoting or installing Serbs in their place. This turned the university into an exclusively Serbian institution. After being barred from university buildings in 1991, the Albanian employees of the university reorganized in alternative makeshift facilities, catering for nearly 20,000 students.[76]

Health Care and the Emergence of Other Parallel Structures

"Emergency measures" that were used against education were also introduced in the field of health care and resulted in the removal of Albanian medical staff from their jobs. The measures were first introduced in 1990 and ended with the closure of clinics and hospitals. Thirty-eight clinics were closed in Prishtina alone.[77] While a complete reorganization of health care following the steps taken by the schools was practically impossible, doctors began engaging in a variety of activities in order to offer medical services to Albanians, who were apprehensive about using Serb-controlled hospitals.[78] While many doctors turned to private practice, the first large-scale organization to offer free medical services was the Mother Teresa Association (MTA), formed in 1990. In 1992 MTA established its first clinic, and by 1998 with the help of international humanitarian organizations nearly 350,000 people relied on MTA for medical assistance and aid.[79]

A variety of cultural and social organizations also continued to operate. While it had its funding discontinued, the Kosovar Academy of Arts and Sciences and the Institute of Albanology continued to function in their original premises until 1994. In addition, several other formerly official institutions, such as the Institute of History and the Institute of Language and Literature, also continued to operate and publish, although in a much smaller capacity. Although oftentimes prevented by police, sports events were organized and leagues were maintained. Albanian-language media also survived efforts to shut them down. After the shutting down of Radio-Television Prishtina there were no longer any Albanian-language broadcasts, but the daily *Rilindja* was resurrected through the transformation of the farmer's magazine *Bujku* into a daily newspaper, while the youth magazine *Zëri i Rinisë* was transformed into a political weekly.[80] The appropriation and transformation of existing institutions at a pace that the state itself could not keep up with became the tactic for resisting Serbia's attempts to fully expel Albanians from institutional life.

Although not necessarily centrally controlled, the activities of parallel institutions were placed under the aegis of the Republic of Kosovo, operating under its ministries and with certain sectors receiving financial support. The instances of institutional resistance were taking place within the context of the Albanian movement and its efforts to deny legitimacy to the Serbian takeover. As collective acts of resistance they derived their rationale and symbolic meaning from that movement. At any rate, it is important to emphasize, as Maliqi does, that "the parallel institutions of Kosovo all pre-date 1990," and that they are "a legacy of the earlier system."[81]

Rounding off the Parallel State: The Elections of 1992

As indicated above, throughout most of 1991, the LDK had an ambiguous policy and was marred by internal disputes. Its ignorance of the Assembly's plans to deprive Serbia of a clean victory in tearing down Kosovo's autonomy by acting defiantly meant that it was the provincial institutions, and not the LDK, which defined the framework of contentious issues and the strategy that would be pursued. And while the LDK dominated politically, it was nonetheless only one among many contenders on the stage of Kosovar Albanian politics. The Assembly continued to consist of LCY-era delegates, while the LDK's only claim to the mantle of legitimacy was through Rugova's chairing of the CCPP—an organization where the LDK nonetheless had to maintain a degree of consensus over general issues of strategy. The elections of 1992 bestowed the LDK—and Rugova personally—with unchallenged control over the shadow Republic of Kosovo, and, therefore, the parallel state and the Albanian movement.

In 1992, Yugoslavia was no more. After the EC's recognition of Slovenia and Croatia in December 1991, the U.S. revised its policy of supporting the maintenance of Yugoslavia and in April 1992 recognized Slovenia, Croatia, and Bosnia-Herzegovina as independent states. During the same year, armed conflict engulfed Bosnia-Herzegovina and the EC boosted its efforts to manage the break-up. The definitive dissolution of the Yugoslav federation opened up the opportunity for the Albanian movement to intensify its claims for Kosovo's independence. The LDK considered Western intervention to be crucial in attaining its goal.

While the Albanian movement's nonviolent posture had gained it sympathy from Western policymakers, they did not support independence. The Kosovar government-in-exile applied for recognition to the EC in December 1991, but its request was refused based on the recommendations of the Badinter commission, which ruled that only republics were eligible for statehood.[82] Nevertheless, through the efforts of a vibrant Albanian-American lobby, it appeared that momentum for independence was gaining ground in the U.S. Congress.[83] In November 1991, and then again in January 1992, Senators Alphonse D'Amato and Larry Presler introduced resolutions in the Senate recommending the recognition of Kosovo's independence and supporting competitive elections in Kosovo.[84] In April, after the U.S. recognition of Slovenia, Croatia, and Bosnia-Herzegovina, several high-ranking senators, including the leading Republican senator Bob Dole, raised the issue of human rights violations in Kosovo. On the same occasion, Senator Pressler called for the inclusion of the Kosovars in the EC's Brussels peace conference, free elections in Kosovo, and the recognition of its independence. Bujar Bukoshi, Kosovo's prime minister in exile, intensified his diplomacy in the first few months of 1992, meeting high-level officials in Denmark, The Netherlands, Austria, Turkey, and the U.S.[85] While elections became important for the consolidation of the Albanian movement, they also became necessary for giving more weight to the demand for recognition and became a legitimate endeavor because they enjoyed international support.[86]

The elections confirmed the LDK's and Rugova's overwhelming popular support and their uncontested position in leading the Albanian movement. In the secret polls held on 24 May 1992, the LDK received 76% of the votes, gaining 96 out of the 140 seats in the shadow parliament.[87] Rugova, running unopposed, received 99% of the vote. The elections were also legitimized by the presence of a number of foreign observers, including U.S. congressional staff and reporters from over 100 foreign media organizations, who stated that the elections had been largely regular. While Serbia did not prevent the vote—the likely reason being that Milošević wanted to avoid additional Western reprimand on top of the condemnation he was receiving because of the violence in Bosnia-Herzegovina—it called the elections illegal and dispersed the meeting of the new parliament a few days later.

Figures in the Albanian movement who differed with Rugova on strategy and other issues, such as the Parliamentary Party leader Veton Surroi and nationalist writer and LDK critic Rexhep Qosja, said the elections were "not free," but stopped short of opposing them, calling them demonstrations of popular will against Serbian rule.[88] However, this did not prevent the LDK from cementing its control over the Albanian movement. Pluralism—in its relative sense—became meaningless as the CCPP ceased to function and other parties were completely marginalized. Contrary to Rugova's statements prior to and immediately after the elections, the parliament and government were never established as standing institutions.[89] This enabled Rugova to wield full personal control, both politically and according to the authority he enjoyed based on the nominal legal norms of the shadow "Republic of Kosovo".[90] The LDK became the sole legitimate authority, both at the central and municipal levels; according to Rugova, "the LDK also functions as the local authority because with the party it is easier to organize life."[91]

Three factors contributed to the LDK's electoral victory. First, the LDK enjoyed massive popular support. Having inherited Kosovo's autonomy-era mass organization structures, it was by far the largest party. In addition, Rugova's personal popularity had soared and was unchallenged by any other individual in the movement. His charisma and soft-spoken demeanor, Western support, and the LDK-controlled media turned him into a cult-like figure within Kosovo. Second, the party controlled the main media outlets, most significantly the daily *Bujku*, which was the only Albanian-language daily in Kosovo. Finally, the LDK was the main organization standing behind the elections. If it were not for the LDK's elaborate organizational structure, there would have been no elections of that scale. However, at the same time, this undoubtedly created a degree of bias in the polls.

The elections completed the institutional framework of the parallel state. After 1992, a series of other steps enabled the parallel state to become sustainable. These included the collection of a voluntary tax from Albanian business people by LDK-controlled financial councils established throughout Kosovo. A voluntary tax was also collected by the government-in-exile from Albanian immigrant communities in Western Europe and the U.S., usually through the efforts of LDK branches formed throughout these communities. The money was used to support the LDK's work and to provide the salaries for teachers and other activists of the parallel state. As the government remained in exile and the new parliament held not a single meeting, the LDK through Rugova, who was now dubbed the President of the

"Republic of Kosovo", became the sole authority in all matters within the Albanian movement.

Conclusion

In her analysis of the collapse of socialist regimes, Valerie Bunce argues that socialism collapsed under its own weight—the institutions that were meant to guarantee socialism's survival ended up subverting the regime.[92] The very same process, it can be argued, caused the emergence of the parallel state in Kosovo: institutions that were meant to guarantee the survival of the state ended up subverting the authority of the state itself. The parallel state was a result of the resilience of autonomy-era institutions much more than of intentional planning by Kosovo's rising political counter-elite, in particular the LDK. Today the territorial claims over Kosovo continue to be cast in a variety of meta-historical terms, with both sides vying to correct ethno-political injustices of previous historical eras. Nevertheless, the particular contours that the conflict took in its earliest stage are most clearly understood in terms of the institutional framework inherited from the socialist era and the specific political dynamic that precipitated and followed the final unraveling of the federal state.

Of the factors discussed in this article, three stand out as crucial in having contributed to the emergence of the parallel state. First, the creation of strong solidarities *within* but not *between* national groups during the late 1980s formed the social bases for parallelism. Second, the political opportunities created by the collapse of state socialism in Eastern Europe and the emerging pluralism in political life made it possible for the first non-state groups to emerge, and these groups were, due to political circumstances, defined by nationally oriented agendas. Finally, the incredible resilience of autonomy-era institutions in spite of severe state repression, spearheaded by the rebellious actions of the provincial Assembly, created the conditions of split sovereignty that became the basis for the parallel state and the Albanian movement's demand for a restoration of autonomy, and, after Yugoslavia's disintegration, independence. These developments structured the dynamics of a conflict that lasted, in the form of the parallel state, throughout the 1990s.

NOTES

1. The arguments found here are in the most part derived from Besnik Pula, "Contested Sovereignty and State Disintegration: The Rise of the Albanian Secessionist Movement, 1988–1992," MA thesis, Georgetown University, Washington, 2001.
2. See, for instance, Susan Woodward, *Balkan Tragedy: Chaos and Dissolution after the Cold War* (Washington: Brookings, 1995).
3. Rogers Brubaker, *Nationalism Reframed: Nationhood and the National Question in the New Europe* (Cambridge: Cambridge University Press, 1996), pp. 13–22.

4. For an example of an analysis of ethnic conflict based on models of strategic action see Roger Petersen, *Resistance and Rebellion: Lessons from Eastern Europe* (Cambridge: Cambridge University Press, 2001). As the reader will notice, the approach taken in this paper does not preclude the possibility of strategic behavior; however, it assumes that such behavior can take place under particular institutional conditions—which must themselves be subject to historical analysis—and that its sphere of possibilities are limited by previously shaped identities and cultural repertoires.

5. For a summary see Doug McAdam, Sidney Tarrow, and Charles Tilly, "Toward an Integrated Perspective on Social Movements and Revolutions," in Mark I. Lichbach and Alan S. Zuckerman, eds, *Comparative Politics: Rationality, Culture, and Structure* (Cambridge: Cambridge University Press, 1997).

6. See Sidney Tarrow, *Power in Movement: Social Movements and Contentious Politics* (Cambridge: Cambridge University Press, 1998), especially pp. 71–80. The quote is from p. 18.

7. McAdam *et al.*, "Toward an Integrated Perspective on Social Movements and Revolutions," p. 155.

8. See *ibid.*; Tarrow, *Power in Movement*. See also Doug McAdam, John D. McCarthy, and Mayer N. Zald, eds, *Comparative Perspectives on Social Movements: Political Opportunities, Mobilizing Structures, and Cultural Framings* (Cambridge: Cambridge University Press, 1996), pp. 1–22. The component of the theoretical edifice that I do not embrace here is the largely social psychological approach to "framing," or identity formation among members of collective movements. In *Dynamics of Contention* (New York: Cambridge University Press, 2001), D. McAdam, S. Tarrow, and C. Tilly make efforts to overcome this problem in the overall framework, but without great success in explicating the cultural and symbolic processes that go into identity construction. I prefer to think of identities themselves being historically embedded and emerging within contexts infused by power relations. For an alternative approach to framing see Marc Steinberg, "The Talk and Backtalk of Collective Action: A Dialogue Analysis of Repertoires and Discourse among 19th Century English Cotton Spinners," *American Journal of Sociology*, Vol. 105, No. 3, 1999, pp. 736–780.

9. The parallel state carried on until the war of 1999; however, the political dynamics of parallelism between 1993 and 1999 are not the subject of this article.

10. In contemporary usage, the geographic term "Kosovo" (Albanian *Kosova* or Serbian *Kosovo-Metohij*) is used to refer to both a current and a historical entity. However, it is important to emphasize that Kosovo as a territorially bounded administrative unit emerged only in 1945. The advent of a regional government in Kosovo was a direct result of the federal territorial arrangements that emerged in post-1945 Yugoslavia ruled by the CPY.

11. Quoted in Radošin Rajović, *Autonomija Kosovo: istorijsko-pravna studija* (Belgrade: Ekonomika, 1985) p. 85.

12. It should be noted that the request for separation from the Communist Party of Montenegro was made at a time when the regional party for Kosovo was dominated by Montenegrins. See Branko Horvat, *Kosovsko pitanje* (Zagreb: Globus, 1988), p. 92.

13. Quoted in Michelé Lee, "Kosovo between Yugoslavia and Albania," *New Left Review*, No. 140, 1983, p. 77.

14. Quoted in *ibid.*, p. 77.

15. Horvat, *Kosovsko pitanje*, p. 92; Lee, "Kosovo between Yugoslavia and Albania," pp. 85–86. The boundaries were reportedly set on "ethnic and historic" criteria. It is clear that the criteria in the case of Kosovo were more or less arbitrary; Albanian-inhabited

parts in Montenegro and western Macedonia were left outside of the frontiers, whereas historically the Ottoman province of Kosovo included large chunks of the Republic of Macedonia and the Sandjak region.

16. Immediately after the war, Kosovo was placed under military administration, to fight Albanian insurgents in the Drenica region and "reactionary elements" active in the province. The military administration was removed in 1946; however, various repressive measures continued to be exercised in Kosovo, with Albanians representing a particular target. An especially brutal episode was the so-called arms collection campaign of 1955–1956, in which hundreds of mostly Albanian homes were raided in the search for weapons. "Ethnic cleansing" was also attempted. During the 1950s, Tito's security chief, Aleksandar Ranković, made efforts to revive a 1938 treaty between Yugoslavia and Turkey to expel 40,000 Muslim (largely Albanian and Turkish) families from Kosovo and Macedonia to Turkey. See in particular Bojan Korsika, *Srbija i Albanci: pregled politike Srbije prema Albancima od 1944. do 1989. godine*, Vols 1–3 (Ljubljana: Casopis za kritiko znanosti, 1989). For an English translation of the text of the Yugoslav–Turkish agreement see Robert Elsie, *Kosovo: In the Heart of the Powder Keg* (Boulder: East European Monographs, 1997), pp. 425–434. According to the Kosovar demographer Hivzi Islami, by 1966 around 230,000 Albanians had left Yugoslavia. For a discussion of the agreement between Ranković and Turkey see Hivzi Islami, "Kërkimet antro-pogjeografike në Kosovë," *Gjurmime Albanologjike: Seria e Shkencave Historike* (Prishtina), Vol. 1, 1971, pp. 115–162.

17. The term *Šiptar* is now considered by Kosovo Albanians a derogatory name. In the 1950s and 1960s Belgrade made attempts to distinguish between Kosovo Albanians and Albanians of Albania, by calling the former *Šiptari* and the latter *Albanci*. This policy ended in the 1960s.

18. For a detailed discussion of Yugoslav federalism see Sabrina Ramet, *Nationalism and Federalism in Yugoslavia, 1962–1991* (Bloomington: Indiana University Press, 1992).

19. Elez Biberaj, "Kosovë: The Struggle for Recognition," in *The Albanian Problem in Yugoslavia: Two Views* (London: Institute for the Study of Conflict, 1982), p. 33.

20. Woodward, *Balkan Tragedy*, pp. 50–57.

21. Dennison I. Rusinow, *The Other Albania: Kosovo 1979*, Part 1 (Hanover, NH: American Universities Field Staff, 1980), p. 10.

22. Patrick F. R. Artisien and R. A. Howells, "Yugoslavia, Albania and the Kosovo Riots," *World Today*, Vol. 37, No. 11, 1981, pp. 421–422.

23. According to Yugoslav census counts taken in 1948 and 1981.

24. For instance, in 1974, out of the 128,000 employees of the state sector, 36% were Serb and Montenegrin, while nearly 39% of managerial positions were held by Serbs. Disproportionate Serb and Montenegrin representation was also evident in administration. Out of 251 presidents of administrative agencies, nearly 38% were Serbs and Montenegrins. See Biberaj, "The Conflict in Kosovo," p. 46. According to statistical data from the 1980s, Kosovo Serbs were still employed in greater proportion to their population than Albanians, their income was higher, and they comprised a smaller percentage of the unemployed. While according to one survey Albanian households in 1989 had on average nine members with only one person permanently employed, Serb households had five members, out of which two had permanent jobs (see Slavko Gaber and Tonči Kuzmanić, eds, *Zbornik: Kosovo—Srbija—Jugoslavija* [Ljubljana: Krt, 1989], p. 288). Official employment data showed that in 1986, when Serbs and Montenegrins constituted less than 15% of the total population, they constituted 25% of the total employed workforce (see Rexhep Ismajli, "Albanski jezik u Jugoslaviji," in Slavko

Gaber and Tonči Kuzmanić, eds, *Zbornik: Kosovo—Srbija—Jugoslavija* [Ljubljana: Krt, 1989], p. 95). In 1981, in terms of per capita income, the income of Serbs was 24% greater than that of Albanians. Albanians were the poorest group in Yugoslavia and, after the Croats, the second poorest in Kosovo itself (based on data in Julie Mertus, *Kosovo: How Myths and Truths Started a War* (Berkeley: University of California Press, 1999), p. 24). In 1970, 1980, and 1981, the vast majority of the unemployed in Kosovo were Albanian. Out of those unemployed in the given years, on average 77% were Albanians, while 16% were Serbs (excluding Montenegrins). Montenegrins were the fewest among the unemployed, with an average of 2% for the years indicated (according to data in Mertus, op cit., p. 28).

25. Author's interview with Fadil Hoxha, Prishtina, July 2000. Hoxha was a leading figure in Kosovo's communist leadership and chaired the committee that drafted the proposals for constitutional amendments in 1968. Hoxha stated that his personal view at the time was that Yugoslavia was not prepared to accept Kosovo as a republic, and rather sought to gain republican powers for the province while maintaining its provincial status. Another Kosovar party leader who was involved in the discussions over Kosovo's status, Mahmut Bakalli, in an interview in 1995 stated that while the Kosovar leadership hoped to gain republic status, they were aware of the constraints. He notes that the stability of Yugoslavia was for them a greater concern than the desire to get republic status (see Momčilo Petrović, *Pitao sam albance šta žele, a oni su rekli: republiku ... ako može* [Belgrade: Radio B92, 1996], pp. 12–20).

26. The paranoia that the riots induced in the party leadership is exhibited by the statement of Stane Dolanc, a member of the Central Committee of the LCY: "behind [the riots] lie the most reactionary forces in the world, fascists, and the most dogmatic [communists], which at this time have probably united and formed a single platform. And that platform is the destabilization of Yugoslavia. ... We will deal in the same manner with any display of nationalism ... [and with] whomever is linked to international reactionary circles of the right or of the left, pro-fascist or pro-dogmatic, pro-Informbureau elements" (quoted in Spasoje Daković, *Sukobi na Kosovu* [Belgrade: Narodna knjiga, 1984], p. 300). The image of an internationally unified reactionary-nationalist-fascist-Marxist-Leninist conspiracy to destroy Yugoslavia was the "sum of all fears," which all combined to signify the "enemy within" who needed to be dealt with forcefully. The *point de capiton*, the bludgeoning stereotype of this discourse which combined an impossible array of conspiracies into a single embodied enemy became "Albanian irredentism," which in 1980s Yugoslav public discourse became the catch-phrase representing all of Yugoslavia's ills, stigmatizing Yugoslavia's Albanian minority as one of the central threats to the integrity of the country and, for Serb nationalists in the CPY, the perpetrators of "genocide" against the Serb minority in Kosovo. The juridical side of this discourse was the persecution of Albanians for the most bizarre reasons, such as for naming children "nationalist names," for not playing non-Albanian music at weddings, or for having expressed admiration for Enver Hoxha's Albania. On the events of 1981 see Mertus, op cit., pp. 17–46. One of the most insightful critiques of the growing discourse of hate against Albanians in public institutions is Fehmi Agani, "Kriticki osvrt na politicki diskurs o Kosovu i Albancima," in Gaber and Kuzmanić, op cit., pp. 111–135. Another discussion is found in Muhamedin Kullashi, "The Production of Hatred in Kosovo (1981–91)," in Ger Duijzings, Dušan Janjić, and Shkëlzen Maliqi, eds, *Kosova/Kosovo: Confrontation or Coexistence* (Nijmegen: Peace Research Centre, 1997), pp. 56–69.

27. Dissatisfaction with the high degree of autonomy the provinces enjoyed surfaced as early as 1977, in the so-called "Blue Book" drafted by the Serbian party leadership. After the

events of 1981, measures were taken to re-establish republican control over provincial governments. In 1984, the Serbian party published an elaborate proposal for reform, which included the revision of the 1974 constitution. In the following year, the Constitutional Court of Serbia annulled a series of decrees that sought to insure the national composition of the provincial leadership was proportional to the population, which had effectively secured Albanian dominance in the provincial government. See Viktor Meier, *Yugoslavia: A History of Its Demise* (New York: Routledge, 1999), especially p. 9.

28. Though there was undoubtedly a perception of intimidation and threat among Kosovo Serbs during the 1970s and 1980s, there is no evidence of systematic, institutionalized attempts to force Serbs to migrate out of Kosovo, as claimed by the Serbian leadership at the time and maintained by some Serbian scholars. A strong but empirically unsupported argument of systematic discrimination of Kosovo Serbs in the period 1970–1989 is found in Marina Blagojević, "The Migration of Serbs from Kosovo during the 1970s and 1980s: Trauma and/or Catharsis," in Nebojša Popov, ed., *The Road to War in Serbia: Trauma and Catharsis* (Budapest: Central European University Press, 2000). Nonetheless, the issue was masterfully exploited by elements of the Serbian party to advance internal power struggles. On those struggles, particularly in relation to the rise of Slobodan Milošević, see Nebojša Vladisavljević, "Institutional Power and the Rise of Milošević," *Nationalities Papers*, Vol. 32, No. 1, 2004, pp. 183–206. For evidence on the connections between Serb protest groups in Kosovo and the Serbian party leadership and the top-down engineering of acts of revolt see Laura Silber and Allan Little, *Yugoslavia: Death of a Nation* (New York: Penguin Books, 1997), pp. 34–35.

29. Sabrina Ramet, *Nationalism and Federalism in Yugoslavia, 1962–1991* (Bloomington: Indiana University Press, 1992), especially pp. 221–3.

30. It took until January 1989 for the provincial party to decide on the character of the miners' protests, and the haggling between local, provincial, and republican party organizations revealed the growing disunity between different segments of the administration in their perception of Albanian protests. See Aziz Abrashi and Burhan Kavaja, *Epopeja e minatorëve* (Prishtina: Koha, 1996), pp. 25–30. See also Miranda Vickers, *Between Serb and Albanian: A History of Kosovo* (New York: Columbia University Press, 1998), p. 233.

31. Howard Clark, *Civil Resistance in Kosovo* (London: Pluto Press, 2000), p. 53.

32. The text of the appeal is found in Harillaq Kekezi and Rexhep Hida, eds, *Ç'thonë dhe ç'kërkojnë kosovarët*, Vol. 1 (Tirana: 8 Nëntori, 1990), pp. 7–14. The list of signatories practically represents a who's who list of Kosovar politics of the 1990s. Out of those who signed the petition, at least 65 were detained and imprisoned in the subsequent months.

33. In its early phase the LDK was an ill-defined organization, it did not have a legal status, since there was no law on opposition parties, and initially its name included the description "Political, Social, and Cultural Association." Rugova's statement to the Voice of America soon after the organization was formed indicates the LDK's untypical position. According to Rugova, the LDK "at the moment is a political and cultural association. In the future we shall see that, when these issues of political pluralism are legalized here in Yugoslavia, it may even become a political, cultural [*sic*] party, etc" (Kekezi and Hida, *Ç'thonë dhe ç'kërkojnë kosovarët*, Vol. 2, p. 16). Rugova later claimed that the LDK was not a party but a movement.

34. Details of the LDK's foundation are found in a book by one of the LDK's founders, Mehmet Kraja, *Vitet e humbura* (Tirana: [no publisher], 1995), as well as Tim Judah, *Kosovo: War and Revenge* (New Haven: Yale University Press, 2000), pp. 66–67. On the

role of official academic associations in the formation of political parties see Shkëlzen Maliqi, *Kosovo: Separate Worlds* (Prishtina: Dukagjini, 1998), pp. 26–27.

35. Jim Seroka and Radoš Smiljković, *Political Organizations in Socialist Yugoslavia* (Durham, NC: Duke University Press, 1986), p. 80.

36. Nikë Gjeloshi, former provincial secretary of the Kosovo SAWP, provides ample evidence that illustrates the extent to which opposition to the constitutional reforms was aired in SAWP chapter meetings throughout the province during 1989. See Gjeloshi, *Kosova në udhëkryq '89* (Gorle, Italy: Editrice Velar, 1997).

37. Albanian police officers were massively laid off from the service in 1990.

38. The move was largely conceived by Kosovar legal scholar Gazmend Zajmi, who authored the text of the "Declaration of Sovereignty" proclaimed that day by the Albanian delegates of the Assembly. Zajmi was not a member of the LDK. See Shkëlzen Maliqi, "Why Did Kosovo's Nonviolent Movement Resistance Fail?" unpublished manuscript, 2001, p. 9.

39. For the text of the document see *Kushtetuta e Republikës së Kosovës* (Zagreb: Dielli, 1990).

40. Maliqi, "Why Did Kosovo's Nonviolent Resistance Movement Fail?" p. 9. Compare the legalist argument for independence in Gazmend Zajmi, *Vepra I* (Prishtina: Akademia e Shkencave dhe e Arteve e Kosovës, 1997), especially pp. 143–164, and the historicist approach in Rexhep Qosja, *Çështja shqiptare: historia dhe politika* (Tirana: Toena, 1998), especially pp. 287–316. Although neither Zajmi nor Qosja was a member of the LDK, their arguments are representative of both schools of thought.

41. Denisa Kostovičová, *Parallel Worlds: Response of Kosovo Albanians to Loss of Autonomy in Serbia, 1986–1996* (Keele, England: Keele European Research Centre, 1997), p. 40.

42. See Woodward, *Balkan Tragedy*, pp. 199–222

43. Gjeloshi, *Kosova në udhëkryq '89*, pp. 143–4; Kostovičová, *Parallel Worlds*, p. 31.

44. See Ibrahim Rugova, *Çështja e Kosovës: bisedë me Marie-Françoise Allain dhe Xavier Galmiche* (Peja, Kosovo: Dukagjini, 1994).

45. For example, in 1995, over 2,324 households had been searched for weapons (Kostovičová, *Parallel Worlds*, p. 53).

46. The LDK's version of the incident is found in "Barbarët në Prekaz," *Illyria*, 4 January 1992, p. 2. In an interview with *Illyria*, Rifat Jashari, one of the family members present during the police raid, confirms that the LDK's and CDHRF's mediation helped avoid bloodshed. See "Rrethimi i tretë," *Illyria*, 22 February 1992, p. 4. Rifat is the brother of Adem and Hamzë Jashari, who in 1998 were massacred together with 28 members of their family by Serb police, in a raid similar to that of 1991. The massacre triggered the rise of the Kosovo Liberation Army and turned the Jasharis into martyrs.

47. Clark, *Civil Resistance in Kosovo*, p. 1.

48. Ample evidence of this is found in *ibid.*

49. Quoted in *ibid.*, p. 59.

50. Tarrow, *Power in Movement*, p. 30.

51. See *ibid.*, pp. 91–105.

52. *Ibid.*, pp. 37–42.

53. *Ibid.*, pp. 103–104.

54. *Ibid.*, pp. 98–103.

55. Although demonstrations in 1989 and 1990 did sometimes contain violence, the overall character of the protests was largely nonviolent. See Clark, *Civil Resistance in Kosovo*.

56. Judah, *Kosovo*, p. 110.

57. As testified by Xhavit Haliti, a key activist in the LPK (interviewed in "Në vitin 1985 nis lëvizja guerile e Kosovës," *Zëri* [Prishtina], 5 February 2001, p. 5).

58. Maliqi, *Kosovo*, p. 32.

59. Gjeloshi, *Kosova në udhëkryq '89*, p. 92.

60. Clark, *Civil Resistance in Kosovo*, p. 76.

61. *Ibid.*, p. 74.

62. Illustrating his fear that nonviolent protest events would provoke a Serbian backlash, Rugova stated in 1994 that "under these circumstances, we cannot organize even peaceful manifestations because it has become exceptionally dangerous to venture out on the streets" (quoted in Rugova, *Çështja e Kosovës*, p. 141).

63. The key protagonists, including the shadow defense minister Hajzer Hajzeraj, were arrested and imprisoned in 1993. On the activities of Hajzeraj's group, see his interview in *Zëri* (Prishtina), 26–27 February 2001.

64. Judah, *Kosovo*, pp. 87–89. On the parallel interior ministry, see also the interview with Avdi Mehmeti, leader of the "interior ministry" group, in *Zëri* (Prishtina), 4–13 December 2000.

65. Judah, *Kosovo*, p. 87–9. See also Rugova's admonishment of organizing armed resistance in Rugova, *Çështja e Kosovës*, pp. 124–9.

66. Maliqi, *Kosovo*, p. 101.

67. Sabrina Ramet, *Nationalism and Federalism in Yugoslavia, 1962–1991* (Bloomington: Indiana University Press, 1992), pp. 70–78.

68. Esat Stavileci, "Ecje përgjatë historisë politike të çështjes së Kosovës," in Esat Stavileci and Pajazit Nushi, *Të vërteta për Kosovën* (Prishtina: Lidhja Shqiptare në Botë, 2000), pp. 34–38.

69. At least this is how dismissed workers *perceived* the rationale behind their dismissal.

70. I.e., with only the manpower available, one cannot reorganize a factory outside of its premises. However, through the maintenance of union organizations, workers maintained organized networks and pressed their claims for reinstatement. The strength of these organizations became apparent in 1999, after NATO forced Yugoslav forces out of Kosovo, when former employees rushed into former workplaces, demanding their jobs back or re-establishing socialist-era enterprises.

71. Prior to 1990, curricula were adopted by the provincial Secretariat for Education. See Pajazit Nushi, "Shkatërrimi i arsimit, i shkencës e i kulturës shqiptare dhe i sistemit institucional të tyre nga sunduesi serbomadh," in Bardhyl Çaushi, ed., *Rrënimi i autonomisë së Kosovës* (Prishtina: Shoqata e Pavarur e Juristëve të Kosovës, 1992), pp. 73–74.

72. Nushi, "Shkatërrimi i arsimit," p. 74–76.

73. Clark, *Civil Resistance in Kosovo*, p. 96–97.

74. Initially, the authorities responded to the setting up of parallel schools by repression. Police actions in the period 1991–1993 resulted in the death of 18 students, two teachers, one principal, and three parents. Two thousand teachers and principals and more than 400 students were maltreated by police, while 140 teachers and six students received jail sentences of 20 to 60 days (Clark, *ibid.*, p. 100). Furthermore, in the early start of parallel schools, teachers worked without pay. In 1993, the government of the Republic of Kosovo began paying teachers token salaries (*ibid.*, pp. 102–104).

75. *Ibid.*, p. 98. A factor that played a role in Serbia's targeting of schools for closure was undoubtedly the sheer number of primary students. There were nearly 300,000 Albanian primary school students, and closing all primary schools down would be an immense task for the authorities. Figure from Denisa Kostovičová, "Kosovo's Parallel Society: The

Successes and Failures of Nonviolence," in William Buckley, ed., *Kosovo: Contending Voices on Balkan Interventions* (Grand Rapids: W. B. Eerdmans, 2000), p. 130.

76. There was a gradual decline in enrolment from 1991 to 1992. In 1996/1997 enrolment fell to 13,805 full-time and part-time students. Figures from Clark, *Civil Resistance in Kosovo*, p. 101.

77. *Ibid.*, p. 106.

78. *Ibid.*, p. 106.

79. *Ibid.*, p. 107.

80. Albanians relied on foreign broadcasts and a satellite TV program broadcast from Tirana, established in 1993 with funding provided by the Kosovar government in exile.

81. Quoted from Maliqi, *Separate Worlds*, p. 182.

82. However, there was skepticism among the Kosovar leaders that the request would actually be granted (see "Kosovo Formally Appeals for EC Recognition," *Illyria*, 28 December 1991, p. 1). A copy of Bukoshi's letter requesting independence was reprinted in "Kosovo Asks EC for Recognition," *Illyria*, 18 December 1991, p. 1, while the text of the formal request is reprinted in "Republika e Kosovës kërkon njohjen e pavarësisë," *Illyria*, 28 December 1991, p. 1. Five U.S. Congresspersons sent a letter to EC envoy Lord Carrington supporting the Kosovars' request (copy in "Republika e Kosovës duhet të njihet," *Illyria*, 15 January 1992, p. 3).

83. For brief background on the Albanian-American community and its political movements see Fron Nazi, "Balkan Diaspora I: The Albanian-American Community," in William Buckley, ed., *Kosovo: Contending Voices on Balkan Interventions* (Grand Rapids: W. B. Eerdmans, 2000), pp. 132–135.

84. "Kërkesë për njohjen e republikave që shpallen sovranitetin," *Illyria*, 16 November 1991, p. 2, and "D'Amato kërkon nga SHBA njohjen e pavarësisë së Kosovës, Kroacisë, Sllovenisë ...," *Illyria*, 1 February 1992, p. 2.

85. "Crowd Hails Bukoshi at JFK," *Illyria*, 23 November 1991, p. 1; "Bujar Bukoshi në Danimarkë," *Illyria*, 22 February 1992, p. 1; "Alois Mock priti Bujar Bukoshin," *Illyria*, 29 February 1992, p. 1; "Bukoshi Meeting U.S. Leaders," *Illyria*, 4 March 1992, p. 7.

86. Besides the support from the U.S. Congress, an April 1992 resolution of the European Parliament also endorsed elections for Kosovo ("Ç'thuhet në rezolutën më të re të Parlamentit Evropian për Kosovën," *Illyria*, 29 April 1992, p. 9).

87. Twenty-three political groups, including two ethnic minority parties, and over 500 candidates contended in the elections. 721,554 voters participated in the polls, comprising 87% of the total number of registered voters. The LDK received 96 seats out of the 98 single-member districts, while the Parliamentary Party of Kosovo (PPK) and the Bosniac Party of Democratic Action (SDA) got one each. The remaining 42 seats were distributed proportionally to the LDK (15), PPK (12), SDA (4), and Turkish People's Party (1). Ten seats were reserved for Serb representatives. See "Nesër në Kosovë mbahen zgjedhjet e lira," *Illyria*, 23 May 1992, p. 1; "Rugova Elected in Massive Turnout," *Illyria*, 27 May 1992, p. 1; "Rezultatet përfundimtare të zgjedhjeve," *Illyria*, 27 May 1992, p. 1; Clark, *Civil Resistance in Kosovo*, pp. 83–84; Vickers, *Between Serb and Albanian*, pp. 259–261; Maliqi, *Kosovo*, pp. 39–40.

88. Surroi's remarks are quoted in Clark, *Civil Resistance in Kosovo*, pp. 83–4, Qosja in "Sulm mbi regjimin militarist," *Illyria*, 27 May 1992, p. 12.

89. See interviews with Rugova in "Ne kemi legjitimitet për zgjedhje të lira në Kosovë," *Illyria*, 16 May 1992, p. 12, and "Bota e di çka do të thotë okupim," *Illyria*, 27 May 1992, p. 12. The government continued to function in exile and wielded no real authority in Kosovo.

90. Weeks prior to the elections, the Assembly had passed a series of amendments to the Kaçanik constitution, giving the president a series of special powers. See "U shpall ligji kushtetues për zbatimin e amandamenteve II–IV në kushtetutën e Republikës së Kosovës," *Illyria*, 16 May 1992, p. 9.
91. Quoted in Clark, *Civil Resistance in Kosovo*, p. 84.
92. Valerie Bunce, *Subversive Institutions: The Design and Destruction of Socialism and the State* (Cambridge: Cambridge University Press, 1999).

The "Mortar Massacres": A Controversy Revisited

Benjamin Rusek and Charles Ingrao

One of the many controversies that survived the war in Bosnia-Herzegovina concerns the responsibility for several of the most deadly artillery attacks against civilians during the three-year siege of Sarajevo. Although indiscriminate artillery fire accounted for a small fraction of the total civilian deaths during the war, graphic video footage of the mass slaughter exercised a disproportionate effect on world public opinion and, therefore, on Western policymakers who felt constrained to "do something." On at least three occasions, individual artillery explosions in the Bosnian capital prompted immediate international intervention that substantially determined the course and resolution of the conflict. The persistence of controversy is informed by a combination of factors, including the substantial consequences of the Western response, the inconclusiveness of some of the forensic data, and the conflicting statements of civilian survivors, journalists, spokesmen for the belligerents, and U.N. officials—all of whom have been accused of some degree of bias by one side or another. Nearly a decade later, testimony and forensic evidence presented at the International Criminal Tribunal for the Former Yugoslavia (ICTY) has shed new light on these incidents, presenting a more comprehensive and authoritative historical baseline account of the "mortar massacres," much as it has for a plethora of criminal acts committed by all sides during the wars of Yugoslav succession. The Tribunal recently released documentation detailing some of the mortar attacks that occurred in the city of Sarajevo, including forensic reports compiled by the U.N. Protection Force (UNPROFOR) which had not been previously made public. The bulk of this information is contained in the Tribunal Judgment[1] and corresponding Dissenting Opinion[2] of the former commander of the Sarajevo Romanija Corps (SRK), Major General Stanislav Galić. Although the reliability of judicial testimony and other evidence is invariably limited by the abilities and resources of both the prosecution and defense, the trial transcript has cleared away at least some of the fog of war, making it somewhat less difficult to apportion responsibility for the disputed attacks. This article integrates the Galić transcript with earlier, wartime U.N. documentation, press releases, and media reports, supplemented by interviews conducted by the authors with military experts familiar with the characteristics of the weaponry employed by the besiegers. It also endeavors to place the most notorious incidents in the broader context presented by the multiplicity of artillery attacks that took place in urban areas across Bosnia between 1992 and 1995.

This is not the place to recount the origin or course of the bloody ethnic conflicts that broke out following the collapse of the Communist Yugoslav state that Marshal Tito had created at the end of World War II. Suffice it to say that independence quickly transformed life for many in the republic of Bosnia-Herzegovina, a region once celebrated as a bastion of diversity, into an unremitting struggle for survival, where former friends and neighbors divided along previously quiescent ethnic lines. The media used the siege in Sarajevo, the mountain-ringed capital city of almost half a million people, to represent the situation in the rest of Bosnia, in large part because it was at once the most visible and accessible part of the country. As a result, the situation in Sarajevo came to symbolize the wider ethnic conflict rampant in the once bucolic and largely inaccessible countryside.

Sarajevo remained under siege for almost the entire conflict, something unseen in Europe since the epic (and incomparably more brutal) siege of Leningrad during World War II. The SRK, buttressed by reinforcements from the Army of Republika Srpska (VRS) waged a protracted campaign against elements of the Army of the Republic of Bosnia and Herzegovina (ARBiH) entrenched within the city. The belligerents divided along opposite sides of the shifting line of control that encircled the city. Since the better-equipped but undermanned VRS could not easily advance without suffering unacceptable casualties, they continued the standard siege tactic developed by the Red Army and subsequently adopted by the Yugoslav military (JNA) of reducing urban areas to submission by stand-off artillery bombardment, which had proven so effective in the opening stages of the Croatian and Bosnian conflicts against defended (and, sometimes, undefended) cities.[3] As a result, the SRK and ARBiH forces entrenched in the steep hillsides around Sarajevo settled into a somewhat regular routine of exchanging fire. This stalemate developed into a three-year-long blockade, while the besieging forces terrorized the population with sporadic rifle fire and artillery bombardment. Snipers regularly shot civilians, including women and children; artillery rounds fell erratically and indiscriminately. The inhabitants of Sarajevo were caught in the middle of this battle. They lived in constant fear of random injury or death. Sarajevans of all ethnicities learned to avoid certain streets, many only ventured outside to search for food and supplies. Meanwhile, the Bosnian government was determined not only to withstand the besiegers, but to keep the remaining, largely Muslim population from advancing the besiegers' agenda of an ethnically cleansed "Serb Sarajevo" by fleeing the city.

In a largely futile effort to minimize civilian casualties and forestall a new, massive wave of ethnic cleansing, the United Nations voted to designate six besieged urban centers as "Safe Areas."[4] Although the U.N. prohibited besieging VRS forces from launching further attacks, its inability to prevent either side from attacking the other ensured that the sieges of all six cities would be punctuated by an unending stream of violations and accusations. Meanwhile the political leaders of both sides regularly manipulated the media—and a worldwide audience—by exaggerating or manufacturing reports of violations by the enemy. In the battle to curry international favor, the stakes were highest in the besieged capital city, if only because the bulk of media resources and personnel were concentrated there. Not that the attention was unmerited. United Nations observers estimated that VRS forces lobbed more than 600,000 rounds of ordinance during the first two years of the siege. One Serbian spokesman even admitted to the firing of 40,000 rounds into Sarajevo during the course of 1993, despite its designation in May of that year as a U.N. Safe Area. [5]

Hence the focus on Sarajevo at the expense of comparably destructive incidents in other Safe Areas, some of which went undocumented by UNPROFOR and unreported by the media. The Bosnian capital provided the setting for seven of the nine artillery incidents—and all three of the disputed attacks—discussed in this paper. Altogether, these attacks generated approximately 900 civilian casualties, including 250 fatalities in the Sarajevo, Goražde, and Tuzla Safe Areas.[6]

At the same time, an important distinction needs to be made between these incidents. In six of the nine cases examined here, Bosnian Serb spokesmen either accepted responsibility for firing the shell(s) or, more typically, chose not to dispute the charges of the Bosnian government and international community. Although some of these six attacks have spawned stories spread by word of mouth that question VRS responsibility, none has been attended by any debate in either official circles or the media.[7] Certainly they were deadly enough to warrant attention and, ultimately, inclusion in the litany of indictments issued by the ICTY. The first "undisputed" attack examined in this paper occurred on 1 June 1993 in Dobrinja, on a hastily prepared football pitch. Two mortar rounds killed more than ten and wounded more than 100. The second occurred on 12 July 1993 near a water queue in Dobrinja, killing more than ten and wounding more than 15. The third occurred in the Alipašino Polje district on 22 January 1994, killing more than six and wounding another four. The fourth occurred on 4 February 1994 near a Dobrinja food aid line, killing eight and wounding more than 20. The fifth and sixth examined attacks, took place outside the capital during a sustained VRS bombardment of Goražde in mid-April 1994 and in Tuzla on 27 May 1995, when a single shell inflicted the highest human toll of the war, killing 71 and wounding more than 150. The Serbs did not publicly deny responsibility for the attacks at the time of these incidents, or seek to refute Bosnian Muslim and international protests. Denial or justification for the Sarajevo attacks occurred only much later as a defense strategy in the trial of SRK General Galić.

By contrast, the three remaining incidents have been surrounded by controversies that began immediately afterward as Bosnian Serb authorities denied responsibility and assigned blame to the Bosnian government forces. In fact, during the conflict, Serb authorities repeatedly accused the outgunned ARBiH of deliberately targeting their own civilians, citing the Bosnian government's desperation to elicit military assistance, if not direct intervention, from the international community. All three cases occurred in Sarajevo during the protracted siege and were readily given names to distinguish among them in the ensuing discussions and debates between the

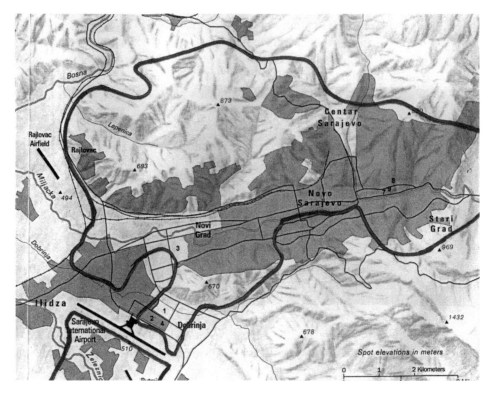

FIGURE 1 Map of Sarajevo: Mortar Attacks[a]

a   Original map appears in the collection: Central Intelligence Agency, *Balkan Battle-grounds: A Military History of the Yugoslav Conflict, 1990–1995*, Vol. 2. (Washington, DC: Office of Russian and European Analysis, 2002). Inserts by Larry Jewell, Purdue University.

belligerents and their advocates. The "Breadline Massacre" occurred on 27 May 1992 at Vaša Miskin, killing 20 and wounding about 100 civilians. The two subsequent "Marketplace Massacres" occurred in Sarajevo's downtown Markale district after the city had been declared a Safe Area (See Figure 1). Both were especially deadly, with the first attack on 5 February 1994 killing 68 people andwounding an additional 200, and the 28 August 1995 explosion killing 37 and wounding 80 others. Quite aside from the Bosnian Serb denials of responsibility that attended them, all three incidents had something in common: the glare of media and hence worldwide attention that prompted international intervention against the Bosnian Serbs.

Undisputed Attacks

Football Pitch, Dobrinja, Sarajevo (1)

On the morning of 1 June 1993, residents of the Dobrinja district[8] were playing and watching a football match. Without warning, at approximately 10:20, soon after the start of the second match of the day, the hastily prepared parking-lot pitch was struck by two mortar shells. Surviving witnesses testified that immediately after the attack the field was strewn with casualties and shrapnel. Both shells landed in approximately the same place only seconds apart, at the center of a gathering of approximately 200 people. Later reports indicate that this attack killed a minimum of ten people and injured another 100.[9]

In an effort to determine the origin of fire and type of shells used in the attack, a local representative of the United Nations Protection Force, widely know by its acronym UNPROFOR, conducted a "crater analysis" immediately after the incident. This report, detailed in the Galić judgment, concluded that the two mortar shells that landed on the pitch that day were "at least 81 mm" in diameter.[10] The author concluded that the shells were fired from an east-southeasterly direction with a minimum impact angle of approximately 45 degrees, which was the minimum necessary for the shells to have cleared buildings during their descent. The analysis placed the origin of fire in SRK-controlled territory approximately "300 meters south of Lukavica."[11] This initial finding is consistent with the reports from UNPROFOR representatives[12] and with additional evidence presented at the ICTY during the Galić trial.

After the attack, responsibility was never in dispute. The SRK forces in the area and the Serb leadership never publicly denied firing the shells that caused these casualties. Years later, the ICTY Galić defense team countered prosecution accusations by attempting to dismiss the UNPROFOR findings as inaccurate and arguing that the area contained legitimate military targets.[13] The prosecution successively convinced the Tribunal majority, or two of the three judges, which concluded that the incident "constitutes an example of indiscriminate shelling by the SRK on a civilian area."[14] The third judge, Rafael Nieto-Navia dissented, writing that "in light of the preceding evidence regarding the ARBiH presence in and near the site of the incident, I conclude that the Prosecution has not established beyond a reasonable doubt that the two shells that exploded on 1 June 1993 in Dobrinja were fired deliberately or indiscriminately by the SRK at civilians." Yet he too harbored no doubts that the deadly rounds had been fired by the besieging forces.[15]

Water Line, Dobrinja, Sarajevo (2)

On 12 July 1993, a single explosion killed more than ten people and wounded another 15.[16] The mortar shell struck at approximately 15:00, landing among a long queue of civilians, many of whom had been standing in line since dawn, waiting to fill water containers in settlement C5 in Sarajevo's Dobrinja district. According to the post-explosion U.N. investigation, an 82-mm mortar caused these casualties.[17]

The high population density of the area surrounding the possible launch sites in ARBiH-controlled territory allowed the ICTY majority to conclude that the fire could not have originated from Muslim-occupied areas, since witnesses would have heard the launch of the mortar. The defense presented no witnesses testifying that the shell originated in Bosnian Muslim held territory. Witnesses who testified at the Tribunal only heard the explosion on impact.[18] Based on witness testimony and post-attack analysis, the Tribunal majority concluded that no military objectives were in the immediate vicinity of the water line and that the civilian water queue "was deliberately targeted on 12 July 1993 by an 82 mm mortar shell fired from SRK-held territory."[19]

During the trial, the defense challenged these claims with a photograph that suggested that the shell had been fired from inside ARBiH lines, but presented tainted impact site evidence in an attempt to shift the blame away from the defendant.[20] Ignoring their initial responsibility argument, the defense also stated that military targets in the vicinity motivated the attack. At the time neither the SRK forces in the area nor the Bosnian Serb leadership publicly denied the attacks or placed blame on the ARBiH after the incident; the responsibility dispute arose as a result of the ICTY Galić investigation and trial. Once again, Judge Nieto-Navia dissented, by arguing that the SRK "may have intended to target one of the nearby ARBiH resources" and that "the Prosecution has not established beyond a reasonable doubt that the 82 millimetre mortar shell which exploded at the water pump in Dobrinja on 12 July 1993 was fired deliberately at civilians by the SRK."[21]

Playground, Alipašino Polje, Sarajevo (3)

On 22 January 1994, three explosions killed six children and injured approximately four others who were among a larger group playing outside in Sarajevo's Alipašino Polje district.[22] A subsequent local investigatory team headed by ballistics expert Mirza Sabljica determined that two 82-mm and one 120-mm mortar shells impacted in the area, leaving large craters consistent with their caliber.[23] Using proven crater analysis methodologies,[24] it determined that the rounds had been fired from a westerly direction from a range well within SRK-controlled territory.[25] The Galić defense team did not dispute Sabljica's testimony. Nor did the SRK or the Bosnian Serbian political leadership publicly deny firing the shells or the casualties they caused.

Since the attack was conducted during an unofficial ceasefire and no military facilities were located in the immediate vicinity, all three of the Tribunal judges concluded that this "incident constituted an attack that was, *at the very least*, indiscriminate as to its target (which nevertheless was primarily, if not entirely a residential neighbourhood), and was carried out recklessly, resulting in civilian casualties."[26] The defense again countered these accusations by denying the prosecution claim that the shells had been fired from SRK-controlled territory, thereby indirectly attributing the attack to ARBiH forces. The imputation found no resonance with the judges, whose judgment declared that "The Defense's assertion that the attack could have been staged by the ARBiH is not supported by any evidence and is therefore dismissed."[27]

Food Aid Line, Dobrinja, Sarajevo (4)

On 4 February 1994, three shells exploded at or about 11:30 in the vicinity of Dobrinja, killing eight and wounding more than 20. The first shell landed among a line of civilians waiting for humanitarian food aid. The second and third landed in a market near Mihajla Pupina and Oslobodilača Sarajeva Streets.[28] An investigation performed approximately one hour later concluded that three 120-mm mortar shells had caused the explosions.[29] Photographs of the shell's tailfins (found intact in the crater) were submitted to the Hague Tribunal on behalf of the prosecution as evidence of responsibility for the attack in the Galić case.[30] It was determined through crater analysis and confirmed by eyewitnesses that the shells had come from an east-northeasterly direction. Although the prosecution's forensics experts conceded that it was impossible to pinpoint the precise origin from rudimentary crater analysis, the number of shells fired in this case made it possible to triangulate both the direction and distance between the impact sight and the mortar.[31]

The defense indirectly claimed that the shells could have originated from ARBiH lines by arguing that the "drop angle" of one of the shells, determined from its tailfin crater position in a photograph, showed that the shell had struck the ground at an almost perpendicular angle, thereby indicating that it could have been fired from within government-held territory.[32] The Tribunal concluded that this single close-up photograph was not consistent with the impact angle of the other shells fired, which had been determined through multiple separate accounts of the attack. In fact, the impact craters were not roughly circular, but elliptical with a footprint that pointed east, indicating that they had been fired at a shallow angle from a greater distance. Hence the ICTY Trial Chamber determined that the shells were more likely fired from a more conventional 45-degree trajectory (as the SRK line of control in this area was only 600 meters from the craters, an extremely high angle of fire would have been necessary for the shells to have been fired by the ARBiH). It therefore concluded that the mortar fire did not originate in ARBiH-controlled territory and could not have been directed against any known military target in what was, at the time, an area predominately inhabited by civilians.[33]

These aforementioned four incidents are very similar with respect to the Serb response and exemplify many of the indiscriminate attacks against civilians that occurred during the siege of Sarajevo. Although the ICTY documents duly note the Galić defense's effort to prove his innocence, the Bosnian Serbs never denied responsibility for the casualties that resulted from these attacks during the war and never publicly accused the ARBiH of firing the shells. Although only two of the three judges characterized all four incidents as examples of SRK forces indiscriminately or purposely shelling civilian targets with no militarily valuable targets in the vicinity, the Trial Chamber was unanimous in its judgment that the incidents at

Alipašino Polje and at the Dobrinja food aid line represented reckless attacks against residential neighborhoods.

The Bombardment of Goražde (5)

On 10 April 1994, British UNPROFOR commander Sir Michael Rose responded to the shelling of civilians in the Goražde Safe Area by ordering the first of three pinprick air strikes against VRS artillery positions. Instead of deterring further attacks, the sorties prompted Bosnian Serb General Ratko Mladić to engage in a test of wills, first by taking U.N. officials hostage, then by ordering a massive ground and artillery assault on the city. The bombardment was particularly intense between 15 and 20 April, during which time 28 people were killed at a first aid station, another ten at a water line, and 20 at the city hospital. Far from denying responsibility, Mladić wanted both the U.N. and the international community at large to know the lengths to which he was willing to go to protect his forces against military intervention. If there was a controversy, it took the form of a debate between General Rose and frustrated Western journalists who had inflated the destruction and casualty count at the hospital to as many as 700 killed and 2,000 wounded. By the 27th, Rose had established a 20-km heavy artillery "exclusion zone" around Goražde, similar to one that was already in place in Sarajevo, but which the U.N. Security Council duly extended to the remaining Safe Areas nine days later.[34] But the hostage taking had also taken a toll on the U.N., which proved reluctant to retaliate against subsequent VRS violations of Security Council resolutions.

Kapija Square, Tuzla (6)

On 25 May 1995, the single worst incident of shelling against civilians during the Bosnian conflict occurred in a small, pie-shaped square in Tuzla, another U.N. designated Safe Area. At dusk VRS forces in the hills surrounding the city fired a single round from a Soviet-era M-46 130-mm cannon (see Figure 2) into a crowd of 500 young people who had assembled at an outdoor café in Kapija Square for the annual celebration of the end of classes. The shell killed 71 and injured more than 150.[35] There never was any doubt who fired the shot, since the ARBiH arsenal did not possess such heavy ordinance. Moreover, on 19 September the Bosnian Army 2nd Corps captured the Cerovo Brdo peak and the M-46,[36] collateral equipment, many of the VRS personnel who had operated the artillery pieces when it was stationed around Tuzla, and the gun's firing logs, which were duly forwarded to the ICTY. A post-attack U.N. investigation concluded that the VRS was likely aiming directly at the square.[37]

Once again, the Serbian authorities did not deny responsibility for the attack at any time after this incident and continued to shell Tuzla periodically. Even though the

Mortar

The mortar is a type of short-barreled muzzle-loaded weapon that can deliver low velocity shells to a target on an elliptical flight path at a steep angle. Militaries use mortars in areas where it is difficult or impossible to fire on a target and where heavy direct fire weapons are impractical. The elliptical flight path allows an operator to utilize a lightweight shell with a smaller amount of propellant to achieve a long range. Because of their smaller size and lighter weight, many mortars are man-portable; the barrel does not need to endure a high firing pressure, can be made out of thin material, and generally emits a much softer report when fired. Unlike some direct fire weapons (see "M-46 130-mm Cannon"), mortars sacrifice some accuracy due to their low firing velocity and the susceptibility of the shell's elliptical flight path to environmental factors, but modern mortars can be very accurate if fielded by well-trained operators.

82-mm Mortar

The majority of the 82-mm mortars in the Sarajevo area were Yugoslav-manufactured type M-69 or derivatives.[a] This weapon has a maximum range of approximately between 3,150 and 5,400 meters and is man-portable with a launcher weight of 62 kg while in use.[b] The standard shell for this weapon weighs between 3.05 and 4.10 kg with muzzle exit velocities between 72 and 297 meters per second. The range of this type of mortar can vary between approximately 90 and 5,400 meters depending on the level of charges attached.[c] The round contains between 680 and 690 grams of explosive. This type of shell caused civilian causalities at the football pitch and water line incidents in Dobrinja, at Alipašino Polje, and at Vaso Mickin.

120-mm Mortar

Many 120-mm mortars were in use during in the Bosnian conflict. Three primary types include the Yugoslav-manufactured 120-mm UBM 52, and the M-74 and M-75 light mortars,[d] all capable of firing similar 120-mm shells. These platforms range in weight from 120 to 400 kg without ammunition and are usually towed behind a vehicle.[e] The 120-mm shell weighs 12.6 kg with 2.25 kg of explosive. Over all charge levels, the shells have a minimum muzzle velocity of 121 meters per second and a maximum muzzle velocity of 297 meters per second. The range of this type of shell varies between 400 and 6,050 meters.[f] This type of shell caused the civilian causalities in Alipašino Polje, at the Dobrinja food aid line, and at Markale.

120-mm M-62P3 Shell

The "P3" or "performance charge" refers to the propellant level attached to the high explosive mortar shell. This part of the system propels the projectile out of the mortar tube and onto the target. The standard charge in this configuration propels the shell to 200 meters per second immediately after exiting the mortar tube. A shell fired at this charge level has a reported standard range between 1,500 and 3,370 meters.[g]

FIGURE 2 Artillery

M-46 130-mm Field Gun
The M-46 is a towed breach-loaded field gun (or cannon) fitted with direct fire sights. Unlike the mortar, it is capable of both indirect and direct fire. One explosion from a 130-mm shell fired by this cannon type caused the civilian causalities at Kapija Square in Tuzla on 25 May 1995. For indirect fire, it fires a 33.4-kg projectile packed with 4.63 kg of high explosive. The shell is traveling at 930 meters per second when it leaves the muzzle.[h] The gun requires a crew of eight operators, can fire at a rate of 5–6 rounds per minute, and has a maximum range of more than 27,000 meters.[i] Since the shell travels at higher velocities, accuracy is not as contingent on environmental conditions. In comparison to a mortar weapon, it is far more accurate in variable situations, but is much less mobile due to its larger size and weight.

FIGURE 2 Artillery

a Central Intelligence Agency, *Balkan Battlegrounds: A Military History of the Yugoslav Conflict, 1990–1995*, Vol. 1 (Washington: Office of Russian and European Analysis, 2002), p. xxvi.
b *Jane's Infantry Weapons, 1990–1991*. Vol. 16 (London: Jane's), p. 530, *Jane's Infantry Weapons*. 1995–1996. Vol. 21 (London: Jane's), p. 403.
c *Jane's Infantry Weapons, 1990–1991*. Vol. 16 (London: Jane's), p. 691.
d Central Intelligence Agency, *Balkan Battlegrounds: A Military History of the Yugoslav Conflict, 1990–1995*, Vol. 1 (Washington: Office of Russian and European Analysis, 2002), p. xxvi.
e *Jane's Infantry Weapons, 1990–1991*. Vol. 16 (London: Jane's), pp. 530–531.
f *Ibid.*, p. 692.
g *Ibid.*
h *Jane's Armor and Artillery, 1990–1991*. Vol. 11 (London: Jane's), pp. 664–665.
i *Jane's Armor and Artillery, 2000–2001*. Vol. 21 (London: Jane's), pp. 712–711.

casualty list was the highest of the war and the shell's origin was never in dispute, the event received little international attention in comparison with the seven mortar salvoes being examined here that were fired into Sarajevo. Perhaps most important, it elicited no tangible response from the international community, aside from a pinprick NATO attack on an ammunition dump in the Bosnian Serb capital of Pale, which the VRS quickly trumped by taking nearly 400 U.N. personnel hostage.

The "Mortar Massacres"

The response or non-response of the Bosnian Serb authorities to the aforementioned incidents was distinctly different than their reaction to the following three incidents. The "Mortar Massacres" are remarkable not only because they inflicted greater human losses than most of the other attacks examined here, but also because official representatives of the Bosnian Serb, VRS, or SRK military forces immediately denied responsibility and have continued to since. Indeed, Bosnian Serb leaders pre-empted or countered accusations of responsibility by assigning guilt directly to the Bosnian Muslim forces. Although their denials either persuaded or raised doubts among UNPROFOR personnel and some Western journalists, each of the attacks brought swift and significant retaliation from key elements of the international community. It is precisely these consequences that inform the continuing debate over who was responsible.

"Breadline Massacre," Vasa Miskin, Sarajevo (7)

On 27 May 1992, barely a month after the start of hostilities, three mortar rounds exploded among a group of civilians waiting to buy bread, killing more than 20 and injuring 100 more. The attack occurred before Sarajevo was designated as a U.N. Safe Area but during a temporary ceasefire between the SRK and ARBiH forces. Although the number of killed would pale by comparison with later artillery attacks, it prompted the U.N. Security Council to impose trade sanctions against Rump Yugoslavia, which was widely perceived as financing and supplying the VRS with men and materiel. The reaction in Republika Srpska was equally noteworthy. Even though VRS forces had already fired thousands of rounds into Sarajevo and other government-controlled cities across Bosnia, this was the first incident to be widely denied by the Serbian authorities, who promptly claimed that ARBiH forces were responsible. Thus was born the hypothesis that the Bosnian government would purposely fire on its own civilians in order to create international sympathy and intervention against the Bosnian Serbs. The charge becomes more plausible in light of at least two incidents of friendly fire recorded by UNPROFOR personnel during the last year of the conflict and subsequent claims by an American general that the ARBiH shot and shelled its own civilians during the siege.[38]

Nonetheless, it is one thing to accuse; quite another to furnish proof. Evidence presented by Belgrade's state-controlled media included claims by a Yugoslav military "explosives expert" that video footage from the scene pointed to a land mine triggered by remote control, since there was no crater and the victims' injuries were all below the waist. This supposition was easily refuted by other photographs showing the impact craters and by hospital records documenting an ample number of head and other upper body wounds. A concurrent assertion that the speedy arrival of media on the scene pointed to a pre-planned explosion ignored the fact that journalists had been filming an unrelated story just blocks away when the mortar shell hit.[39] Three months later, in *The Independent*, Leonard Doyle further fueled the charge that the Bosnian Muslims were systematically killing themselves to boost international sympathy in an effort to foster international intervention. It claimed that the "Bosnian bread queue massacre was a propaganda ploy"[40] on their behalf. Yet Doyle's assertion that Sarajevo's defenders were attacking their own people only cited unnamed "confidential UN reports," "UN officials," and a "classified briefing to U.S. policy makers". All of this actually boiled down to the conjecture of a single source, U.N. commander Major General Lewis Mackenzie. Nevertheless, when Mackenzie was confronted by journalist Tom Gjelten with the available evidence, he distanced himself from the statements he had made to Doyle.[41] In response to a subsequent mortar attack in Sarajevo on 9 November 1993, Gjelten observed that "through twenty-one months of war in Sarajevo ... no physical evidence has ever been found that suggests Muslims purposely shoot themselves."[42]

Yet discrediting specious evidence does not, in itself, prove that the opposite is true. Hence the frustration of many observers, like Gjelten, who endured the reality of continuous VRS shelling launched from the hills around Sarajevo without having the means to prove conclusively that a specific round emanated from the same source. The charge that the ARBiH fired on its own civilians survives to this day, both as an article of faith among Bosnian Serb apologists, and also as an element of doubt in the minds of some in the West whose sense of fairness demands keeping an open mind in the absence of conclusive proof. Thus the explanation given by one UNPROFOR official that "we had been blaming the Serbs for everything, and it was uncomfortable for MacKenzie. He felt this need to balance it."[43] That the General and other international officials made such a choice has been characterized by sociologist Keith Doubt as a Weberian "iron cage of rationality" that entices neutral parties into adopting a strict regimen of impartiality at the expense of "substantive justice" and sheer common sense.[44]

First "Marketplace Massacre," Markale, Sarajevo (8)

Even though no credible evidence of ARBiH responsibility for the "Breadline Massacre" was ever produced, the notion that "Muslims were capable of killing their own people" had taken on a life of its own that would be reincarnated two years later in the most widely known—and hotly debated—shelling incident of the war. On 5 February 1994, one explosion from a single 120-mm mortar round killed 68 people and injured approximately 200 others at the Markale market in downtown Sarajevo. It happened the day after the aforementioned Dobrinja food aid line incident in which three 120-mm mortar shells had killed eight civilians and wounded 20 in Sarajevo's residential Dobrinja district. Taken together, the two attacks constituted the single largest civilian shelling death toll during the war and raised the specter of a steady tally of civilian deaths at the hands of VRS artillery.

Within hours the Bosnian Serbs issued the first of many denials of responsibility. In a letter[45] dated 5 February 1994, the VRS command demanded a joint committee of all parties involved to examine the incident.[46] The U.N. ignored this request, echoing a prevailing consensus that the VRS had fired the shell. Nonetheless, the outrage within the international community over the "Marketplace Massacre" was so intense that U.N. commander General Michael Rose recommended the creation of the aforementioned 20-km heavy artillery exclusion zone around Sarajevo. The NATO Council quickly endorsed this proposal, issuing an ultimatum to the VRS, demanding that it withdraw all artillery beyond a 20-km-wide "total exclusion zone" or face air strikes. Although the VRS complied with the demand, the siege continued. Meanwhile, the political and military consequences of the "Marketplace Massacre" gave the Bosnian Serbs additional incentive to establish their innocence—and the ARBiH's complicity—in the attack.[47]

Indeed, the controversy had only begun, fueled as it was by continued Bosnian Serb denials, inconclusive and sometimes contradictory reports released by UNPRO-FOR investigators, and, perhaps, an underlying commitment to neutrality that sustained among outside parties a willingness to entertain the notion that the ARBiH was capable of firing on its own civilians.

The UNPROFOR investigations All three elements played a role in the numerous investigations that UNPROFOR performed at the impact site. Upon first arriving at the scene one hour after the incident, a unit from the French battalion FreBat 4 discovered a large crater, clearly the result of a recent explosion and a tailfin embedded in the center determined to belong to a 120-mm mortar shell. The team concluded only that the mortar round had come from a "northerly direction" (a bearing of 35 degrees),[48] but left open the identity of the attacker, since it was unable to determine the precise distance from which the round had been fired. Moreover, in the process of removing the tailfin with a knife, the team irrevocably altered the shape of the shell's fuze well, thereby limiting the potential for subsequent forensic examination. An examination one hour later by another French officer, Captain Verdy, arrived at a radically different direction of 79 degrees (almost due east), owing to a mathematical error that placed the shell's origin squarely behind ARBiH lines. Ninety minutes later British Major John Russell conducted a somewhat more thorough examination before removing the tailfin and shell fragments from the scene for closer analysis. His report readily dismissed Verdy's assessment, confirming instead the admittedly inconclusive findings of the first forensic team. Even here, however, it revised the initial report by ascertaining that the deadly mortar round had been fired at a bearing of 25 degrees, while descending at between 67 and 73 degrees and exploding upon contact with the asphalt.[49] Nor was UNPROFOR finished. A fourth study completed a total of seven crater analyses on 11–12 February,[50] establishing in the process a new shell origin of between 18 and 23.6 degrees with an approximate angle of descent between 53 and 62 degrees. Except for Verdy's miscalculation, the wide variation was at least partly the result of crater damage and further deterioration during the week after the attack, together with additional testimony gathered from victims near the blast and technical information about VRS and ARBiH mortar batteries employed in the area.[51] Although the final, official report[52] released to the U.N. Security Council on 15 February 1994 takes all four of the UNPROFOR investigations into account, it essentially confirms the last report, stating that the devastation of 5 February 1994 stemmed from a single 120-mm mortar shell that had originated from a northeasterly direction between 18.5 and 23.6 degrees and had descended on the marketplace at an angle of between 53 and 62 degrees.[53] This conservative analysis placed the firing position of the mortar anywhere between approximately 300 and 5,550 meters from the impact site. As a result the final U.N. report concluded that "there was insufficient physical evidence to prove that one party or the other fired the mortar bomb. The mortar bomb could have been fired by either side."[54]

Since four of the five UNPROFOR reports left open the question of responsibility, they did very little to resolve the controversy surrounding the first "Marketplace Massacre." Meanwhile, Verdy's discredited assessment remained a weapon in the hands of not only Serb apologists but international officials seeking to justify their continued neutrality and disengagement. Its potential was borne out by one British UNPROFOR commander, who successfully extracted concessions from the ARBiH command simply by threatening to make Verdy's report public.[55] Not surprisingly, some interpreted the sudden ARBiH compliance with this threat as an admission of guilt in the Markale attack. In any event, word of Verdy's report did leak out, thereby further complicating an already insoluble debate over the origin of the explosion.

And so the debate continued. Apologists for the Bosnian Serbs began circulating "new" evidence that pointed the finger at the ARBiH. One of the most active participants in this campaign was Bosnian Serb President Radovan Karadžić, who asserted that media vans equipped with satellite dishes and ambulances were already parked at the marketplace, a claim repudiated by U.N. officers who were at the scene moments before and after the explosion.[56] Less credible yet was his claim that several of the Markale dead were refrigerated corpses trucked in from the morgue with ice still clinging to their ears.[57] Such claims of defrosting (but, presumably, fully clothed) corpses mingling among the victims enjoyed credence principally with "true believers" in Serbia and the Serbian diaspora. At the same time, however, news reports began to appear in the Western media that cast doubt on Serb responsibility, with some officials privately hinting that the ARBiH forces had triggered the explosion to raise international support for the Bosnians' plight. U.N. Secretary-General Boutros Boutros Ghali even went so far as to conclude that the ARBiH was "most likely" the source.[58]

The Galić trial The Stanislav Galić Judgment and Dissenting Opinion released on 5 December 2003 details the extensive ICTY investigation of the incident and the subsequent Tribunal decision.[59] Having determined that no international team had conducted an accurate and thorough investigation on the scene after the attack, both the prosecution and the defense teams commissioned "experts" to examine the evidence around the attack and testify in the Galić case.[60] The prosecution's case combines extensive technical evidence as well as expert and eyewitness testimony in an attempt to place the origin of fire "beyond a reasonable doubt" behind SRK lines.

This ultimately included a local team working independently that presented a report that elaborated on the earlier U.N. findings.[61] This investigation also determined the angle of descent and penetration depth of the incoming round. Before the U.N. removed the shell fragments, they observed that the tailfin on the device had penetrated into the ground to a depth between 200 and 250 mm (this measurement

---

Fuze

An artillery fuze is a device, usually located in the nose cone section of the shell triggering the projectile's warhead. The fuze activates after the operator drops the shell into the mortar tube and the shell leaves the mortar muzzle. There are different types of fuze: The *point-detonating* or *impact* fuze triggers the mortar warhead to explode on impact with the ground or an object. A *proximity* fuze can also detonate on impact, but is typically triggered by radar to explode a given distance from an object. A *delay* or *time-delay* fuze (or *point-detonating delay* fuze) triggers the mortar explosion a set time period after the projectile contacts the target.[j]

Tailfin Tunnel

This is a cylindrical depression (aka "fuze well" or "fuze furrow") left by a shell in the impact crater after its explosion.[k] In the case of the crater caused by the 120-mm shell in the Markale attack, a significant impression remained to measure the distance the shell penetrated into the ground (see "Tailfin Depth"). The defense used this measurement[l] to estimate the velocity of the shell and ultimately to determine the approximate distance of the explosion from the firing point.

Tailfin

Unlike high explosive cannon rounds, standard 82-mm and 120-mm mortars often use stabilizing fins in flight to insure accuracy due to the shell's relatively low speed in the air and susceptibility to environmental conditions. After the Markale attack, several witnesses reported that the tailfin of the 120-mm mortar shell remained imbedded in the crater. The prosecution cited this as proof that the shell in question was fired at a sufficient velocity to overcome the force of the high explosive warhead detonation. Experts for the defense and the prosecution agree that the shell must have been traveling faster than 150 meters per second for the tailfin to embed into the surface of the market.[m]

Charge Level

The "charge level" of the mortar refers to the amount of propellant utilized to propel the shell out of the tube and to the target. The text refers to mortar charge levels as low, mid, and high. The operators of the Yugoslav 120-mm mortars in and around Sarajevo had access to shells with different charge levels. Mortar shells are equipped with a standard "0" charge level; the operator attaches additional charges to the tailfin prior to launch depending on the desired range. This alters the minimum and maximum distance that the shell can travel.[n] The M62 120-mm high explosive mortar shell has six standard "performance charge" levels. The minimum range of these shells (P1–P6) is 400 meters from launch to target to 6,050 meters from launch to target.[o]

FIGURE 3 Artillery terms

Elliptical Flight Path
Although all forms of artillery are capable of "indirect fire," mortars are designed to fire a projectile at a much steeper angle relative to the ground than "direct fire" artillery. They achieve a long range by using gravity to assist a generally low-powered projectile. This creates a lightweight "man-portable" weapon easily fired covertly in areas that would obscure direct fire weapons. Since the projectile follows this elliptical path, the speed at launch and angle of assent are relative to the speed at impact and angle of decent. The ICTY Galić prosecution determined the speed and angle of impact of the Markale market shell to improve the accuracy of the original UNPROFOR shell origin estimate. These measurements could not determine the exact origin of the shell but did rule out the possibility that the shell was fired from within ARBiH-controlled territory.
Tailfin Angle
In conjunction with charge level and tailfin depth, tailfin angle is useful to estimate and approximate shell origin. The Markale shell was traveling at a sufficient velocity for the tailfin to overcome the force of the warhead explosion and imbed itself into the crater to a substantial depth. Evidence presented at the ICTY stated that the tailfin to ground angle was between 53 and 65 degrees.[p] Due to a mortar shell's elliptical trajectory, the angle of the tailfin relative to the impact surface is similar to the angle of the mortar on firing.
Tailfin Depth
In the case of the Markale attack, an intact 120-mm mortar tailfin was found imbedded to a depth of between 200 and 250 mm in the center of the impact crater.[q] A measurement of penetration into a known surface can be used to estimate the speed of the mortar shell on impact. Due to the nature of a mortar's elliptical flight path, the velocity of the shell on impact is similar to the shell's initial muzzle velocity. Witnesses at the ICTY testified that the shell was traveling at a velocity greater than 200 meters per second to embed to the depth measured.[r] The prosecution at the ICTY used the tailfin depth measurement to estimate the initial charge level of the shell. The prosecution used this information in conjunction with tailfin angle to drastically improve the accuracy of the original UNPROFOR shell origin estimate.
Counter-Battery Radar
Counter-battery radar is useful for pinpointing the location of artillery launchers by tracking shells during their flight path. The British UNPROFOR contingent was operating counter-battery radar in Sarajevo at the time of the first Markale attack, but the system was outdated and not used to monitor the Markale district.[s] A modern counter-battery radar could have determined the exact origin of the shells fired against the Markale markets and other civilian groups in Sarajevo during the conflict.

FIGURE 3 Artillery terms[t]

j   For further detail see *Jane's Infantry Weapons, 1990–1991*. Vol. 16 (London: Jane's), pp. 693–694.

k   ICTY, "Prosecutor v. Stanislav Galić, Judgment and Opinion," paragraphs 467, 484.

l   "The Majority is convinced that the crater caused by the explosion was approximately 9 centimetres deep and that the depth of the tunnel of the tail-fin and the depth of the crater were together 200–250 mm." ICTY, "Prosecutor v. Stanislav Galić, Judgment and Opinion," paragraph 484.

m   *Ibid.*, paragraph 476.

n   Range is also variable by barrel angle if the shell does not need to clear an obstacle in front of the operator or the target.

o   *Jane's Infantry Weapons, 1990–1991*. Vol. 16 (London: Jane's), p. 692.

p   ICTY, "Prosecutor v. Stanislav Galić, Judgment and Opinion," paragraph 466 and note 1676.

q   *Ibid.*, paragraph 484.

r   *Ibid.*, paragraph 478.

s   Interview with Bill Stuebner, a former advisor to the Prosecutor for the International Criminal Tribunal for the Former Yugoslavia and a senior staff member of the Organization for Security and Cooperation working in Bosnia & Herzegovinia, 12 December 2003.

t   The authors wish to acknowledge the assistance of Professor Christopher Bassford, Colonel Mark D. Hanson and Colonel James E. Harris III of the National War College, Washington, for their assistance.

was not used in any U.N. report) with the tailfin forming a 60-degree angle with the asphalt surface (with a five-degree margin of error). The shrapnel blast pattern combined with the surrounding height of the buildings which the round had to clear correlated with and confirmed these measurements. Through these measurements and by utilizing the propellant range firing tables of 120-mm M62P3 mortars (see Figure 2) utilized by the SRK forces stationed in the surrounding area, the team estimated the possible range of the shell. Taking into account the 400-meter elevation variation between the probable sites of fire and impact, they concluded that, contingent on the power level of the 120-mm mortar charge, the shell originated at a minimum of 1,650 meters and a maximum of 6,550 meters from the point of impact (see Figure 3). This allowed for six possible firing origins along the approximately 18-degree trajectory of the mortar shell. Their report states that of the six possible locations for shell origin, only one was positioned in ARBiH-held territory.[62]

The main author of this report, Dr Berko Zećević, went a bit further in his trial testimony about the tailfin measurements taken in the crater. Since this part of the mortar shell embedded between 200 and 250 mm into the ground, the shell had to be traveling at a speed in excess of 200 meters per second to overcome the explosive force of the mortar and embed in the asphalt at the reported depth (see Figure 3). Given the characteristics of the mortar weapon in question, this velocity requires a high initial "charge level" that would alter the trajectory of the elliptical flight path, necessitating a further revision of the estimates contained in the U.N. and independent forensic reports. Indeed, a shell fired at the necessary velocity to penetrate the ground to this depth could only have originated between 4,900 and 6,000 meters from the impact site, placing the source of the mortar in SRK territory.[63]

The prosecution utilized the reported penetration depth of the tailfin to estimate the range of the mortar and determine a more accurate estimation for origin of fire. In previous U.N. analysis of the attack, this evidence was recorded but overlooked and not utilized. This information is useful to determine the approximate speed of a projectile in flight and can further minimize the possible points of origin. Since the velocity of the shell at impact is related to the velocity of the shell at firing, the impact velocity can be determined by the distance the tailfin penetrates into the asphalt[64] and initial velocity can be extrapolated accurately (see Figure 3). The impact velocity of the shell must be greater than 150 meters per second for the tailfin to overcome the explosive force of the mortar and penetrate the ground at all.[65] The force of the explosion reduced the velocity by 150 meters per second but, since the shell actually penetrated into the ground, the actual velocity was significantly greater than this figure. Experts testified that in order for the shell to penetrate the asphalt surface of the marketplace to a depth of 20 cm the impact velocity of the shell must have been approximately 260 meters per second. This velocity, combined with the agreed impact angle of the mortar, is consistent with the flight characteristics of a 120-mm shell with a mid- to high-level charge and fired from a distance greater than 4,500 meters.[66] This calculation places the shell origin past the 2,600-meter zone controlled by the ARBiH at the time of the incident, and in SRK-controlled territory.

The prosecution also presented non-technical evidence to the Tribunal. At the ICTY, several witnesses in the area testified that they heard a shell fired from the vicinity and direction of Mrkovici (Serb-controlled territory at the time) on the day of the attack. Their testimony is consistent with the location of known SRK mortars in Serb territory at the time of the shelling. In addition, the nearest Bosnian brigade headquarters was approximately 300 meters from the impact site and U.N. officers testified that no military facilities existed near the market. Although an adjacent building was used to manufacture uniforms for police and military defense forces, the factory was not operational at the time. In addition, SRK representatives stated to U.N. report authors that several SRK 120-mm mortars were stationed near Mrkovici along the north-northeast bearing estimated as the direction of fire in the U.N. final report. On the morning of the incident, the U.N. final report stated that "four mortar rounds were fired into the grid square beside the Markale area."[67] Since the likelihood of hitting a small area with one round is so low, this activity increases the probability that the party was attempting to target the market. [68]

Galić's defense team attempted to rebut these assertions by characterizing the prosecution's evidence as insufficient and unreliable, most of it having been provided second-hand. It showed pictures of blast damage and shrapnel from the site that it claimed did not correspond to the damage caused by a 120-mm mortar. It also stated that measuring the tailfin angle relative to the ground—especially after its initial removal—results in a speculative and therefore inaccurate measurement for angle of descent. Measuring an exact angle of descent is necessary to determine origin. It should be noted that the defense refuted the testimony of Berko Zećević by rejecting his tailfin depth assessment. They did this through faulty calculations based on the measurement of tailfin depth impact penetration data for concrete surfaces, and not for the thin layer of asphalt that applied to the Markale marketplace at that time. When confronted with this, the defense experts reassessed their calculations with results congruent with the findings in the prosecution's reports.[69] In addition, they argued that if in fact the explosion was caused by a mortar, the probability of deliberately hitting such a small target is very low. They also introduced the possibility that the ARBiH fired on the market "to attract international sympathy for the Muslim population of Sarajevo," since the final U.N. report concludes that the possibility exists that the shell originated in ARBiH-controlled territory. The ARBiH utilized 120-mm mortars, and the defense speculated that certain units of the ARBiH were capable of firing into their own territory.[70]

After considering the evidence, the Tribunal unanimously concluded that a single 120-mm mortar shell was fired from a north-northeasterly direction and exploded upon impacting the ground, resulting in the death of more than 60 people and the injury of at least 140 more.[71] But the prosecution was able to persuade only two of the three Tribunal judges that the round had originated from SRK-controlled territory and had deliberately targeted civilians at the marketplace. Once again, Judge Nieto-Navia dissented because the prosecution had failed to prove "beyond a reasonable doubt that this projectile was fired from SRK-controlled territory."[72]

At no point did Nieto-Navia intimate that the ARBiH was responsible for the attack. Rather, his dissent was informed by the extreme difficulty of fixing the precise location of indirect-fire ordnance such as the 120-mm mortar employed in the Markale attack. Crater analysis is at best also an inexact science; attempts to determine speed, range, or direction are exponentially exaggerated by any slight miscalculation at the scene, as can be seen from the differences between the four UNPROFOR investigations. Most expert analysis teams require at least three craters to triangulate and verify the direction of the attack in an attempt to determine origin although one crater is suitable to determine an approximate direction.[73] Moreover, even in instances where it is possible to determine the location and identity of the attacker, the margin of error in directing fire is often greater than the distance that separated civilian from military targets.

Admittedly, a more thorough, authoritative forensic investigation immediately after the explosion might have removed much of the ambiguity that arose around the incident. The pre-positioning of appropriate monitoring equipment, such as modern counter-battery radar, would have pre-empted the ensuing debate altogether. The British U.N. forces did have some rudimentary counter-battery radar units in Sarajevo, but these obsolete systems were too inaccurate to be suitable for the pinpoint type of analysis needed to determine culpability in a contested war zone like Sarajevo—even if it was officially a Safe Area.[74] Although Sarajevo's new 20-km heavy weapon exclusion zone was never strictly enforced and did not foreclose the positioning of mortars around Sarajevo, it did reduce somewhat the severity of artillery attacks on the besieged capital. As a result, 18 months passed after the first "Marketplace Massacre" without any high-casualty incidents comparable to those examined here.

During that time, much of the media attention and consequent accusations of VRS violations switched to the other Safe Areas, such as the aforementioned attacks in Goražde and Tuzla, and major VRS assaults on Bihać, Srebrenica, and Žepa, the last two of which fell in July 1995. There were, however, two instances in which French UNPROFOR commanders accused Sarajevo's ARBiH defenders of firing on their own civilians. The first concerned an 8 November 1994 mortar attack on the capital's Kosevsko Brdo neighborhood which injured a child. After analyzing two impact craters, "artillery specialist" Lieutenant Colonel Jacques Lechevallier gave a tele-vised press briefing during which he presented an array of maps, charts, and photographs taken at the scene to demonstrate that both shells could only have been fired from "well within Bosnian Army lines."[75] If Lechevallier's work was persuas-ive, a subsequent, six-week investigation by another French team equipped with night vision equipment presented definitive evidence that a group of ARBiH snipers positioned inside the 40-storey Bosnian parliament building had repeatedly fired on civilians during the first half of 1995. Once again, the number of casualties had been small, consisting of only two civilians "hit" (but, presumably, not killed), together with a number of near misses.[76] Not surprisingly, the Bosnian government rejected responsibility for the attacks, which even the French accusers publicly intimated were likely the work of isolated renegade elements, perpetrated without the knowl-edge of ARBiH commanders. Yet the government never attempted to refute the evidence of the mortar and sniper attacks (although it may have had some role in the sudden end of sniper activity emanating from the parliament building). Quite aside from the hard evidence presented, UNPROFOR's accusation of incidental acts that left few casualties was plausible enough, especially coming at a point late in the war when Bosnia and its advocates despaired of ever securing international intervention, particularly from VRS military actions in Sarajevo. On the other hand, neither incident rises to the level of depravity necessary for soldiers to direct heavy ordnance against large concentrations of their own civilian population.

Second "Marketplace Massacre" at the City Market, Sarajevo (9)

All speculation about "self-inflicted" casualties and continued international indiffer-ence ended abruptly on 28 August 1995 when a single mortar round exploded next to the Habsburg-era City Market building, killing 43 civilians and injuring over 80. This incident has since become known as the "second" Markale attack, because the round landed less than 100 meters from the site of the 5 February 1994 explosion. Yet the incident was linked most closely to events just six weeks earlier in the Srebrenica Safe Area, where thousands of Bosniak men and boys had been executed by the VRS following the town's capture. Amid the horror of the Srebrenica massacre, NATO leaders had resolved to retaliate militarily the next time the VRS attacked one of the country's Safe Areas. Hence, as soon as UNPROFOR commander Admiral Rupert Smith had confirmed that a forensic team had reported that this second Markhale attack had originated from behind VRS lines, NATO launched Operation "Deliberate Force." The sustained, 11-day air bombardment of VRS positions that commenced on 30 August 1995 was the largest operation ever conducted by the alliance and proved decisive in ending the Bosnian war.[77]

NATO intervention came despite the expected denial of responsibility from the Bosnian Serb leadership. Moreover, on this occasion UNPROFOR conducted only a single and still secret crater analysis to confirm VRS complicity, after which the short, successful career of "Deliberate Force" rendered further discussion moot.[78] Although the VRS continued to blame the ARBiH for the attack, much of the ensuing controversy centered around Russian UNPROFOR Colonel Andrei Demurenko, who called for an extensive U.N. investigation, claiming that the initial determination had been incorrect and that the ARBiH had fired the shell.[79] Moreover, he repeated these charges in a lengthy television interview, which elicited harsh criticism from the U.N. and his immediate transfer. Meanwhile, U.N. officials dismissed his claims, citing inaccuracies in his own statements, while reaffirming the firm conclusions of a panel of French, British, Spanish, and American forensics experts who had assigned responsibility to the VRS.[80] Yet U.N. officialdom's united front in defense of its secret report has not laid the debate fully to rest, thanks to a series of closely confidential interviews that Dutch scholar Cees Wiebes conducted with a dozen military and intelligence officers from as many countries who insist that the ARBiH was, indeed, responsible.[81]

Conclusions

The quick and unequivocal response to the second Markale incident represented an evolution not only in technique but in the understanding and resolve of U.N. and other international officials. At the time of the breadline attack in 1992 they were unprepared to evaluate the Bosnian Serb countercharge of ARBiH responsibility. By 1995 they had sufficiently anticipated the inevitable controversy in the wake of the second Markale attack to conduct a prompt and adequate forensic examination, while refusing to accept counterclaims in the absence of supporting evidence. This skepticism toward Bosnian Serb accusations was still evident eight years later in the Hague Tribunal's judgment against Stanislav Galič, which dismissed claims that the ARBiH had targeted its own civilians with the rejoinder "that a mere hypothesis is not a basis for reasonable doubt. Some fact or allegation must be relied on to turn a mere possibility into a reasonable one."[82]

This change in mindset represented the adoption of inductive reasoning to modify what had been a commitment to impartiality so dogged that it had denied the distinction between unsupported claims or hypotheses and credible, verifiable evidence. Induction can be a powerful vehicle for judging *probability*. Certainly JNA military doctrine and the widespread commission of atrocities across Bosnia suggested a lack of sensitivity to the rights of civilians. This included numerous artillery assaults, such as the six incidents cited here that were not disputed by the Bosnian Serb leadership, together with a plethora of anecdotal, eyewitness accounts of crimes intentionally committed against individual civilians. Hence General Smith's observation on the morrow of the second Markale attack that a conclusive judgment by the forensics team was unnecessary in light of the plethora of artillery salvoes that the VRS had unleashed on Sarajevo's civilian population during the course of his tenure as UNPROFOR commander.[83] In this vein, some of the most damaging evidence was provided by the Bosnian Serbs themselves through their presentation of arguments and evidence that was subsequently exposed as fraudulent, most notably claims of a land mine at the breadline, Karadžić's eyewitness accounts of news vans and frozen corpses pre-positioned at the Markale marketplace, and persistent Serb denials of atrocities for which there is irrefutable evidence, such as the Srebrenica massacre or the later expulsion of 800,000 Albanians from Kosovo. By 1995, many in the international community had been disposed to dismiss their counterclaims as untrue.

Of course, inductive logic alone is never sufficient to establish absolute proof, certainly not in a court of law. The "dissenting judge" Rafael Nieto-Navia correctly stood for the primacy of positive evidence by refusing to rule that hundreds of VRS attacks conclusively established its responsibility for specific attacks in the absence of firm evidence. But scholars are not a jury that must render a clear-cut judgment that determines the fate of individual defendants. Rather, they are afforded the latitude—and obligation—to weigh probabilities from the evidence at hand. It is on the basis of what we know that we feel comfortable in concluding that the VRS was responsible for the first six "uncontested" mortar attacks and, in default of a single shred of credible contrary evidence, that there is a very high probability that it was also behind the "Breadline Massacre" of 27 May 1992, as well as the first and second "Marketplace Massacres" of 5 February 1992 and 28 August 1995. As with much scholarship, this assessment does not foreclose the possibility that additional evidence—perhaps even the testimony of those individual soldiers who launched the attacks—will either definitively reaffirm or refute it. Until then, historical scenarios around the hypothesis that the ARBiH committed one or more of these crimes would appear to be without merit.

NOTES

1. Case No. IT-98-29-T, "Prosecutor v. Stanislav Galić, Judgment and Opinion." In Trial Chamber I, Before: Judge Alphons Orie, Judge Amin El Mahdi, Judge Rafael Nieto-Navia. Released 5 December 2003.
2. Case No. IT-98-29-T, "Prosecutor v. Stanislav Galić, Separate and Partially Dissenting Opinion of Judge Rafael Nieto-Navia." In Trial Chamber I, Before: Judge Alphons Orie, Judge Amin El Mahdi, Judge Rafael Nieto-Navia. Released 5 December 2003.

3. Citation from a JNA manual?
4. Bihać, Goražde, Sarajevo, Srebrenica, Tuzla, Žepa.
5. P2261 (U.N. report) p. 43.
6. United Nations Security Council Resolution (UNSCR) 819 (1993) designated the city of Srebrenica and its surrounding area as a Safe Area. UNSCR 824 designated Žepa, Goražde, and Bihać and their surroundings as Safe Areas.
7. These attacks were only disputed long after the incident by General Galić's defense team as reported in the Judgment and Opinion and Separate and Partially Dissenting Opinion of the ICTY Trial Chamber.
8. Dobrinja is in southwest Sarajevo adjacent to the international airport and close to the line of control at the time.
9. Eyewitnesses at the ICTY testified that between 11 and 16 people were killed because of the explosions. ICTY, "Prosecutor v. Stanislav Galić, Judgment and Opinion," paragraph 376. The post-attack Canadian UNPROFOR investigation determined that the attack killed 13 people and injured 133. William J. Fenrick, Annex VI.A, "Incident Study Regarding Mortar Shelling, Dobrinja, Sarajevo on 1 June 1993." UNSC. 28 December 1994.
10. ICTY, "Prosecutor v. Stanislav Galić, Judgment and Opinion," paragraph 376. "81 mm" refers to the diameter of the mortar shell and barrel. This paper discusses 82- and 120-mm mortar shells, and 130-mm artillery shells. For additional information, see Figures 2 and 3.
11. *Ibid.*, paragraph 377.
12. The post-attack analysis states that "the shells came from the Serbian side, approximately 300 meters south of the Lukavica Barracks." See Figure 1 for the general location of the Lukavica Barracks relative to the Dobrinja district. William J. Fenrick, Annex VI.A, "Incident Study Regarding Mortar Shelling, Dobrinja, Sarajevo on 1 June 1993." UNSC, 28 December 1994.
13. ICTY, "Prosecutor v. Stanislav Galić, Judgment and Opinion," paragraph 382.
14. *Ibid.*, paragraph 388.
15. ICTY, "Prosecutor v. Stanislav Galić, Separate and Partially Dissenting Opinion of Judge Rafael Nieto-Navia," paragraph 65.
16. The UNPROFOR incident investigator stated, "the mortar shell killed 11 persons and wounded 13 others." ICTY, "Prosecutor v. Stanislav Galić, Judgment and Opinion," paragraph 389.
17. ICTY, "Prosecutor v. Stanislav Galić, Judgment and Opinion," paragraph 391.
18. *Ibid.*, paragraph 388–389.
19. *Ibid.*, paragraph 397.
20. The defense conclusion "that the direction of fire of the shell was most probably from an 'East-Southwest direction' was based on inverted pictures." ICTY, "Prosecutor v. Stanislav Galić, Judgment and Opinion," paragraph 393.
21. ICTY, ' "Prosecutor v. Stanislav Galić, Separate and Partially Dissenting Opinion of Judge Rafael Nieto-Navia," paragraph 70.
22. "Six children had been killed by the explosions and another three children and one adult had been seriously injured." ICTY, "Prosecutor v. Stanislav Galić, Judgment and Opinion," paragraph 333.
23. ICTY, "Prosecutor v. Stanislav Galić, Judgment and Opinion," paragraph 335.
24. "The Trial Chamber finds that Mirza Sabljica employed the correct methodology to determine the direction from which the shells had landed." ICTY, "Prosecutor v. Stanislav Galić, Judgment and Opinion," paragraph 341.

25. Sabljica testified "that all three shells originated in Nedarići, in the vicinity of the Institute for the Blind," an area occupied by the SRK forces. ICTY, "Prosecutor v. Stanislav Galić, Judgment and Opinion," paragraph 335.
26. *Ibid.*, paragraph 345.
27. "The Trial Chamber reiterates that a mere hypothesis is not a basis for reasonable doubt. Some fact or allegation must be relied on to turn a mere possibility into a reasonable one. Moreover, concerning the alleged possibility that the ARBiH mistakenly hit Alipašino Polje while aiming at Nedarići, for which there is not the slightest factual basis, the fact that the two locations are about a kilometre apart, would necessarily exclude such allegation." ICTY, "Prosecutor v. Stanislav Galić, Judgment and Opinion," paragraph 342.
28. *Ibid.*, note 1351.
29. "The investigation team into the incident was headed by Zdenko Eterović, a judge and investigative magistrate." ICTY, "Prosecutor v. Stanislav Galić, Judgment and Opinion," paragraph 403.
30. *Ibid.*
31. *Ibid.*, paragraph 404.
32. *Ibid.*, paragraph 406.
33. The attack "was, at the very least, indiscriminate as to its target (which nevertheless was primarily if not entirely a residential neighborhood), and was carried out recklessly, resulting in civilian casualties." *Ibid.*, paragraph 410.
34. Chuck Sudetic, *Blood and Vengeance: One Family's Story of the War in Bosnia* (New York: Penguin Books, 1998), pp. 232–234; Steven L. Burg and Paul S. Shoup, *The War in Bosnia-Herzegovina: Ethnic Conflict and International Intervention* (Armonk, NY and London: M.E. Sharpe, 1999), pp. 147–150.
35. Central Intelligence Agency, *Balkan Battlegrounds: A Military History of the Yugoslav Conflict, 1990–1995*, Vol. 1 (Washington, DC: Office of Russian and European Analysis, 2002), p. 385.
36. *Ibid.*, p. 387.
37. Alexander G. Higgens, "Tuzla, First Anniversary," Associated Press World Stream, International News, 25 May 1996.
38. Shoup and Burg, *War in Bosnia-Herzegovina*, pp. 162, 165; Sudetic, *Blood and Vengeance*, p. 248; Charles G. Boyd, "Making Peace with the Guilty: the Truth about Bosnia, *Foreign Affairs*, Vol. 74, 1995, pp. 22–38.
39. Tom Gjelten, *Professionalism in War Reporting: A Correspondent's View* (Washington, DC: Carnegie Corporation of New York, June 1998), < http://www.wilsoncenter.org/subsites/ccpdc/pubs/gj/gjfr.htm >.
40. Leonard Doyle, "Muslims Slaughter Their Own People," *The Independent*, 22 August 1992, p. 1.
41. Mackenzie tells Gjelten, "It will take other investigations, other than somebody who saw it from afar or only saw bits and pieces of the evidence, to come to a conclusive finding." Tom Gjelten, "Blaming the Victim," *New Republic*, 20 December 1993, pp. 14–16.
42. *Ibid.*
43. Gjelten, *Professionalism in War Reporting*, p. 17.
44. Keith Doubt, *Sociology after Bosnia and Kosovo: Recovering Justice* (New York: Oxford University Press, 2000).
45. Letter presented as evidence item D138.1. ICTY, "Prosecutor v. Stanislav Galić, Judgment and Opinion," paragraph 440.
46. Bosnian Muslim representation refused to comply with this request. ICTY, "Prosecutor v. Stanislav Galić, Judgment and Opinion," paragraph 440.

47. Central Intelligence Agency, *Balkan Battlegrounds: A Military History of the Yugoslav Conflict, 1990*–1995, Vol. 1 (Washington, DC: Office of Russian and European Analysis, 2002), pp. 229–230.
48. The origin of incoming fire is calculated in degrees, beginning with true North (0°) and proceeding clockwise in a 360-degree arc, with East 90°, South 180°, and West 270°.
49. ICTY, "Prosecutor v. Stanislav Galić, Judgment and Opinion," paragraph 445–447.
50. This team comprised Major Sahaisar Khan, Commandant John Hamill, and Captain Jose Grande.
51. ICTY, "Prosecutor v. Stanislav Galić, Judgment and Opinion," paragraph 446–449.
52. P2261 (U.N. report).
53. With an absolute minimal angle of 49.15 degrees due to structures blocking lower flight paths.
54. P2261 (U.N. report) p. 4. ICTY, "Prosecutor v. Stanislav Galić, Judgment and Opinion," paragraph 449 and note 1628.
55. David Binder, "Anatomy of a Massacre," *Foreign Policy*, Vol. 97, 1994–1995, pp. 70–78.
56. Interview with British UNPROFOR Captain Ken Lindsay.
57. Mark Danner, "Bosnia: the Turning Point," *New York Review of Books*, 5 February 1998, p. 34–41.
58. Binder, "Anatomy of a Massacre," pp. 77–78.
59. In addition, the ongoing Slobodan Milosevic Hague trial is re-examining this incident.
60. ICTY, "Prosecutor v. Stanislav Galić, Judgment and Opinion," note 1560.
61. Principal local investigators: Mirza Sabljica, and Berko Zečević had investigated prior mortar incidents in Sarajevo. At the time Hamdija Čavčić, was "a police investigator in the Department for Criminal and Technical Investigations in Sarajevo" (ICTY, paragraph 391). ICTY, "Prosecutor v. Stanislav Galić, Judgment and Opinion," paragraph 441.
62. ICTY, "Prosecutor v. Stanislav Galić, Judgment and Opinion," paragraph 443.
63. *Ibid.*, paragraph 444.
64. Reported by multiple sources to be between 200 and 250 mm
65. The fact that the tailfin was present in the crater proves that the shell was moving at a velocity greater than 150 meters per second. See Figure 3.
66. ICTY, "Prosecutor v. Stanislav Galić, Judgment and Opinion," paragraph 481.
67. *Ibid.*, paragraph 459.
68. *Ibid.*, paragraph 454–460.
69. *Ibid.*, paragraph 453.
70. *Ibid.*, paragraph 449.
71. ICTY, "Prosecutor v. Stanislav Galić, Separate and Partially Dissenting Opinion of Judge Rafael Nieto-Navia," paragraph 73.
72. Case No. IT-98-29-T. "Prosecutor v. Stanislav Galić, Separate and Partially Dissenting Opinion of Judge Rafael Nieto-Navia." In Trial Chamber I, Before: Judge Alphons Orie, Judge Amin El Mahdi, Judge Rafael Nieto-Navia. Released 5 December 2003. Paragraphs 92, 94, 98–101, 488, 493, 495–496.
73. The U.S. Army field manual for artillery states, "It is possible to do the following: verify as confined locations, suspected locations that have been obtained by other means. Confirm the presence of enemy artillery and obtain an approximate direction to it. Detect the presence of new types of enemy weapons, new calibers, or new ammunition manufacturing methods." This manual ignores the possibility of determining range estimates through post-impact analysis. Although it does state, "often, tail fins are found in the fuze tunnel of the crater," it does not elaborate on a method for extrapolating range

from the tailfin. U.S. Military Field Manual FM 6-50, Appendix J "Crater Analysis and Reporting," Section J-4.

74. Interview with Bill Stuebner, former advisor to the Prosecutor for the International Criminal Tribunal for the Former Yugoslavia and a senior staff member of the Organization for Security and Cooperation, working in Bosnia-Herzegovina, 12 December 2003. See Figure 3.

75. Chuck Sudetic, "Bosnia Army Said to Shell Its Own Area," *New York Times*, 11 November 1994, p. 10.

76. Mike O'Connor, "Investigation Concludes Bosnian Government Snipers Shot at Civilians," *New York Times*, 1 August 1995, p. 6.

77. Central Intelligence Agency, *Balkan Battlegrounds: A Military History of the Yugoslav Conflict, 1990–1995*, Vol. 1 (Washington: Office of Russian and European Analysis, 2002), pp. 377–378.

78. The forensic report has never been released, even at the Galić trial. According to Burg and Shoup, who interviewed a source close to the investigation, the shell was one of five salvoes, the other four had definitely originated from VRS positions, but the origin of the all-important fifth shell that inflicted the casualties could not be ascertained, probably because it had been deflected just before impact. *War in Bosnia-Herzegivina*, p. 168.

79. Andrei Naryshkin, "Russian Commander Question UN Probe into Sarajevo Attack," *Tass*, 3 September 1995.

80. Central Intelligence Agency, *Balkan Battlegrounds: A Military History of the Yugoslav Conflict, 1990–1995*, Vol. 1 (Washington: Office of Russian and European Analysis, 2002), p. 417.

81. Cees Wiebes, *Intelligence and the War in Bosnia, 1992–1995* (Munich, Hamburg, Berlin, Vienna and London: Lit Verlag, 2003), p. 68; 5 October 2004 interview with the author.

82. ICTY, "Prosecutor v. Stanislav Galić, Judgment and Opinion," paragraph 342.

83. Interview with UNPROFOR Captain Ken Lindsay, who employed parallel logic in giving responsibility for the 5 February 1994 Markale salvo, which he recounted as one of an estimated 600 that fell on Sarajevo that day.

The Effects of the Dissolution of Yugoslavia on the Minority Rights of Hungarian and Italian Minorities in the Post-Yugoslav States

Matjaž Klemenčič and Jernej Zupančič

Introduction

Thousands of books have been written on Yugoslavia's dissolution and the wars that followed in the 1990s. Most of them, however, deal with relations among the main ethno-nations of Yugoslavia, *i.e.*, Serbs, Croats, Slovenes, Bosniaks (Muslims), Montenegrins, Macedonians and Albanians, and the effects on them of the dissolution and wars. Hungarians and Italians of Yugoslavia also suffered, and the wars affected their destiny; but these peoples have rarely been mentioned in the context of this history. It is the aim of this article to fill the gap.

The international boundaries of Yugoslavia as they were formed after World Wars I and II were not identical with ethnic borders. This was also true of the international boundaries created in the region in the 1990s. Therefore, parts of numerous ethnic groups lived as "national minorities" outside the boundaries of their homelands. These groups were defined as "nationalities" in the 1974 Constitution of Yugoslavia, because the term "minority" meant something less; and the politicians and ideologists who wrote the Constitution wanted to prove that nationalities constituted equally important parts of the society.[1]

Among the minorities in Yugoslavia, Italians and Hungarians deserve special attention; the Hungarian group because of its size, the Italian because after World War II—after almost all of the Germans left—it remained the only Western European ethnic minority in the country. Due to historical reasons, numerous Hungarians live as ethnic minorities outside Hungary in neighboring countries; and the Hungarian state is concerned about their welfare.[2]

Soon after World War II, the Italian and Hungarian minorities became the subject of attention and partners in political and economic cooperation within Yugoslavia itself as well as in cooperation with their motherlands (this distinguishes them from the Albanian minority of Yugoslavia, which was the object of inter-ethnic conflict throughout the post-1945 period).

Areas of Settlement of Italians and Hungarians in Yugoslavia

The boundary between Hungary and Yugoslavia was determined by the Peace Treaty of Trianon in 1920, drawn without regard to the ethnic situation in the region.[3] This boundary remained unchanged after World War II. There were almost 500,000 Hungarians living in Yugoslavia. Things were different with Italy, which after World War I in accordance with the secret Treaty of London of 1915 gained extensive territories of what is today western Slovenia (so-called "Primorska"), and Istria and parts of Dalmatia in today's Croatia. After World War II, Italy lost these territories. For different reasons, most of the Italians of Istria and Dalmatia migrated to Italy after the boundaries were redrawn in 1947 and later finally in 1954.[4]

Italians settled on the coast of Istria (and in the hinterland), in the Kvarner Islands (Cres and Lošinj) and on the Dalmatian coast between Zadar and Split. Within Istria, people changed their ethnic identity; and today it is possible to talk about an Istrian regional identity.[5] Italians settled the cities and were historically, from the Middle Ages on, employed in the non-agrarian sector. Due to the economic power of the bourgeoisie, even Slavic immigrants to the cities from the hinterland became Romanized as early as the first generation. Most of the Italians of the former Yugoslavia live today in Croatia, with approximately 90% of them on the coast and the remainder in the continental area. While the Italians in the coastal belt of Croatia are part of an old historical (autochthonous) group, the Italians in the continental part of Croatia are exclusively migrants.[6]

Hungarians in Yugoslavia settled mainly on the Pannonian Plain and surrounding low hills, *i.e.*, eastern Prekmurje in today's Slovenia, Eastern and Western Slavonia and Baranja in today's Croatia, and Vojvodina in today's Serbia & Montenegro. Most of them live in Bačka, including Novi Sad. Villages especially were historically mostly ethnically homogeneous. In Slovenia the villages are smaller; the area of settlement was, however, homogeneous. More Hungarians live in Croatia. Their settlements are dispersed, however, and—with the exception of Baranja—they form spatially divided "ethnic islands." A similar situation may be found also in Vojvodina, where the Hungarian ethnic islands are larger and in close proximity.

In the 1990s, the economic situation of the regions where Hungarians were settled worsened. Most of the regions where Hungarians lived in Croatia were in the war zones. Therefore, they had numerous victims of war among them; they lost most of their economic potential, which—in addition to political pressures—stimulated their emigration. The number of ethnic Hungarians in the region had fallen even before the fighting began, due to low natural increase.

The regions of settlement of Italians and Hungarians in the former Yugoslavia are part of the periphery, where negative demographic and economic processes prevailed even before the 1990s. Minorities shared the destiny of their areas of settlement: it means, that if, for example, the war devastated the region then also members suffered, if there is economic crisis, also minority members were affected. Therefore a decrease in their numbers is not surprising, nor is the poor economic structure of the minority populations.

Demographic Development of Hungarians and Italians in Slovenia, Croatia and Serbia and their Population According to the Censuses of 1991 and 2001/2002

Italians in Slovenia and Croatia and Hungarians in Slovenia, Croatia and Vojvodina represent an old component of the ethnic structure of these regions. The demographic development of the Italian and Hungarian minorities in the regions of their settlement is very complex and we could explain it—in spite of the trend of slow decrease in numbers in all the states that developed after the dissolution of Yugoslavia—as a result of both outside factors (geographic features of their settlement areas, *e.g.*, natural change, migration) and internal factors (statistical methods of census taking, national policy of the state, mixed marriages, changes in the identity of the population, and non-coerced assimilation).

Italians in Slovenia and Croatia

The majority of the Italians in Slovenia and Croatia are partially an autochthonous and partially a subsequently resettled population that settled in 1918–1943, when Primorska and Istria, Rijeka, parts of Dalmatia and the islands of Cres, Krk, Lastovo and Palagruža became part of Italy.[7] Italian Fascists were also forcefully assimilating Slovenes and Croats or forcing them to leave.[8] The Italian 1936 census[9] indicated approximately 230,000 persons who listed Italian as their language of communication in the territory of contemporary Slovenia and Croatia, which was then part of the Italian state (*c.* 194,000 in today's Croatia and *c.* 36,000 in today's Slovenia). Most of them left after the above-mentioned territory became part of Yugoslavia in accordance with decisions of the Paris Peace Conference in 1947.

From the end of World War II until 1953, according to different data, 250,000–350,000 persons emigrated from the above-described regions. Two-thirds of them were ethnic Italians; one-third of them were Slovenes and Croats who opposed the Communist regime in Yugoslavia.[10] Approximately 15% of all emigrants left without migration permits, while the majority left with the approval of the authorities. These are the so-called *optanti* emigrants, *i.e.*, those who lived permanently in this region on 10 June 1940 and who expressed their wish to obtain Italian citizenship and emigrated to Italy. The emigration of Italians reduced the total population of the region and altered its ethnic structure.[11]

So, in 1953 only 36,000 Italians lived in Yugoslavia, *i.e.*, 16% of their population before World War II. Italians also emigrated in later decades (most of them to the U.S. and other overseas countries). Therefore their population declined during each subsequent census until 1981 (see Table 1).

We have to emphasize that the data of the Yugoslav censuses are unreliable in relation to the real number of Italians, since many members of the Italian minority, because of various reasons, chose "Nationality Undeclared" or their regional identity (mostly as "Istrians").

The number of Italians changed also in the last two decades of the twentieth century. In the 1991 census there was a relatively large increase in Italians, compared with the 1981 census. Many Italians who in previous censuses did not declare

TABLE 1 The Italian population in Yugoslavia, 1953–2001/2002

		1948[1]	1953[5]	1961	1971	1981	1991	2001/2002
Slovenia	No.	25,451[2]	n.a.	3,072	3,001	2,187	3,063	2,258
	%	1.77		0.19	0.17	0.12	0.17	0.11
Croatia	No.	85,803[3]	n.a.	21,103	17,433	11,661	21,303	19,636
	%	2.27		0.51	0.39	0.25	0.45	0.44
Former Yugoslavia	No.	113,278[4]	n.a.	25,615	21,791	15,132	26,108	No data
	%	0.72		0.14	0.11	0.07	0.11	

[1] Data for Slovenia and Croatia are recounted for these regions after the final boundaries were drawn in 1954
[2] The data for Slovenia are counts of the results of the 1953 census of population of Slovenia (1,458) and data of the Statistical Office of the Istrian Regional People's Committee in Koper County (23,993), which was then part of the Free Territory of Trieste.
[3] The data for Croatia are counts of the results of the 1953 census of population of Croatia (76,093) and data of the Statistical Office of the Istrian Regional People's Committee in Buje County (9,710), which was then part of the Free Territory of Trieste.
[4] The data for the former Yugoslavia are counts of the results of the 1953 census of population (79,575) and data of the Statistical Office of the Istrian Regional People's Committee in Koper County (33,703), which was then part of the Free Territory of Trieste.
[5] There are no data for the regions that were part of the Free Territory of Trieste for 1953 and therefore there are no data for ethnic affiliation for Slovenia and Croatia and also for the former Yugoslavia.

Sources: Statistika prebivalstva Istarskega okrožja po stanju z dne 15. decembra 1947 (Koper, Slovenia: Statistični urad Istarskega okrožnega ljudskega odbora, 1948)—Arhiv Inštituta za narodnostna vprašanja v Ljubljani; Statistički ljetopis Istre, Primorja i Gorskog Kotara 1992 (data only for former Buje Commune); Konačni rezultati popisa stanovništva od 15 marta 1948. godine, Knjiga IX: Stanovništvo po narodnosti (Belgrade: Savezni zavod za statistiku, 1954); Popis stanovništva 1953. Knjiga XIII: Stanovništvo i domaćinstva (Belgrade: Savezni zavod za statistiku, 1959); Popis stanovništva 1961. Knjiga VI: Vitalna, etnička i migraciona obeležja—rezultati za opštine (Belgrade: Savezni zavod za statistiku, 1967); Popis stanovništva i stanova 1971. Statistički bilten 727: Nacionalni sastav stanovništva po opštinama (Belgrade: Savezni zavod za statistiku, 1972); Popis stanovništva, domaćinstava i stanova u 1981. godini. Statistički bilten 1295: Nacionalni sastav stanovništva po opštinama—konačni rezultati (Belgrade: Savezni zavod za statistiku, 1982); Prvi rezultati popisa stanovništva, domaćinstava i poljoprivrednih gazdinstava 1991. godine. Statistički bilten broj 1934: Nacionalni sastav stanovništva po opštinama (Belgrade: Savezni zavod za statistiku, 1995); Popis stanovništva 2001. Stanovništvo prema narodnosti, po gradovima/općinama (Zagreb: Državni zavod za statistiku, 2002), <http://www.dzs.hr/Popis%202001/Popis/H01_02_02/ H01_02_02.html> (16 November 2003); Popis prebivalstva, gospodinjstev in stanovanovanj, Slovenija, 31. marca 2002. Statistične informacije no. 93: Prebivalstvo (Ljubljana: Statistični urad Republike Slovenije, 2003), p. 23; Popis stanovništva 2002 (Belgrade: Savezni zavod za statistiku, 2004), <http://www.kanjiza.co.yu/nepszamlalas2002/popisst2002.htm > (20 January 2004).

130

themselves as such declared themselves "Italians" in 1991 because they counted on the help of Italy in forthcoming crises in the region. Once the situation in Slovenia and Croatia pacified after they became independent (and especially after the end of the war in Croatia), there followed a decrease in the numbers of "Italians" in both countries.

According to the Croatian census of 2001, most of the Italians lived in communes of the Istrian county (županija)—c. 14,300, or 6.92% of the whole population. In the communes that belonged to the Free Territory of Trieste until 1954, they still today form a significant percentage of the population: Grožnjan (51.21%), Brtonigla (37.37%), Buje (29.72%), etc. More then 3,000 Italians live in Rijeka and surroundings (see Figure 1).

The Italians live also in continental Croatia, in several settlements in the Pakrac (559 persons or 6.31%) and Lipik (208 persons or 3.12%) municipalities in Western Slavonia. They came from Upper Tagliamento during the period from 1880 to 1909. They were stock farmers. In the new homeland each family got eight acres of land from a count who owned the land (generally forests), which they had to clear within 30 years. They proved quite industrious and paid off their debts in a shorter period.[12] Like the members of other nationalities of this region, the Italians were subject to the process of urbanization, but even today most of them are still involved in agriculture. They blended into life in the area and did not, like the Italians of coastal Croatia, emigrate after the Second World War.[13] During the period of war in Croatia (1991–1995) their number decreased by only 10%, in spite of the fact that their settlement areas were war zones. In comparison, the number of Hungarians who lived in approximately the same region of Western Slavonia decreased by almost 42% (see Table 2).

During the war in Croatia there were no military battles in Istria. Therefore the Croatian government brought to Istria ethnic Croatian refugees from the regions that were under control of the Republic of Srpska Krajina, Herzegovina and central Bosnia. Many of those refugees settled permanently in Istria. These settlements were politically motivated, to "strengthen the Croatian stock" in Istria, because in the decade 1981–1991 the number of Italians in Istria increased by more than 80%. The Croatian political leadership was then worried because of political pressures from Italy, where demands for revisions of the Treaties of Osimo surfaced in extreme nationalist circles. On the other hand, the Croatian leadership was also worried because Istrians—both Croat and Italian—demanded autonomy within Croatia. That politics was involved with the settlement of ethnic Croatian refugees in Istria could be ascertained also from the fact that the number of Croats increased the most in the region where the percentage of Italians was the highest, i.e., in the region of the former Buje commune (from 9,422 to 14,411). In all of Istria the number of Croats increased from 111,516 to 148,328 (i.e., by 32.9%).

131

Map 1: **ITALIANS IN SLOVENIA AND CROATIA IN 2001/02**

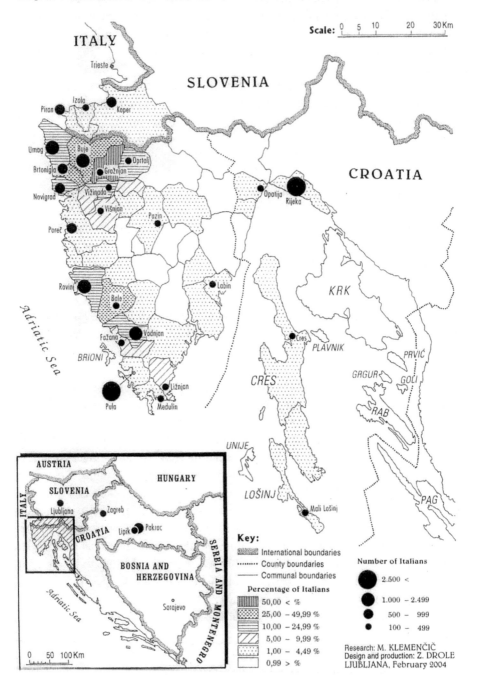

FIGURE 1 Italians in Slovenia and Croatia, in 2002

TABLE 2 Changes in the size and percentage of the Croatian and Italian population, by regions of settlement in the Republic of Croatia, 1991–2001

Regions	Croats					Italians			
	1991	2001	Changes in number	Index 2001/1991		1991	2001	Changes in number	Index 2001/1991
Istria	111,596	148,328	+ 36,732	132.92		15,306	14,284	– 1,022	100.98
Rijeka and surroundings	180,537	192,678	+ 12,141	106.72		3,907	3,478	– 429	93.57
Regions of autochthonous settlement of Italians—total	292,133	341,006	+ 48,873	116.72		19,213	17,762	– 1,451	96.92
Continental Croatia	9,896	10,954	+ 1,058	110.69		869	767	– 102	56.29
Regions of settlement of Italians—total	302,029	351,960	+ 49,931	116.53		20,082	18,529	– 1,553	94.58

Sources: Popis stanovništva 1991. Narodnosni sastav stanovništva Hrvatske po naseljima (Zagreb: Republički zavod za statistiku, 1992); *Popis stanovništva 2001. Stanovništvo prema narodnosti, po gradovima/općinama* (Zagreb: Državni zavod za statistiku, 2002), <http://www.dzs.hr/Popis%202001/Popis/H01_02_02/H01_02_02.ıtml> (16 November 2003).

Hungarians in Slovenia, Croatia and Vojvodina

After World War II, Hungarians represented (after Albanians) the second-largest minority in Yugoslavia. Most of them lived in Vojvodina, some also in Slovenia and Croatia (see Table 3).

Approximately 87% of the Hungarians in Slovenia lived in Prekmurje (Hungarian: Muravidék or Murántúl). The majority of them were peasants who lived in the economically less-developed countryside along the Slovene–Hungarian border. Socialist industrialization, urbanization and change in lifestyle accelerated the mobility of the population, although, unlike in other socialist countries, most agricultural land remained in private ownership.[14] The Hungarian population of Prekmurje suffered from a declining natural increase, because of emigration from its ethnically mixed settlement areas. The migrants were seeking better job opportunities in central Slovenian cities and abroad. The number of ethnic Hungarians living in Slovenia outside the Prekmurje rose from 195 in 1948 to 814 in 2002. During the 1960s, 1970s and 1980s, with the possibility to work in and migrate to the countries of Western Europe, the number of Hungarians fell further.[15] Due to natural decrease, aging, emigration, the ongoing process of assimilation, or loss of linguistic and ethnic identity, the Hungarians of the Prekmurje lost more than 40% of their population between 1948 and 2002; from 10,384 to 5,212 in 2002 (see Table 4).

At the time of the last census, in 2002, 5,429 people in Prekmurje declared themselves to be ethnic Hungarians. Most of them lived in the communes of Lendava (Hungarian: Lendva—3,917), Dobrovnik (Hungarian: Dobronak—616) and Moravske Toplice (351).[16]

Today, most of the ethnic Hungarians in Croatia live scattered along the Hungarian border in the northeast and in large cities. The territory inhabited by Hungarians specifically includes the area of the Baranya and some Eastern Slavonian settlements around the confluence of the Danube and Drava rivers, near the city of Osijek (Hungarian: Eszék).[17] A larger number of Hungarians live also in Western Slavonia in the surroundings of Bjelovar and Daruvar (see Figure 2).

Since World War II, an accelerating fall in the number of Hungarians in Croatia has been recorded by the censuses. A particularly important factor was subjective considerations, including ethnic identity. According to Kocsis,[18] Hungarians of Croatia were disguised by the ideology of proletarian internationalism. Dictated by a national policy to make the country "Yugoslavian-Serbian-Croatian," emphasis was placed on developing an inferiority complex among Hungarians, stemming from their minority situation, emphasizing their footlessness and lack of opportunity. Factors promoting natural assimilation were a change of language, a loss of national identity and mixed marriages in ever increasing numbers, especially by the Hungarians in Slavonia. Due to the above-mentioned reasons, the number of Hungarians in Croatia decreased between 1948 and 1991 by almost 57%.

TABLE 3 The Hungarian population n the former Yugoslavia, 1948–2001/2002

Region		1948	1953	1961	1971	1981	1991	2001/2002
Slovenia	No.	10,579	11,019	10,498	9,785	9,496	8,499	6,243
	%	0.76	0.75	0.66	0.57	0.50	0.43	0.32
Croatia	No.	51,399	47,711	42,347	35,488	25,439	22,355	16,595
	%	1.37	1.22	1.02	0.80	0.55	0.47	0.37
Vojvodina	No.	428,932	435,345	442,561	423,866	385,356	340,945	290,207
	%	25.79	25.42	23.86	21.71	18.94	16.94	14.28
Former Yugoslavia	No.	496,492	502,175	504,369	477,374	426,867	377,700	No data
	%	3.15	2.97	2.72	2.33	1.90	1.59	

Sources: See Table 1.

TABLE 4 Hungarians in the Republic of Slovenia, 1991–2002

Commune/region	1991			2002			Changes 1991–2002	
	Total population	Hungarians		Total population	Hungarians		No.	Index
		No.	%		No.	%		
Dobrovnik/Dobronak	1,561	931	59.64	1,307	616	47.13	– 315	66.17
Hodoš/Hodos	459	316	68.84	356	159	44.66	– 157	50.32
Lendava/Lendva	12,326	5,323	43.19	11,151	3,917	35.13	– 1,406	73.59
Moravske Toplice	6,798	514	7.56	6,151	351	5.71	– 163	68.29
Šalovci	2,147	244	11.36	1,718	169	9.84	– 75	69.26
Communes on the ethnically mixed areas*	23,291	7.328	31.46	20,683	5,212	25.20	– 2,116	71.12
Other regions of Prekmurje	66,596	309	0.46	62,216	217	0.35	– 92	70.22
Prekmurje—total	89,887	7.637	8.50	82,899	5,429	6.55	– 2,208	71.09
Other regions of Slovenia	1,876,099	866	0.05	1,881,137	814	0.04	– 52	94.00
Slovenia—total	1,965,986	8.503	0.43	1,964,036	6,243	0.32	– 2,260	73.42

Sources: Prvi rezultati popisa stanovništva, domaćinstava i poljoprivrednih gazdinstava 1991. godine. Statistički bilten broj 1934: Nacionalni sastav stanovništva po opštinama (Belgrade: Savezni zavod za statistiku, 1995); *Popis prebivalstva, gospodinjstev in stanovcnovanj, Slovenija, 31 marca 2002. Statistične informacije no. 93: Prebivalstvo* (Ljubljana: Statistični urad Republike Slovenije, 2003), p. 23.

*Those communities where members of more than one ethnic group live. In Slovenia the ethnically mixed areas where autochthonous minorities live are defined in the statutes of these communes. On these areas Slovene Constitution defines special rights of autochthonous minorities.

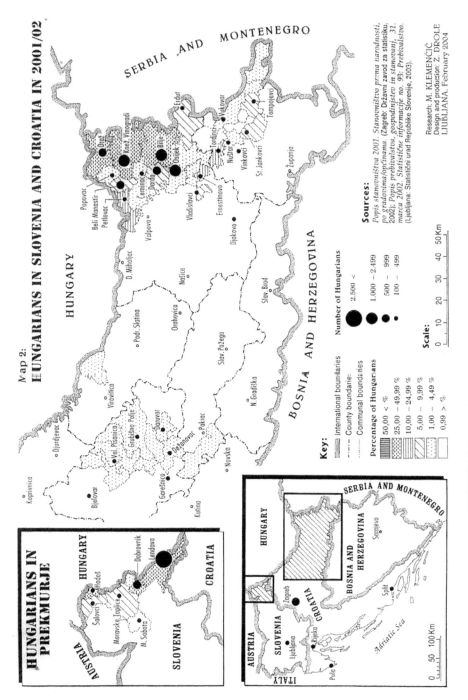

FIGURE 2 Hungarians in Slovenia and Croatia, in 2002

The number of Hungarians in Croatia decreased also in the 1991–2001 period (by more than one-quarter). The reasons for mass emigration could be found in the fact that most members of the Hungarian minority lived in the regions that, during the period 1991–1998, were part of the Republic of Srpska Krajina (Baranja, Eastern Slavonia) or bordered it and were therefore in the war zone (Western Slavonia) (see Table 5).[19]

At the time of the last census in 2002, 16,595 people in Croatia declared themselves to be ethnic Hungarians. The largest numbers were found in the communes of Kneževi Vinogradi (Hungarian: Hercegszölös—2,121) and Belje (Hungarian: Bellye—1,921) in Baranja and in the commune of Osijek (Hungarian: Eszék—1,154) in Eastern Slavonia.[20]

Vojvodina, the province north of the Sava and Danube rivers, today belongs to the state community Serbia & Montenegro. At the time of the last Yugoslav census, in 1991, 340,946 people declared themselves to be ethnic Hungarians. The majority of Hungarians live in the northern Bačka, along the Tisa river, where they represent over 56% of the local population (See Figure 3). The demographic situation and the ethnic identity of Hungarians in Vojvodina have been influenced by many factors. First we have to mention natural increase, which fell from + 8.3% in 1953 to –6.6% in 1991, and in connection with it also the growing percentage of the older population. The old age index (number of persons over 60 years compared with 100 persons under 14 years) of the Hungarians in Vojvodina increased between 1961 and 1991 from 63.9 to 155.2.

Historical events at the end of the 1990s also influenced the decrease in size of the Hungarian minority in Vojvodina. According to some data, more than 40,000 ethnic Hungarians left Vojvodina. They left due to the economic crisis, poverty, soured relations and the tense atmosphere between the Serbs—particularly Serbian refugees (242,340 persons in 1996[21]) from Croatia and Bosnia—and the Hungarian and other minorities. According to the census of 2002, only 290,207 Hungarians lived in Vojvodina, or some 50,000 (or 14.88%) less than in 1991. During the same period, the number of Serbs increased by more than 170,000 (or 14.80%) (see Table 6).

The largest changes in ethnic structure between 1991 and 2002 took place in Bačka, which is still today the center of Hungarian settlement in Vojvodina. From there 28,000 Hungarians emigrated, while 110,000 Serbs—mostly refugees from Croatia and Bosnia and Herzegovina—moved in.

Until 1996, Serbian refugees were settled in limited numbers (5,891 persons) in the Hungarian ethnic area of northern Bačka. At the same time, significant numbers of Serbs found new homes in traditionally Hungarian towns with good transportation links, e.g., Subotica (Hungarian: Szabadka), 6,401; Temerin (Hungarian: Temerin), 3,444; and Bcčcj (Hungarian: Óbecse), 1,471.[22]

Among communes that experienced the largest changes in size and percentage of Hungarian population between 1991 and 2002, we should mention especially those

TABLE 5 Hungarians in the Republic of Croatia, 1991–2002

Commune/ region	1991			2002			Changes 1991–2002	
	Total population	Hungarians		Total population	Hungarians			
		No.	%		No.	%	No.	Index
Baranja	54,265	8,956	16.50	42,633	7,114	16.69	−1,842	79.43
Eastern Slavonia	544,169	6,662	1.22	432,641	4,717	0.93	−1,945	70.80
Western Slavonia	144,042	2,022	1.40	133,084	1,188	0.89	−834	58.75
Regions of authochthonous settlement— total	742,476	17,640	2.38	608,358	13,019	1.95	−4,621	73.80
Other regions of the Republic of Croatia	4,041,789	4,715	0.12	3,769,102	3,576	0.09	−1,139	75.84
Republic of Croatia—total	4,784,265	22,355	0.47	4,437,460	16,595	0.37	−5,760	74.23

Sources: Prvi rezultati popisa stanovništva, domaćinstava i poljoprivrednih gazdinstava 1991. godine. Statistički bilten broj 1934: Nacionalni sastav stanovništva po opštinama (Belgrade: Savezni zavod za statistiku, 1995); *Popis stanovništva 2001. Stanovništvo prema narodnosti, po gradovima/opčinama* (Zagreb: Državni zavod za statistiku, 2002), <http://www.dzs.hr/Popis%202001/Popis/H01_02_02/H01_02_02.html > (16 November 2003).

Map 3: **HUNGARIANS IN VOJVODINA IN 2002**

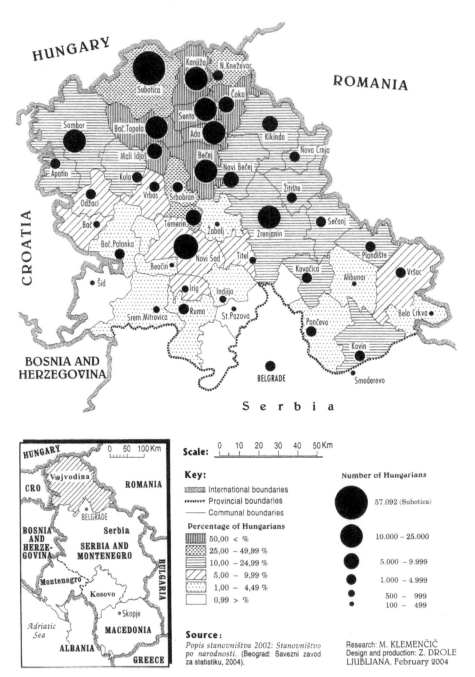

FIGURE 3 Hungarians in Vojvodina, in 2002

TABLE 6 Changes in the size and percentage of the Serb and Hungarian population, by regions of settlement in Vojvodina, 1991–2001

Regions	Serbs				Hungarians			
	1991	2002	Changes in number	Index 2002/1991	1991	2002	Changes in number	Index 2002/1991
Bačka	483,726	594,269	+ 110,543	122.85	192,596	164,134	− 28,462	85.22
Banat	431,303	443,677	+ 12,374	102.87	143,493	121,837	− 21,656	84.91
Srem	236,324	283,861	+ 47,537	120.12	4,857	4,236	− 621	87.21
Vojvodina—total	1,151,353	1,321,807	+ 170,454	114.80	340,946	290,207	− 50,739	85.12
Serbia proper	5,081,766	4,891,031	− 190,735	96.25	4,430	3,092	− 1,338	69.80
Serbia and Vojvodina—total	6,233,119	6,212,838	− 20,281	99.67	345,376	293,299	− 52,077	84.92

Sources: Prvi rezultati Popisa stanovništva, domaćinstava, stanova i poljoprivrednih gazdinstava 1991. godine. Statistički bilten broj 1934: Nacionalni sastav stsnovništva po opštinama (Belgrade: Savezni zavod za statistiku, 1992), str. 32–33; *Popis stanovništva 2002: Stanovništvo po narodnosti* (Belgrade: Savezni zavod za statistiku, 2004), <http://www.kanjiza.co.yu/nepszamlals2002/popisst2002.htm > (20 January 2004).

in which the percentage decrease was more then 20% (Odžaci, 27.32%; Apatin, 21.31%; and Novi Sad, 22.43%) and those in which the decrease was more then 3,000 persons (Subotica, 7,182; Novi Sad, 4,536; Bačka Topola, 3,969; Bečej, 3,423; and Sombor, 3,058). At the same time the number of Serbs increased in some communes: Novi Sad (52,214 persons or 30.05%), Subotica (13,363 or 59.49%), Sombor (10,545 or 21.41%), Bačka Palanka (5,113 or 11.95%) and Temerin (4,952 or 36.47%).[23]

Only on a slightly narrower scale were the changes in Banat, a region east of the Tisa river. The difference results from a significantly smaller number of Serb immigrants. The Serb population increased only by 2.87% or c. 12,000 persons. Most of the Serb refugees settled in Pančevo, which is actually a suburb of Belgrade on the left bank of the Danube.

The number of Hungarians of Banat decreased in largest numbers in the communes of Zrenjanin (3,376 persons or 19.20%), Kanjiža (3,346 or 12.33%), Sečanj (2,890 or 12.31%) and Ada (2,157 or 12.90%). Due to the mass emigration of Hungarians and members of other ethnic minorities, the total population of Banat decreased by 5.63% or 41,000 persons[24] (see Figure 4).

Significant changes in ethnic structure of the population during 1991 to 2002 took place also in Srem, a region between the Sava on the south and the Danube on the north and east. The already low number of members of the Hungarian minority decreased by 12.79%, while at the same time the number of Serbs increased by more than 47,000 persons (21.12%)—mostly in the communes of Stara Pazova (13,490 persons or 32.62%), Indjija (10,049 or 31.34%) and Šid on the Croatian border (8,352 or 38.14%).[25]

The above-mentioned large-scale immigration of Serbian refugees and the increasing emigration of Hungarians (and members of other minorities) resulted in an important change in the ethnic structure of the population of Vojvodina. According to the 2002 census, the proportion of Serbs had reached 65.05% (compared with 57.21% in 1991) and that of Hungarians had fallen to 14.28% (compared with 16.94% in 1991).[26]

This was the result of the process that started in 1991, after the Serbs began to move as refugees from Croatia and Bosnia and Herzegovina into Vojvodina, while the Hungarians chose refugee status in Hungary rather than participate in Yugoslavia's war. The fact is that the Yugoslav government was forcibly mobilizing Hungarians. The magnitude and extent of this forced conscription is evident from the appeal addressed to Lord David Owen and Cyrus Vance, co-chairmen of the Conference on Yugoslavia in Geneva, by András Agoston, the president of the Democratic Alliance of Hungarians in Vojvodina (*Vajdasági Magyarok Demokratikus Közössége*—VMDK). This letter, dated 7 December 1992, indicates "The government mobilized 2.5 times more Hungarians into front-line battalions than the Hungarians' percentage in Serbia's population warrants."[27]

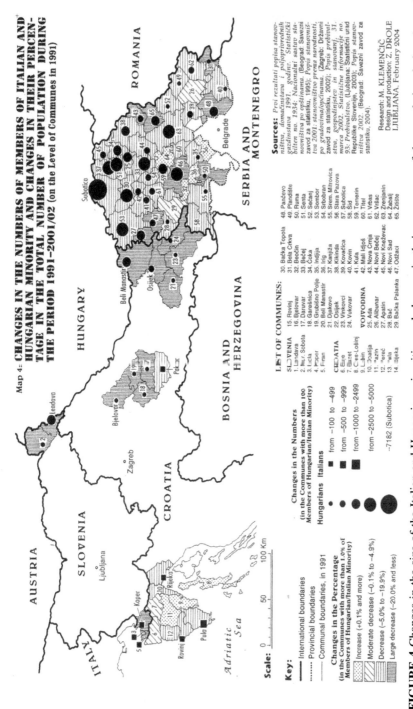

FIGURE 4 Changes in the size of the Italian and Hungarian minorities and changes in their percentage of the population during the period 1991–2002 (on the level of communes on 1991)*

*Communes are the lowest administrative entities shown on this map. It is important to note that borders of communes changed after 1991 in Slovenia and Croatia so that communes became smaller. Therefore it was possible to compare the data for 1991 and 2001/2002 on the level of administrative divisions of 1991.

143

Italians and Hungarians also lived in the other Yugoslav republics. A significant number of Hungarians lived in Belgrade. Their numbers decreased in the period 1991–2002 from *c.* 2,900 to *c.* 2,100. Italians lived also in northern Bosnia and Herzegovina. More than two-thirds lived in the commune of Prnjavor (*c.* 18 miles northeast of Banja Luka). According to general statistical data, we can assume that their number decreased because it followed the patterns in Slovenia and Croatia from 1961 to 1991, when their number decreased first from 717 in 1961 to 616 in 1981, and then increased to 732 in 1991. Before the wars in Yugoslavia in the 1990s, in the village of Šibovska, Italians had their own school with Italian as the language of instruction. In the mid-1980s the school had 91 pupils and employed eight teachers.[28] There were only a few scattered individuals of Italian and Hungarian nationality who lived outside Slovenia, Croatia, Vojvodina and the above-mentioned regions.

While in other parts of the former Yugoslavia the conditions of war prevailed throughout the 1990s, Slovenia maintained "normal" conditions and, we should emphasize, also the standard techniques and methodology of the census. Thus, the decreases found in the number of minorities in the war areas resulted not only because of forced assimilation and war conditions, but also because of the techniques and methodology used for the counts.

The last census of population (2002) in Slovenia, which shows a significant decrease in the numbers of members of the Italian and Hungarian minorities, caused unrest among members of those minorities as well as in the general populace of the country. According to that census, even the number of Slovenes had significantly decreased. However, we have to search for the reasons for the statistical decrease in numbers of the two minorities mostly in the changed methodology of the census rather than in sociological factors. There was no significant emigration of members of minorities and no significant pressures for emigration.

For example, in 1991 and previous censuses, one member of the family identified nationality for the whole family; while in 2002 every person who was more than 15 years old had to tell the enumerators his or her nationality. At the time of the census many people were not available to tell their nationality to the enumerators. It was possible to send a statement on their nationality, but many did not send it to the census commission. Therefore, more than 126,000 persons (6.42% of the population of the Republic of Slovenia) are included under the rubric "nationality unknown." Also emigrants who were temporary workers abroad were not taken into account in the 2002 census. In previous censuses, someone who had his or her residency formally in Koper or Lendava was counted even though he or she had lived for a decade in Trieste or Hungary or any place else in the world. The census of 2002 counted only those who really lived in the place of their permanent settlement.

There is a problem also with having to choose one nationality at the census, because many people in ethnically mixed territories are from ethnically mixed families. It is possible, therefore, that some minority members did not want to (or could not) answer the question on their nationality. In the Slovenian census of 2002, more than 60,000 did not answer this question. The census of 2002 asked also for mother tongue, and the number of persons whose mother tongue was Italian (3,762 persons) or Hungarian (7,713 persons) was significantly higher than those who identified as Italians (2,256 persons) or Hungarians (6,253) by nationality. The decrease in ethnic identity was significantly lower if mother tongue is taken into account.

This example shows that we have to be careful when talking about and explaining the results of the population censuses according to nationality, so that we do not explain the reduction of an ethnic group only in terms of assimilation or emigration but instead look at all factors.

Minority Rights in the former Yugoslavia (Different Approaches in the Socialist Republics of Slovenia, Croatia and Serbia) and in the Post-Yugoslav States

During the period of Communist Yugoslavia (1945–1991), the equality of ethno-nations and national minorities and how to handle inter-ethnic relations were key questions of Yugoslav internal politics. With the creation of the multi-ethnic autonomous regions (Kosovo and Vojvodina) in Serbia, the federation of Yugoslavia was proclaimed by the second Anti-Fascist Council of National Liberation of Yugoslavia (AVNOJ) Assembly in November 1943. The fourth paragraph of the proclamation stated, "National minorities in Yugoslavia shall be granted all national rights." These principles were codified in the 1946 and 1963 constitutions and reaffirmed again, in great detail, by the last federal constitution of 1974.[29] It declared that the nations and nationalities should have equal rights (Article 245). It further stated that "each nationality has the sovereign right to freely use its own language and script, to foster its own culture, to set up organizations for this purpose, and to enjoy other constitutionally guaranteed rights" (Article 274).[30]

In spite of the fact that the federal constitutions (1946, 1953, 1974) and the constitutions of the republics and autonomous provinces, as well as various laws, emphasized the protection of national minorities, there was—as in other East Central European socialist states—an ever widening gap between theory and practice.[31] In theory, Yugoslav standards were even higher than the standards in other European states.

Slovenia

This country has been an example of how to protect autochthonous national minorities. Already the Constitution of the Socialist Republic (SR) of Slovenia of 1963 guaranteed the Italian and Hungarian minorities equality and the possibility of development and progress in all fields; equality of their languages in ethnically mixed territories; and care for the development of education, printing presses, radio and cultural education (Article 77).[32] The importance of both minorities was emphasized also in a chapter on the special rights of Italians and Hungarians in the last

145

Slovenian Constitution in the former Yugoslavia (1974, Articles 250 and 251). Both articles guaranteed to both minorities free usage of their languages, expression of their national culture, usage of symbols and establishment of special organizations. In ethnically mixed territories, the languages of minorities were proclaimed equal with the Slovene language, and members of minorities were guaranteed the right to bring up and educate their children in their own language.[33]

Slovenia put special emphasis on protection of its autochthonous minorities, in part because of its international obligations after World War II, but also because that was in keeping with the process of decentralization and democratization of the then Yugoslav federation and the "opening of frontiers" (*i.e.*, Yugoslav citizens were given the right to travel abroad and tourism became one of most important Yugoslav industries) at the end of the 1950s and beginning of the 1960s. Slovenians started to see "ethnic minorities on both sides of the frontier as a connecting factor."[34] An especially important factor in determining the levels of protection of autochthonous minorities was also the care for the well-being of Slovene minorities in neighboring countries, in spite of the fact that the level of minority protection was then and is still today significantly lower in those countries than in Slovenia.[35] This could be proved by the example of Slovenes in Italy and Italians in Slovenia, comparing 24 categories of special rights, privileges and protection enjoyed by both minorities after the Special Protection Law was passed by the Italian parliament in February 2001.

As one can ascertain from Table 7, Slovenia gives its Italian minority all 24 categories of special rights, privileges and protections. On the other hand, Italy gives the Slovene minority in the Trieste Region and Gorizia Region only 14 categories of rights, of which only four are 100% fulfilled, with partial rights in ten categories. In the Udine Region, Italy fulfills protection measures in only four categories, and only one category of minority protection is 100% fulfilled.[36]

The Constitution of independent Slovenia (1991) kept and upgraded the level of protection of the Italian and Hungarian minorities. Two rules were new: (a) the level of protection and rights is not dependent on the number or size of a minority group in proportion to other groups, and (b) laws and other ordinances that deal with granting constitutional rights and the situation of national minorities cannot be accepted or changed without the consent of representatives of the national minorities. It is a type of "absolute" veto in the hands of representatives of the national minorities referring to the above (both deputies in the Slovene parliament and municipal council members).[37] Compared with the other Council of Europe member states, Slovenia enacted very wide minority protection.

Minority protection in Slovenia is based on two principles: the principle of territoriality and the principle of collectivity. The first determines the territory of autochthonous settlement, which includes all the settlements where Italians and Hungarians have been settled for centuries. The second emphasizes the collective nature of minorities and their needs in addition to general and special individual rights. In those territories, the official language in addition to Slovene is Italian or

TABLE 7 The rights, benefits, and protections enjoyed by the Slovene minority in Italy and Italian minority in Slovenia

The rights, benefits and protections	Slovenia	Trieste Region and Gorizia Region	Udine Region
The level of protection not dependent on minority's percentage of population	Yes	No	No
Assured representation in the national parliament	Yes	No	No
The right to veto decisions that affect minority rights at all levels of governments	Yes	No	No
Assured protection on the local level of government	Yes	No	No
The language of the minority is an official language in the territories of autochthonous settlement	Yes	No	No
The right of minority language usage in the national parliament	Yes	No	No
The right of minority language usage on the local level of government	Yes	Partially	No
The right of minority language usage in relations with local government	Yes	Partially	No
The right of minority language usage in relations with judicial authorities	Yes	Partially	Partially
The right of minority language usage in relations with administrative bodies	Yes	Partially	No
The duty of the authorities to use the minority language at official ceremonies	Yes	Partially	No
The duty of the authorities to provide bilingual official inscriptions	Yes	Partially	No
The duty of the authorities to fly the national flag of autochthonous minorities in addition to the Slovene	Yes	No	No
The duty of private enterprises to put up bilingual signs	Yes	No	No
Mandatory bilingual local signs in the ethnically mixed territories	Yes	Partially	No
The right of the minority organization—official representatives of minorities—to veto decisions of local governments which affect minorities	Yes	No	No
Radio program in minority language	Yes	Yes	Yes
TV program in minority language	Yes	Yes	No
Bilingual official forms	Yes	Partially	No
Bilingual IDs	Yes	Partially	No
Compulsory learning of the minority language for pupils/members of majority nation	Yes	No	No
Kindergartens, elementary schools and high schools in the minority language	Yes	Yes	No
State subsidies of daily and periodical minority press	Yes	Partially	Partially
Financing of cultural activities	Yes	Yes	Partially

Hungarian.[38] These ethnically mixed territories are recognizable on first sight because of bilingual signs and inscriptions for names of settlements, towns and cities. Visible bilingualism is not restricted to signs on the streets and official buildings like courts, county and municipal buildings, *etc.*; this right is ensured also for the buildings of private and state-owned enterprises.[39]

Bilingual documents are compulsory for all inhabitants of ethnically mixed areas, irrespective of their ethnic affiliation. In addition to personal identity cards and passports (which are trilingual in Slovene, English, and Italian or Hungarian), the following documents are bilingual: drivers' licenses, vehicle registration documents, medical insurance booklets and army service booklets.[40]

Bilingual procedures are also prescribed for judiciary institutions; courts are obliged to guarantee the equality of the minority language. The court proceedings may be conducted monolingually if only one party appears or if both parties in the proceedings use the same language. Once the judicial process has been started on a bilingual basis, it will be conducted bilingually in higher courts also, even when the seat of the higher court lies outside an ethnically mixed area. Of course, members of the minorities must demand the right to have the court proceedings in their languages or bilingually, as well as other administrative procedures and correspondence. Employees are entitled to higher pay for their knowledge of the Italian or Hungarian language.[41]

Members of the Hungarian or Italian minority in the ethnically mixed territories also have the right to use their language in municipal administration. It is important to stress again that the above-mentioned rights are on paper; the actual use of them depends on everyday practice by the members of elected bodies and other citizens. Similarly, the right to use Italian and Hungarian mother tongues is ensured by the Catholic and Evangelical churches. On the bilingual territories, religious services in Hungarian or Italian are held weekly in both Evangelical and Catholic churches. These services are said by Slovene priests and ministers, for the simple reason that at this moment there are no Hungarian or Italian minority priests or ministers in Slovenia.[42]

Slovenia is implementing the right to education in a minority mother tongue in two different ways. The compulsory bilingual education system in the ethnically mixed area of Prekmurje and the monolingual schools for members of the Italian ethnic minority area have developed as a result of two totally different historical situations.[43] In the ethnically mixed area of Prekmurje there are 11 bilingual kindergartens, five central bilingual primary schools, six affiliated bilingual primary schools and one bilingual secondary school. Learning material on Hungarian history, culture and geography is added to the appropriate Slovene curriculum. Most of the books are bilingual, as are the school administration, public relations and conversations with parents.[44]

For the Italian minority a monolingual school system was developed. In the 2000/2001 school year, 264 children were enrolled in Italian-language kindergartens,

435 students were in nine central and affiliated primary schools, and 278 students were in three secondary schools. In schools where Italian is used for instruction, it is also the language of communication with parents and the language of administration. In these schools, learning Slovenian is compulsory; Italian is compulsory in the ethnically mixed territory on the Slovene coastland for students who are attending schools where Slovenian is the language of instruction. Schools with Italian as the language of instruction are not limited to members of the Italian minority. The parents decide which school their children will attend; there are already quite a few children whose mother tongue is not Italian who are attending the "Italian" schools.[45]

Due to the small number of members of the Hungarian and Italian minorities, it is not possible to organize university education in their mother tongue in Slovenia. It is possible to study the Hungarian language and culture at the Universities of Maribor and Ljubljana; also bilingual kindergarten governesses and teachers of bilingual primary schools are being educated at the two universities.

Study of Italian language and culture is possible at the University of Ljubljana and at the University of Primorska (in Koper). At the University of Primorska education of kindergarten governesses and primary school teachers in the Italian language is taking place.

Because of the limited opportunity to study in the languages of autochthonous minorities in Slovenia, Slovenia signed agreements with Hungary and Italy that enable members of minorities on both sides of the border—Slovenes from Italy or Hungary, as well as Italians from Slovenia and Hungarians from Slovenia—to study at universities in all three countries.[46]

Among the important rights of the national minorities is also the right to be informed in their own language.[47] For the members of the Hungarian ethnic minority, a weekly, *Népujság*, has been published since 1958 with a circulation of 2,000 copies. It has an independent editorial board. Since 1960 the editors have also prepared an almanac entitled *Naptár*, and since 1988 a literary magazine. Radio broadcasts in the Hungarian language are also worth mentioning. An eight-hour daily program in Hungarian is transmitted from its own studio in Lendava. On national TV, a twice-weekly 30-minute program in Hungarian with Slovenian subtitles, called *Hidak-Mostovi* (*Bridges*), is transmitted by Slovene National Television.[48]

A radio station in the Italian language was established in 1949. It transmits 14 hours of broadcasting in Italian. In 1971 a TV station was added. It broadcasts 11 hours a day in Italian and one hour a day in Slovenian. Both provide information for the Italian population in Slovenia and Croatia. The Italian-language radio and TV stations function as part of the organizational framework of National Radio and TV but have broad autonomy in programming as well as organizational matters.[49]

The Italians in Slovenia and Croatia publish their own newspapers together. The publisher is EDIT, located in Rijeka (Croatia) with a special correspondence office in Koper. Its chief publications are the daily *La Voce del Popolo*, with a print run of 3,750 copies; the weekly *Panorama* with 2,200 copies; the trimonthly literary magazine *La Battana* with 1,000 copies and a children's newsletter, *Arcobaleno* (2,500 copies). Since 1992 the newspaper *La Voce del Popolo* has been sold together with the Triestine daily paper *Il Piccolo* in a sandwich arrangement: two papers for the price of one. The Republic of Slovenia supports the publishing of printed media with suitable financial grants. The amount represents 20% of the sum allocated for these activities in the Republic of Croatia.[50]

With the help of different grants-in-aid on the initiative of the members of both minorities, the minorities are making use of their right to their own cultural development[51] in six Italian and 22 Hungarian cultural societies.[52] The Republic of Slovenia also financially supports the cultural exchange of minority organizations and institutions. The Italian and Hungarian minorities also have the constitutional right to fly their flags on the territories of their autochthonous settlements.[53]

According to the Constitution of Slovenia, minority members have the right to two votes in the elections of members of the State Assembly as well as in elections of the organs of local self-government (city councilors).[54] They may use the first vote in accordance with their political affiliation and the second vote to elect special minority representatives. In the State Assembly, a body with 90 seats, two seats are reserved for the representatives of the Hungarian and Italian national minorities. The Republic of Slovenia has authorized the self-governing ethnic communities to compile electoral registers of citizens who are their members. The deputies of the Italian and Hungarian minorities are elected by all members of the ethnic minorities who have voting rights, irrespective of whether they live in the ethnically mixed areas or elsewhere in Slovenia. In the National State Assembly a Permanent Commission for Minorities has been established as one of its four permanent commissions.[55] A similar situation exists on the local level.[56]

Self-governing ethnic communities were established in every municipality inhabited by members of the autochthonous ethnic minorities.[57] The municipal ethnic communities then join together to form the Italian or Hungarian ethnic community. The two communities are the key partners in relations with the Republic of Slovenia. When they decide on matters affecting the status of ethnic minorities, state bodies must acquire the prior opinion of the self-managing ethnic communities. A similar provision also applies on the local level. The members of self-governing ethnic communities also cooperate with international organizations and participate in the preparation of international agreements relating to their status at the local, state and even international level.[58]

As a member of the Council of Europe and a member of the European Union, Slovenia also has to obey all of the rules and different regulations that are part of European laws.[59]

In spite of the fact that Slovenia is legally giving its autochthonous minorities more rights than prescribed by European standards, in enforcing those laws of minority protections, problems are surfacing that are primarily explainable by the lack of a culture of law enforcement. Measures to cut state spending on all levels also extend to minority protection. The high level of minority protection has created numerous minority institutions that are financially more or less dependent on state support. In this sense, the minorities have become part of the market economy, and this has been a shock for them. Both minorities are quite small in numbers and do not have the economic base to self-finance their institutions and activities.

Representatives of both minorities in the State Assembly have therefore many times called attention to their troubles and urged recognition that the situation of the Italian and Hungarian minorities is extremely critical.[60] In early January 2004, when the state and its special organs did not react properly, the deputy of the Italian minority in the Slovene parliament, Roberto Battelli, decided to resign as president of the special Commission of the State Assembly for Nationalities.[61] The resignation of Battelli also echoed in neighboring Italy. The former Italian foreign minister Gianni de Michelis—who, at the end of the 1980s, was already against Slovene independence—issued a statement:

> In Slovenia I recognize very negative things ... The protest of the deputy of the Italian minority, Roberto Battelli, represents a very bad sign. I knew Slovenian circumstances very well, I criticized them and I did not change my opinion and what is happening is a continuation of the shortsighted vision of the Slovene political class, which does not realize the new reality it is entering.[62]

Other representatives of the Italian minority in Slovenia also emphasized the problems of non-implementation of minority protection laws.[63] The debate in the Slovene parliament showed that the Hungarian deputy also thinks the same with regard to the situation of Hungarians in Slovenia.

Members of the Slovene minority in Italy showed solidarity with the Italian minority in Slovenia, although their legal situation as well as the actual enforcement of the law are much worse than that of the Italian minority in Slovenia.[64]

Croatia

Even before it became independent, Croatia had relatively good laws in place to protect its national minorities. In addition to the Hungarians and Italians, the Czechs, Slovaks, Ruthenians and Ukrainians also enjoyed protection of their minority rights (Serbs enjoyed the status of a constitutive nation of Croatia). All the above-mentioned national minorities had their special institutions in the fields of education and culture, which helped them to retain their identities.[65]

Croatian politicians tried to regulate inter-ethnic relations on their territory. In 1990, when Croatia was still a part of Yugoslavia, they declared in a special resolution that Croatia would protect its national minorities.[66] The 1990 Constitution of the Republic of Croatia (amended 1997)[67] declared that Croatia "is the national state of the Croatian nation and members of the other nations and minorities who are its citizens: Serbs, Muslims, Slovenes, Czechs, Slovaks, Italians, Hungarians, Jews, and others to whom equality with citizens of Croatian nationality is guaranteed." The Constitution also declared Croatian to be the official language and the Latin alphabet the official alphabet, except in the regions of settlement of minorities, where their languages and alphabets are official in addition to Croatian. This statement was repeated in the Declaration on Independence and Sovereignty of the Republic of Croatia[68] and in the special Decree on the Rights of Serbs and Other Minorities in Croatia.[69]

Protection of minorities is also treated in the Constitutional Law of December 1991 (amended in 2000). Regulations in it are general and deal with all minorities in Croatia. The law cites international obligations of Croatia and generally valid international norms, and specifically regulates the protection of minorities, including their right to development and cultural autonomy; prohibits discrimination; regulates the rights of members of minorities to be adequately represented in representative and other bodies of the Republic of Croatia; defines regions with special status; allows for international surveillance on implementation of regulations of this law with the aim to ensure that human rights will be respected; and prohibits all activities that would threaten general human rights and the rights of minorities.[70] A special law defines official usage of languages and alphabets in the Republic of Croatia.[71] Croatia also signed and ratified some bilateral and multilateral agreements aimed at protection of minorities. In 1992 it concluded a Memorandum on Understanding with Italy. It signed similar agreements with Hungary and Ukraine, and in 1997 it accepted and ratified the European Charter on Regional and Minority Languages and other international documents as part of its accession to the Council of Europe.

Croatian protection of national minorities is still today a struggle, with many problems due to war and the occupation of parts of its territory (1991–1995). This is especially valid for the Hungarian minority, because its main region of settlement (Baranja and Eastern Slavonia) was re-integrated into the Croatian state only in 1998.

It was much easier to give minority rights to the Italian minority in the region of Istria and Rijeka, where that minority was well organized. Partially financed by the Italian state, it developed very effective programs in the fields of culture, education and media. Nevertheless, there were quite a few problems between the Croatian state and local authorities in Istria. The Croatian Constitutional Court in February 1995 declared null and void 18 of 36 articles of the Statutes of Istria County (Statut Istarske županije); most of them dealt with the question of Italian language usage. In its explanation, the Constitutional Court wrote that those articles were not under the jurisdiction of local authorities.[72]

On the other hand, Italians in the Lipik and Pakrac communes do not enjoy any protection from the Croatian state.

The Italian minority actually felt neglected; and the fact that, after Yugoslavia's dissolution in 1991, its unified territory of autochthonous settlement was divided between the Republic of Slovenia and the Republic of Croatia created more problems. Once the new Slovene–Croatian border was established, the seats of most of the organizations of the Italian minority remained in Croatia (the publishing house EDIT, the editorial offices of the daily *La Voce del popolo* and the weekly *Panorama*, the quarterly literary publication *La Battana* and the special publication for children *Arcobaleno* and the most important political organization of the Italian minority, the Italian Federation [Unione Italiana]).[73] Members of the Italian minority in Slovenia remained without a substantial number of their organizations, which they could not—due to small numbers—replace with new ones. Therefore they tried to continue to act as one entity. This would be the only way to sustain a critical mass necessary to be able to operate their organizations and to continue their necessary cultural and economic projects in order to sustain the Italian culture and language in both countries.

The coordination of members of the Italian minority in Slovenia and Croatia was taken over by Unione Italiana. Because it had its seat in Rijeka, in Croatia, its registration in Slovenia was a long and difficult process. The authorities claimed that Unione Italiana wanted to become the "exclusive" representative of the Italian minority in Slovenia and Croatia and at the same time forget that Slovenia and Croatia are two sovereign states. The authorities could not prove that, however. Some also claimed that Unione Italiana had a privileged status in connection with its financial support by Italy. We have to emphasize, however, that Unione Italiana is not the final recipient of the money it gets. It serves only as a middleman. The final recipients have been minority schools, minority media, other minority organizations and those members of the Italian minority who received stipends.[74]

Due to the above-mentioned problems, Unione Italiana took many years to get registered in Slovenia. Representatives of Unione Italiana first reached an agreement on a division of responsibilities with the representatives of the Coastal Self-Management Community of the Italian Nationality (Comunitá autogestita costiera della nazionalitá Italiana). The community would take care of political and other basic questions concerning the fulfillment of the rights of the Italian minority, while Unione Italiana would take care of unification on the basis of interests. Later Unione Italiana wrote into its constitution some amendments with respect to Slovene law, and thus it finally got registered in August 1998 as a federation of societies.[75] However, it did not better the situation of the Italian minority in Slovenia.

Serbia & Montenegro

Until the dissolution of the Federal Socialist Republic of Yugoslavia (FSRY), minorities in Serbia and especially Vojvodina at least formally enjoyed wide protection of their minority rights. In Vojvodina alone, before 1988, 20 laws attempted to ensure the equal use of all the five local languages (Serbian, Croatian, Hungarian, Slovak and Rusyn-Ukrainian) in the fields of education, information and socio-political organizational activities, along with economic and administrative units of "self-management." Some of these laws were implemented, especially in education and information, but most of them have never materialized.[76] In spite of this, Vojvodina, as an autonomous province within Serbia, could legally regulate minority rights and also had wide autonomy.

The new 1990 Constitution of the Republic of Serbia, which strengthened the power of Slobodan Milošević, did away almost completely with the autonomy of Vojvodina (and Kosovo). The provincial parliament of Vojvodina lost all legislative rights and decision making, and law creation became the exclusive right of the Parliament of Serbia in Belgrade (Skupština). The provincial parliament of Vojvodina became a consultative body, which had the right to submit proposals to the Serbian parliament. The situation of the Hungarian minority as well as that of other minorities worsened after the dissolution of the SFRY. In spite of the fact that the Serbian Constitution of 1990 and the new Constitution of the Federal Republic of Yugoslavia of 1992 gave ethnic minorities special collective rights in the field of education, culture and media, the implementation of those rights in praxis was rendered more difficult.[77]

On the basis of the Law on the Official Usage of Language of 1991, the Hungarian language was used in addition to Serbian in 31 communes of Vojvodina. In accordance with this law, in these communes topographic signs and signs on public institutions are supposed to be written in both Serbian and Hungarian. This law is still today neither respected nor implemented. Under the regime of Slobodan Milošević, discrimination against individuals, especially in the public sector, was the rule. Because jobs in the judiciary, police and public administration were "reserved" for members of the Serb majority, the use of the Hungarian language in communication with official authorities was practically impossible.[78]

There were many problems in the field of education. Members of the Hungarian and other minorities were rarely named as principals of primary and secondary schools because decisions on appointments were made in Belgrade. Education in the Hungarian language did not fulfill the wishes of the Hungarian minority because curricula and textbooks were unified for all pupils in the Federal Republic of Yugoslavia. Educational materials for minorities were verbatim translations of Serb textbooks, in which no Hungarian literature, culture and history were taught. In spite of all the troubles in the school year 2000/2001, there were 11 elementary schools in Vojvodina in which the language of education was exclusively Hungarian. In 69 elementary schools in Vojvodina there were Serb as well as Hungarian classes. There were classes in which Serb or Hungarian was the language of education in 30 secondary schools also. After the fall of the regime of Slobodan Milošević in 2000, discussions began on inclusion of "national" content in curricula for national minorities in special subjects such as the mother tongue, culture and history.[79]

After the fall of Slobodan Milošević, the Serb and federal governments, in principle, supported minority rights. In reality the conditions of minorities did not change. Nationalism and xenophobia are still very present. Numerous incidents continue to take place in which the victims are members of minorities. The Serb nationalists' attacks are aimed not only at random individuals but also at well-known leaders of nationality groups, *e.g.*, Joszef Kasza, former vice-president of the Serbian government and president of the Union of Hungarians of Vojvodina (Savez vojvod-janskih Madjara/Vajdasági Magyar Szövetség—VMS), and Bela Tonković, former vice-president of the commune of Subotica and the president of the Democratic Union of Croatians of Vojvodina. Kasza received an email in which he was threatened with hanging on the Terazije (one of the best-known squares in Belgrade). Tonković was described in the media as "the Ustaša who is maltreating the Serbs." In June 2001, Mihail Kocsis, a member of the Hungarian minority and the principal of the Subotica elementary school Grof Isztvan Szeczenyi, was beaten at a gas station. The beating was connected with the fact that the above-mentioned elementary school changed its name; formerly it was named after Ivo Lola Ribar, who was a Serb World War II hero.[80] Members of the Hungarian minority in Vojvodina were also upset by vandals who demolished ethnic Hungarian tombs in the Catholic cemetery in Novi Sad in January 2003. Laszlo Galambasz, president of the City Commitee of VMS, made a statement in which he described this "as an act not worth a human being and a primitive act ... which happened already once before in the first half of 2002 ... These and numerous other acts of ethnic violence prove that there are still many people who live in Novi Sad who want to instigate quarreling among members of different nationalities, who have lived here for many centuries."[81]

Minority protection did not have a priority in government programs even before the elections in 2004. It did not have any public support either. This was the standpoint of the president of the Federal Republic of Yugoslavia, Vojislav Koštunica, who, at the beginning of March 2001, declared that "now is not the time for Vojvodina" and "the economic autonomy of Vojvodina does not make sense now"[82] The Serb Radical Party of Vojislav Šešelj was also against any renewal of autonomy for Vojvodina, declaring, "Serbian Vojvodina is the most threatened Serbian region."[83] And Serbian Academy of Sciences member Vasilije Krestić declared, "Vojvodina's autonomists ... have gone the same way as Montenegrin separatists; therefore their traitorous work must be hindered."[84]

The reactions of the parties that fought for a renewal of autonomy and rejected the reproaches of separatism were very sharp. The VMS declared that autonomy is the exact counterweight to separatism.[85]

In the late spring of 2004 inter-ethnic relations in Vojvodina began to worsen again. The political atmosphere after the parliamentary elections of November 2003 was characterized not only by a strengthening of Serb nationalism but also by anti-Semitism and an escalation of worsened relations between the Serbs and the Hungarian minority. As in the past the ethnic Hungarians were the victims of threats of physical violence; they were beaten up, some of their houses were put on fire again, and tombs in their cemeteries were demolished. The attacks on individual minority members and their properties alarmed diplomats in neighboring countries—especially in Hungary. The Hungarian government demanded that the attacks stop;

otherwise it threatened to bring these events to the attention of the Council of Europe.[86] In the heated atmosphere of interethnic relations in Serbia today even criminal acts can be interpreted as inter-ethnic violence. According to reports in *Politika*, a Serb was attacked by a group of Hungarians in late June 2004 in Temerin, a small town near Novi Sad.[87] The incident was compared to Albanian attacks on Serbs in Kosovo in the 1980s.[88] The members of Šešelj's Serb Radical Party used the case to start an anti-Hungarian campaign[89] and looting of Hungarian houses followed. Later *Politika* explained that the attack on the Serb in Temerin was a purely criminal act.[90]

Because the situation in Vojvodina is not getting better, even the future existence of the Hungarian minority is in question. Due to the emigration of more then 40,000 Hungarians—mostly younger intellectuals—its economic and reproductive demographic power has fallen.

The Positions of Hungary and Italy towards Their Minorities in the Former Yugoslav Lands and in the Post-Yugoslav States

Hungarian–Yugoslav relations were rocky during the 1950s, but improved afterwards and were free of major problems until 1990. The more than 400,000 Hungarians living in Yugoslavia were treated better than any other Hungarian minority in the other former socialist countries surrounding Hungary (Romania, Ukraine, Slovakia).[91] With the change of the political regime in Hungary in 1989/1990, an interest in the living conditions of and a respect for minority rights of Hungarians in neighboring countries became major components of Hungarian foreign policy. With the widening of the Yugoslav conflict and the potential threat to the Hungarian minorities living in that region, Hungary offered a new approach in its continuous effort to make minority rights a priority issue for the Conference on Security and Cooperation in Europe process.[92]

From the outset of the Yugoslav conflict, Budapest adopted a very cautious stance out of concern for Vojvodina's large Hungarian minority, choosing to align its policy with that of the European Community (EC) and recognize the independence of Croatia and Slovenia only in January 1992. Since then, Hungary has upgraded its relations with the two new states. Croatia joined the 1991 Hungarian–Ukrainian declaration on minority rights in the spring of 1992 and agreed to the establishment of a joint minority commission to work out a minority protection agreement for the 30,000 ethnic Hungarians in Croatia and the estimated 80,000 Croats in Hungary.[93] In November 1992, Hungary signed with Slovenia a special bilateral treaty,[94] and in 1993 also a treaty on friendship and cooperation that defines protective measures for the status of Hungarians in Slovenia and Slovenes in Hungary.[95]

Trying to solve the status of Hungarian national minorities outside Hungary's borders, the Hungarian parliament passed an Act on Hungarians Living in Neighboring Countries (Törvény a szomszédos országokban élo magyarokról).[96] The so-called

"Status Law" offered members of Hungarian minorities in neighboring countries—
with the exception of the Hungarians of Austria—many benefits during their sojourns
in Hungary and even financial aid (to promote their education in the mother tongue)
in the states where members of Hungarian minorities have permanent residence. The
law also foresaw the possibility of employment in Hungary for three months a year.
With this Status Law, the then Hungarian center-right government of Viktor Orban
tried to show its concern for Hungarian minorities, strengthen their national consciousness and confirm the awareness of all Hungarians that they belonged to the
same cultural community.

Hungary, as a state concerned with the fate of Hungarians living abroad, considered it a political and moral duty to help Hungarians, especially those living in the
bordering countries. Until then, the Hungarian state principally supported the institutions of the national minorities; after this law was passed, it supported also the
individual members of the Hungarian ethnic group. The Hungarian government
considered that the existence of such a law, and the facilities offered by this law,
would both encourage Hungarians to refrain from emigration and could moderate the
process of assimilation of Hungarian ethnic minorities abroad.[97]

The Hungarian government of Viktor Orban expressed the following goals
regarding its national policy towards Hungarians abroad and especially in the
neighboring countries:

> The Government's policy on the ethnic Hungarian minorities in neighboring countries
> aims to build and develop political, cultural, and economic ties between Hungary and
> Hungarian communities abroad as part of the general process of European unification,
> as well as to help Hungarians living in neighboring countries to live and prosper in
> their own homeland. In order to achieve this, the bonds between ethnic Hungarian
> minorities and Hungary must be settled within a framework of legislation and
> government, so as to preserve the organic ties of Hungarian communities to Hungary,
> even after its accession to the European Union.[98]

This program reinforces Hungary's special relationship with the Hungarian minorities in the neighboring countries, but emphasizes the importance of settling this
relationship within the legislative framework. In addition, for the first time it is stated
that the "organic ties" between the Hungarian communities abroad and Hungary are
of primary importance. George Schöpflin describes the arguments for such a law as
follows:

> In broader terms, the status law can be said to have two dimensions. One of these is
> the aim to regulate Hungary's relations with the Hungarian communities in the
> neighboring states, a problem that was not created by Hungary but by the victorious
> powers after 1918. The hard reality is that the very existence of the Hungarian state
> generates tension between Hungary and the minorities living in the neighboring states,
> given the intimacies of the shared culture ... Second, the broader context of the law
> is the historic drive to establish a new narrative for the Hungarian nation in its cultural
> dimension as a modern community. The loss of empire in 1918 was a catastrophe for
> the Hungarian model of modernity and ever since, Hungary has been struggling to

find a new narrative that would reestablish the model in the new context. Indeed, this model is essential for Hungary's return to Europe and for Hungary's membership in the European Union. The law, therefore, is intended to reflect the requirements of democracy, of the European environment and the needs of the Hungarian state.[99]

The official argument for framing the Status Law was as follows:

The main aim of this law is to ensure special relations of the Hungarians living in neighboring countries to their kin state, the promotion and preservation of their national identity and well-being within their home country; therefore to contribute to the political and economic stability of the region, and through this to contribute to the Euro-Atlantic integration process of Hungary in particular and the Central and Eastern European region in general. In this context the law promotes the preservation of the cultural and social cohesion as well as the economic consolidation of Hungarian communities abroad.[100]

The Status Law soon became the target of many critics, including the Hungarian opposition, which defined it as a "deception" of Hungarians,[101] and the international community. Some thought of this law as a new source of conflicts. Others warned that the protection of national minorities is a duty of the states in which minorities are living and that it is a precondition for a successful government, especially in multicultural states.[102] The so-called "Venetian Commission" of the Council of Europe dealt with the Status Law and emphasized that the interest of the mother countries for their minorities in neighboring countries is legitimate, but that these countries should not pass measures addressed to groups outside their territories without prior consent of the states in which these minorities are living.[103] The Status Law was criticized also by the European Commission in its report in 2001 on the progress of Hungary as an accession candidate to the EU. This report stated that the Status Law contradicted prevailing European standards of protection of national minorities. Therefore it would be better for Hungary if it solved the question of protection of its minorities in neighboring countries with bilateral agreements with the neighboring countries. The way in which this question was treated in the agreement between Slovenia and Hungary in 1992 was cited as an example.[104]

Neighboring countries were also critical of the Status Law. Especially critical was the opinion of the Romanian government, which thought that the law was "discriminatory" towards non-Hungarian citizens of Romania, "that it is in opposition to the European norms and that it had 'validity only in space.'"[105] Because of the sharp Romanian criticism, which even caused disruptions in Hungarian–Romanian bilateral relations, Hungary agreed to some concessions to Romania. It signed a special memorandum of understanding with Romania on 22 December 2001.[106] The Slovak government also reproached Hungary, accusing it of an intention to interfere with the legal system of Slovakia and violation of international law. The reaction of Serbia & Montenegro was mild.[107]

All these international criticisms and the electoral victory of the socialists and the liberals in Hungary in April 2002 placed the question of the Status Law in a new light: in June 2003, the Hungarian parliament passed an amendment to it. Of the major changes made, two are relevant. The first has to do with usage of the concept of the Hungarian nation. The original law defines its goals as follows: "In order to ensure that Hungarians living in neighboring countries form part of the Hungarian nation as a whole and to promote and preserve their well-being and awareness of national identity within their home country." The modification of the law defines the goal as follows: "In order to ensure the well being of Hungarians living in neighboring states in their home-state, to promote their ties to Hungary, to support their Hungarian identity and their links to the Hungarian cultural heritage as an expression of their belonging to the Hungarian nation." The modified law dropped its reference to the "Hungarian nation as a whole" and moved toward support for "Hungarian cultural heritage."

The other modifications of the law changed entitlements. The modified law puts the emphasis on Hungarian culture and not on Hungarian individuals. Moreover, it supports Hungarian culture specifically and not—as intended by the framers—Hungarian individuals living in the neighboring states.[108] Among others things, the amendment stated that Hungary would (financially) help Hungarian minorities in neighboring countries in education and culture only on the basis of bilateral agreements with those countries. In spite of passing the amendment, the articles of the Status Law that dealt with privileges of the members of Hungarian minorities in neighboring countries remained almost unchanged.

Even with the changes, Slovak Prime Minister Mikuláš Dzurinda declared that Slovakia would not respect this law, because it still discriminated against the majority Slovak population.[109]

The most disappointed with the changes in the status law were Hungarians from economically devastated Vojvodina, who "expected from this law more than only humanitarian aid," as the vice-president of VMS Szandor Egereszi stated.[110] They counted—as did Hungarians from Ukraine—on getting dual citizenship, especially because they were afraid that after Hungary entered the EU they would have trouble retaining contacts with their homeland due to the "Schengen regime"[111] at the border.

There have been attempts to pass similar laws in Slovenia, Croatia and Ukraine, but the legislators there are more cautious because of the problems Hungary had with its neighboring countries after the Status Law was passed.

Yugoslav–Italian relations after 1945 were marked with a long history of disputes and attempts to solve them. Among the most problematic were: (1) demarcation of the frontier between Italy and former Yugoslavia; (2) emigration of members of the Italian minority from territories annexed to Yugoslavia; and (3) the property of emigrant members of the Italian minority. All these questions—of which the question of the property of individuals, which remained in Yugoslavia (it is the property of individuals, who left Yugoslavia, and left their property behind them and did not sell it, before they left), is still open today—also affected the minority rights of Italians in Yugoslavia and Slovenes of Italy.[112] The status of the Italian minority in Slovenia and Croatia and the Slovene minority of Italy after World War II was

159

regulated by the Paris Peace Treaty[113] and the Special Statute of the Free Territory of Trieste, which was added to the Memorandum of Understanding between the Governments of Italy, the United Kingdom, the United States and Yugoslavia.[114] The Special Statute ceased being valid when the Agreement between SFRY and the Republic of Italy, agreed upon in Osimo in 1975, was put into force.

This treaty, known as the "Osimo Treaty," in general regulated legal issues of sovereignty and citizenship and related questions of wealth in the region of the former Free Territory of Trieste. In addition it declared in Article 8 that Italy and Yugoslavia (or Slovenia and Croatia) "shall preserve the validity of internal measures that were adopted during the implementation of the Statute mentioned, and shall, with the framework of its internal legislation, guarantee to the members of the concerned minorities the same level of protection as was provided by the Special Statute, which is hereby terminated." The Special Statute remained valid as far as the minority rights of the Slovenes of Italy and the Italians of Slovenia and Croatia were concerned.[115]

Article 8 of the Osimo Treaty was always subject to different interpretations and a source of trouble in relations between Yugoslavia and Italy. The Slovenes of Italy, with the help of Slovenia until 2001, tried to compel the Italian parliament to pass a "global protection law" for them.[116] In June 1992, as one of the successor states of Yugoslavia, Slovenia accepted all the latter's treaties with Italy.[117] At the same time, in a special diplomatic note, Italy notified Slovenia that it knew that Slovenia accepted those 46 treaties. Soon after the above-mentioned diplomatic exchange, in July 1992, Italian politicians started (at least indirectly) to ask for a revision of treaties, especially of the Osimo Treaty, which Italian nationalist politicians and parties defined as an "unjustified dictate from outside."[118] Therefore the question of protection for the Slovenes of Italy and for the Italians in Istria remained one of the most important unfulfilled parts of the Osimo agreements.[119] The minority question remained open in spite of the fact that passing of the Special Protection Law (in February 2001) meant a great improvement in relations between Italy and Slovenia.[120]

Political and Cultural Organizations of the Hungarian and Italian Minorities in the Former Yugoslav Lands and in the Post-Yugoslav States

In spite of the fact that members of national minorities in Slovenia have the right to be elected, to vote and to form their own parties, members of the Italian and Hungarian minorities have not established their own political parties. The reason for this may be found in their small size. Members of both minorities are successfully included in Slovene political parties. As already mentioned, the Hungarians of Slovenia have their own organization, the Hungarian National Self-Management Community of Pomurje, with its seat in Lendava. Italians are organized in a similar organization, *i.e.*, the Coastal Self-Management Community of the Italian

Nationality. In addition, Italians are organized in the Union of Italians, which joins the Italians of Slovenia with the Italians of Croatia.

In Croatia since 1949 the Hungarians have had an independent organization that has maintained a unique form of minority cultural autonomy. Within the one-party state framework of Communist Croatia, the Association of Hungarians in Croatia (AHC)—known as the "Hungarian Cultural and Educational Federation of Croatia" until 1969—attempted to address issues regarding Hungarian schools, arts groups, book publishing, the media, language cultivation and relations with the mother nation.[121] Because the AHC could not fulfill a political interest-protecting role, the Hungarian People's Party of Croatia (HPPC) was founded in the spring of 1990 after the multi-party elections. Because of its smaller size and structure, this party soon became isolated from most of the Hungarians of Croatia. The ethnic wars practically eliminated the institutions of the Hungarians of Croatia and forced its prominent members to flee to Hungary. Internally, the organization was characterized by a dual legitimacy: in February 1992, the presidium relieved Jósef Csörgits, president of both the AHC and HPPC, of his office; however, neither he nor his supporters were willing to accept his dismissal. The elected director of the reform wing was Arpád Pasza. The August 1992 parliamentary election reinforced the credibility of the reformers when their vice-president, Ferenc Faragó, won the majority of the Hungarian-speaking population's support. Faragó was the only representative of the Hungarian minority in the Croatian parliament (Sabor).[122]

In Vojvodina until the end of the SFRY, the Hungarian minority had political rights in the socialist system. As a consequence of the fall of the "autonomist" regional leadership in October 1988 and the introduction of a new constitution in Serbia in March 1989, Vojvodina and Kosovo lost their former quasi-republican status. Since then, matters of crucial and vital importance have been determined by the Serb leadership in Belgrade. In 1989 the Democratic Alliance of Hungarians in Vojvodina (Vajdasági Magyarok Demokratikus Közössége—VMDK) was founded. It is a grassroots social organization, not a political party. Its goal is the assertion of individual and collective human rights for Hungarians in Vojvodina, including improving the right of proportional representation in the elected, administrative and judicial bodies; the free use of the mother tongue; a provision for public information in the mother tongue; equal opportunities in economic and social life; education in the mother tongue in elementary and secondary schools; and establishment of ties with institutions in the mother country and with international minority organizations.[123]

When the Yugoslav army attacked Slovenia in June and Croatia in July–August 1991, the VMDK was among the first to protest against this cruel and self-destructive war. The VMDK leaders were accused of being CIA and Vatican agents and working for the reunion of Vojvodina with Hungary. In spite of all the pressures of Milošević's regime, the VMDK has become the sole viable and legitimate mass organization representing the interests of the Hungarian minority.[124] In spring 1992

161

it presented the so-called "three-tiered program," which aimed to ensure personal–cultural autonomy, local self-government and, possibly, territorial autonomy. The Serbian authorities rejected this program as an attempt at secession.[125] Because the VMDK tried to internationalize the problems of the Hungarians of Vojvodina and addressed its demands to the international community, part of its members in 1994 established the VMS, which tried to work on its demands inside the Yugoslav political system. This party soon became larger than the VMDK.[126]

Minority Functions along the Borders

Minorities have settled for the most part in frontier regions. The structural disadvantages of frontier regions are bad for the minorities: those regions are demographically disadvantaged and also economically worse off than the central areas of the states. Minorities were and are potential targets of conflicts. In more developed regions, especially in the most recent decades, members of minorities have been accepted as an asset because of their bilingualism, biculturalism and knowledge of people and situations in frontier regions. Members of minorities are often bearers of transborder activities and connections, from various trade and cultural activities to economic cooperation in the fields of business, management, banking, *etc.* For those activities, there is a need for highly qualified and motivated minority individuals who are integrated in the majority environment and who also have connections in their mother state.

Minority protection could show positive economic results here also. This was evident in the case of the Slovenes in Italy and Austria. Italians and Hungarians in Slovenia have not experienced such good results in the promotion of economic cooperation between Slovenia and their mother states. A high level of minority protection could, however, be counterproductive if educational, cultural and political minority organizations that are state funded gave jobs to a majority of the qualified members of the minorities. This could mean that few people from the minorities would be left to work in the field of economics.

At a moment when language and culture also became part of the market economy, the Italian and Hungarian minorities lived through a shock for which they were not ready. Cutbacks in state funds are a trend occurring throughout Europe. If minorities want to survive, they will have to develop more civil service institutions and will have to develop their initiative at home and become better partners there. The state has to give them institutionalized support as well. In the context of today's information society, the human factor is more important than ever in history.

Conclusions

During the course of the twentieth century three crises took place on the territory of Yugoslavia. After World War I, Yugoslavia was established as a state of three constituent nationalities. During World War II, the occupiers used Yugoslavia's complicated ethnic structure to divide the country and to establish puppet states. After the war Yugoslavia was re-established as a federation with a socialist socioeconomic system. In the 1990s, the Socialist Federal Republic of Yugoslavia disappeared from the political map of Europe. All these political changes and wars affected the fate of minorities. This article has informed the reader about the destiny of two ethnic minorities of Yugoslavia that are little known in contemporary literature, namely the Hungarians and Italians.

The borders of Yugoslavia and its successor states with Hungary were drawn after World War I (in the Treaty of Trianon, 1921). Almost 500,000 ethnic Hungarians living in the then Yugoslav part of the Pannonian Basin became an ethnic minority. The destiny of the Italians was different, since the territories of Istria, Rijeka, Zadar and some islands became part of Italy after World War I. They became a minority only after World War II, when Yugoslavia, as a member of the winning coalition, enlarged its territory to the west to encompass the above-mentioned territories. In a short period, 1945–1955, more than 200,000 ethnic Italians migrated to Italy, responding to strong propaganda by the Italian state, political pressure by the new Communist regime in Yugoslavia and worsened economic circumstances. The Italians became a small minority, which was divided among several territories in the Slovene and Croat parts of Istria, Rijeka and some places in Dalmatia. They also lived in Western Slavonia and in northern Bosnia.

From the 1960s, both minorities in the Socialist Federal Republic of Yugoslavia enjoyed very wide minority protection. The legal and real level of this protection varied in the different republics and autonomous provinces. The level of protection of both minorities was the highest in the Socialist Republic of Slovenia, even though both minorities were the smallest in size there.

The process of dissolution of Yugoslavia brought another phase in the history of both ethnic communities in the region. In Slovenia the legal level of protection increased, and both minorities profited from the process of Slovenia's entering the EU and from the enhanced performance of the economy and the general rise in the standard of living of the population. The Italian minority especially in Slovenia did not like the fact that the border was established between Slovenia and Croatia. Most of the Italians in Croatia did not suffer from the consequences of the war. Those living in Western Slavonia did, however. The Hungarians of Croatia suffered terribly, since their territories of settlement were destroyed by the ravages of war. The Hungarians of Vojvodina also suffered. During Milošević's reign, Vojvodina lost most of the autonomy it had enjoyed under the Yugoslav Constitution. In the last decade of the twentieth century and in the first years of the twenty-first century they have even been victims of physical persecution. They were forced to migrate to Hungary in large numbers, and thus their numbers in the Vojvodina decreased significantly.

The authors believe that minorities will play a significant role in building ties among states in contemporary Europe. Italians and Hungarians in Slovenia already serve as a bridge in various forms of cross-border cooperation among the states of the enlarged EU. Their example might serve as a good practice not only for Italians and Hungarians in Croatia and Serbia & Montenegro but also for example of good practice in minority protection in general in East Central and South-eastern Europe.

NOTES

1. Matjaž Klemenčič and Vladimir Klemenčič, "The Role of the Border Region of the Northern Adriatic in Italy, Croatia and Slovenia in the Past and in the Process of European Integration," *Annales*, Vol. 7, No. 10, 1997, pp. 285–294.
2. Andrew Ludanyi, ed., "Hungary and the Hungarian Minorities," Special Topic Issue, *Nationalities Papers*, Vol. 24, No. 3, 1996.
3. David Turnock, "Hungary," in Francis W. Carter and David Turnock, eds, *The States of Eastern Europe. Volume 1: North-Eastern Europe* (Aldershot, England: Ashgate, 1999), pp. 110–119; Pál Péter Tóth, "Hungarians in the Successor States: From World War I to World War II," *Nationalities Papers*, Vol. 24, No. 3, 1996, pp. 425–437.
4. Matjaž Klemenčič and Mitja Žagar, *Former Yugoslavia's Diverse Peoples: A Reference Sourcebook* (Santa Barbara, Denver, and Oxford: ABC–CLIO, 2004), pp. 217–218; Ivan Crkvenčić: "Emigration of Italians and Germans from Croatia during and Immediately after the Second World War," *Društvena istraživanja*, Vol. 45, 2000, pp. 19–39.
5. Jernej Zupančič and Peter Repolusk, "Regionalism in Istria," *Region and Regionalism*, Vol. 2, 1995, pp. 110–112.
6. Crkvenčić, "Emigration of Italians and Germans from Croatia," p. 23.
7. *Ibid.*, p. 24.
8. Milica Kacin-Wohinz and Jože Pirjevec, *Zgodovina Slovencev v Italiji 1866-2000* [History of the Slovenes in Italy 1866–2000] (Ljubljana: Nova revija, 2000).
9. *VIII. Censimento della popolazione 21 aprile 1936.* Vol II, *Fasc. 24: Provincia del Friuli; Fasc. 31: Provincia del Carnero; Fasc. 32: Provincia di Gorizia, Fasc. 22: Provincia dell'Istria, Fasc. 34: Provincia di Trieste; Fasc. 35: Provincia di Zara* (Rome: Istituto Centrale di Statistica del Regno d'Italia, 1936).
10. Crkvenčić, "Emigration of Italians and Germans from Croatia," p. 18; Vladimir Klemenčič, "Jugoslawien—Zerfall und Bildung neuer Staaten," *Europa: neue Konturen eines Kontinents* (Karl Ruppert, ed.) (Munich: Oldenbourg Verlag, 1993), p. 220.
11. Crkvenčić, "Emigration of Italians and Germans from Croatia," p. 28.
12. M. Kuzle, "Porijeklo Talijana i njihovih naselja u Zapadnoj Slavoniji" [Ancestry of Italians and Their Settlements in Western Slavonia], *Geografski horizont*, Vol. 4, 1995, p. 15.
13. Crkvenčić, "Emigration of Italians and Germans from Croatia," pp. 23–24.
14. Vladimir Klemenčič, "Prekmurje kot nerazvito obmejno območje v Sloveniji" [Prekmurje as Less Developed Frontier Region in Slovenia], *Dela*, Vol. 8, 1991, pp. 108–124.
15. Vladimir Klemenčič, "Sodobni regionalni problemi madžarske in italijanske narodnosti v procesih družbeno-ekonomske preobrazbe" [Contemporary Regional Problems of Hungarian and Italian Nationality in Processes of Socioeconomic Development], *Razprave in gradivo*, Vol. 23, 1990, pp. 52–61; Kocsis and Kocsis-Hodosi, *Ethnic Geography of the Hungarian Minorities*, pp. 187–193.

16. *Popis prebivalstva, gospodinjstev in stanovanj, Slovenija, 31 marca 2002. Statistične informacije No. 93: Population* (Ljubljana: Statistični urad Republike Slovenije, 2003), p. 23.

17. András Bertalan Székely, "The Hungarian Minority in Croatia and Slovenia," *Nationalities Papers*, Vol. 24, No. 3, 1996, p. 483.

18. Kocsis and Kocsis-Hodosi, *Ethnic Geography of the Hungarian Minorities*, p. 181.

19. Klemenčič and Žagar: *Former Yugoslavia's Diverse Peoples*, p. 309.

20. *Republika Hrvatska: Popis stanovništva 2001. Stanovništvo prema narodnosti, po gradovima/općinama*, < http://www.dzs.hr/Popis%202001/Popis/H01_02_02/ H01_02_02.html >, 16 November 2003.

21. Census of Refugees and Other War-Affected Persons in the Federal Republic of Yugoslavia, UNHCR Commissioner for Refugees of the Republic of Serbia, Belgrade, 1996.

22. Kocsis and Kocsis-Hodosi, *Ethnic Geography of the Hungarian Minorities*, p. 160.

23. *Prvi rezultati Popisa stanovništva, domaćinstava, stanova i poljoprivrednih gazdinstava 1991. godine. Statistički bilten broj 1934: Nacionalni sastav stsnovništva po opštinama* (Belgrade: Savezni zavod za statistiku, 1992), str. 32–33; *Popis stanovništva 2002: Stanovništvo po narodnosti* (Belgrade: Savezni zavod za statistiku, 2004), < http:// www.kanjiza.co.yu/nepszamlalas2002/popisst2002.htm >, 20 January 2004.

24. *Ibid.*

25. *Ibid.*

26. *Popis stanovništva 2002: Stanovništvo po narodnosti* (Belgrade: Savezni zavod za statistiku, 2004), < http://www.kanjiza.co.yu/nepszamlalas2002/popisst2002.htm), 20 January 2004.

27. András Agoston's letter to Lord Owen and Cyrus Vance, co-chairmen of the Conference on Yugoslavia, 7 December 1992, quoted in Andrew Ludányi, "The Fate of Magyars in Yugoslavia: Genocide, Ethnocide or Ethnic Cleansing," *Canadian Review of Studies in Nationalism*, Vol. 28, Nos 1–2, 2001, p. 134.

28. Sonja Novak-Lukanović, "Some Yugoslav Experiences in Asserting Equality of the Nations and Nationalities in the Field of Education," *Razprave in gradivo*, Vol. 18, 1986, p. 75.

29. *The Constitution of the Federal People's Republic of Yugoslavia* (Belgrade: Secretariat for Information, 1963); *The Constitution of the Socialist Federal Republic of Yugoslavia* (Belgrade: Secretariat for Information of the Federal Executive Council, 1963).

30. *The Constitution of the Socialist Federal Republic of Yugoslavia* (Belgrade: Jugoslovenska stvarnost and Jugoslovenski pregled, 1989).

31. Žagar Mitja, "Yugoslavia: What Went Wrong? Constitutional Aspects of the Yugoslav Crisis from the Perspective of Ethnic Conflict," in Metta Spencer, ed., *The Lessons of Yugoslavia* (Amsterdam: Elsevier Science, 2000), pp. 65–96; Lajos Arday, "Hungarians in Serb-Yugoslav Vojvodina since 1944," *Nationalities Papers*, Vol. 24, No. 3, 1996, p. 473.

32. *Ustava Socialistične republike Slovenije* (Ljubljana: Uradni list SRS, 1963).

33. *Ustava Socialistične republike Slovenije* (Ljubljana: Uradni list SR Slovenije, 1974).

34. Vladimir Klemenčič, "Državna meja no območju SR Slovenije in obmejna območja kot nov geografski fenomen" [State Border in the Region of SR Slovenia and Frontier Regions as a New Geographic Phenomena], *Razprave in gradivo*, No. 20, 1987, p. 58.

35. Ciril Ribičič, "Italijanska in madžarska narodna skupnost v Republiki Sloveniji: Ustavnopravni položaj. Posebna skrb Slovenije za obe manjšini že pred osamosvojitvijo" [Italian and Hungarian Nationality Group in Republic of Slovenia: Constitutional Legal Situation. Special Care of Slovenia for Both Minorities Already before Independence], *Republika*, Vol. 6, No. 4, 1997, p. 4.

36. Milan Gregorič, "Zakonska zaščita Slovencev v Italiji včeraj, danes in jutri" [Legal Protection of Slovenes in Italy Yesterday, Today, and Tomorrow], *Primorska srećanja*, No. 243, 2001, pp. 454–459.

37. Lojze Ude, Franc Grad and Miro Cerar, Jr, *Ustava Republike Slovenije: z uvodnim komentarjem dr. Lojzeta Udeta, dr. Franca Grada in Mira Cerarja ml. in stvarnim kazalom* [Constitution of Republic of Slovenia: With Introduction ...] (Ljubljana: Uradni list Republike Slovenije, 1992).

38. Miran Komac, "Varstvo narodnih skupnosti v Sloveniji" [Protection of Minorities in Slovenia], in Miroslav Polzer, Liana Kalcina, and Mitja Žagar, eds., *Slovenija in evropski standardi varstva narodnih manjšin/Slovenia and European Standard for the Protection of National Minorities* (Ljubljana: Informacijsko dokumentacijski center Sveta Evrope pri NUK, Inštitut za narodnostna vprašanja, and Avstrijski inštitut za vzhodno in jugovzhodno Evrope, 2002), p. 17.

39. Pravilnik o določanju imen naselij in ulic ter o označevanju naselij, ulic in stavb [Regulations on Determining the Names of Settlements and Streets and the Marking of Settlements, Streets and Buildings], *Uradni list SRS,* No. 11/80, Ljubljana, 1980; Zakon o imenovanju in evidentiranju naselij, ulic in stavb [Law on the Naming and Registering of Settlements, Streets and Buildings], *Uradni list SRS*, No. 8/80, Ljubljana, 1980.

40. Miran Komac, *Protection of Ethnic Communities in the Republic of Slovenia* (Ljubljana: Institute for Ethnic Studies, 1999), p. 43.

41. Zakon o sodiščih [Law on Courts], *Uradni list RS*, No. 19/94, Ljubljana, 1994; Zakon o notariatu [Law on Notaryship], *Uradni list RS*, No. 13/94, 48/94, Ljubljana, 1994; Zakon o državnem tožilstvu [Law on the Office of Public Prosecutor], *Uradni list RS*, No. 63/94, Ljubljana, 1994.

42. Komac, *Protection of Ethnic Communities*, p. 45.

43. The international legal obligations of Slovenia towards the education of members of ethnic communities in their own language may be found in the following: (1) Special Statute of the Memorandum of Understanding, 1954, points b and c of Article 4; (2) Sporazum o zagotavljanju posebnih pravic slovenske manjšine v Republiki Madžarski in madžarske narodnc skupnosti v Republiki Sloveniji [Convention on the Providing of Special Rights of the Slovenian Ethnic Minority in the Republic of Hungary and the Hungarian Ethnic Community in the Republic of Slovenia], *Uradni list RS*, No. 6/93, Ljubljana, 1993; (3) Framework Convention for the Protection of National Minorities, Article 12–14; European Charter for Regional or Minority Language, Article 8.

44. Komac: *Protection of Ethnic Communities*, pp. 46–47.

45. Komac, "Varstvo narodnih skupnosti v Sloveniji," pp. 38–39.

46. Memorandum o soglasju o vzajemnem priznavanju slovenskih in italijanskih diplom in strokovnih naslovov [Memorandum on Agreement on Mutual Acceptance of Slovene and Italian Diplomas and Titles], *Uradni list Republike Slovenije–Mednarodne pogodbe*, No. 4/96, Ljubljana, 1996; Sporazum o sodelovanju na področju kulture, izobraževanja in znanosti med Republiko Slovenijo in republiko Madžarsko [Agreement on Cooperation between Republic of Slovenia and Republic of Hungary in the Fields of Culture, Education, and Science], *Uradni list Republike Slovenije–Mednarodne pogodbe*, No. 6/93, Ljubljana, 1993; Zakon o posebnih pravicah italijanske in madžarske narodne skupnosti na področju vzgoje in izobraževanja [Law on Special Rights of Italian and Hungarian Nationality Groups in Field of Education], *Uradni list republike Slovenije*, No. 35/2001, Ljubljana, 2001.

47. Zakon o javnih glasilih [Law on Mass Media], *Uradni list RS*, No. 18/94, Ljubljana, 1994.
48. Komac, *Protection of Ethnic Communities*, pp. 51–52.
49. Statut Javnega zavoda Radiotelevizije Slovenija [Statute of the Public Institution RTV Slovenia], *Uradni list RS*, No. 66/95, Ljubljana, 1995.
50. Komac, *Protection of Ethnic Communities*, pp. 52–53; "Varstvo narodnih skupnosti v Sloveniji," p. 56.
51. Zakon o uresničevanju javnega interesa na področju kulture [Law on the Realization of Public Interest in the Area of Culture], *Uradni list RS*, No. 75/94, Ljubljana, 1994.
52. Komac, *Protection of Ethnic Communities*, pp. 53–54.
53. Zakon o grbu, zastavi in himni Republike Slovenije ter o slovenski narodni zastavi [Law on the Coat of Arms, Flag and Anthem of the Republic of Slovenia, and on the Slovenian National Flag], *Uradni list RS*, No. 67/94, Ljubljana, 1994.
54. See Article 64 of the *Constitution of the Republic of Slovenia*.
55. Zakon o evidenci volilne pravice [Law on the Records of Voting Rights], *Uradni list RS*, No. 46/92, Ljubljana, 1992; Zakon o volitvah v državni zbor [Law on Elections to the National Assembly], *Uradni list RS*, No. 44/92, Ljubljana, 1992.
56. Zakon o lokalni samoupravi [Law on Local Self-government], *Uradni list RS*, No. 72/93, Ljubljana, 1993.
57. Zakon o samoupravih narodnih skupnostih [Law on Self-Governing Ethnic Communities], *Uradni list RS*, No. 65/94, Ljubljana, 1993.
58. *Ibid.*
59. Zakon o ratifikaciji Evropske listine o regionalnih in manjšinskih jezikih [Law on Ratification of European Charter of Regional and Minority Languages], *Uradni list Republike Slovenije–Mednarodne pogodbe*, No. 17/2000, Ljubljana, 2000; Zakon o ratifikaciji Okvirne konvencije za varstvo narodnih manjšin [Law on Ratification of Provisional Convention for the Protection of National Minorities], *Uradni list republike Slovenije—Mednarodne pogodbe*, No. 4/98, Ljubljana, 1998.
60. Boris Šuligoj, "Bolje Slovenec v Italiji kot Italijan v Sloveniji" [It Is Better to Be Slovene in Italy than an Italian in Slovenia], *Delo* (Ljubljana), Vol. 46, No. 3, 2004, p. 2.
61. Boris Šuligoj, "Ne vprašaj, kaj lahko država stori zate" [Do Not Ask What the State Can Do for You], *Delo* (Ljubljana), Vol. 46, No. 6, 2004, p. 5.
62. Lojze Kante, "Solidarni z manjšino" [We Express Solidarity with Ninority], *Delo* (Ljubljana), Vol. 46, No. 8, 2004, p. 2.
63. Interview with representatives of Obalna samoupravna skupnost italijanske narodnosti (Comunita' autogestita costiera della nazionalita italiana), 30 January 2004.
64. Kante, "Solidarni z manjšino," p. 2.
65. Nikola Radačić, "Odgoj, Obrazovanje, kultura i informiranje na jezicima nacionalnih manjina u Republici Hrvatskoj" [Education, Culture, and Informing in the Languages of National Minorities in Republic of Croatia], in Peter Vencelj, Vladimir Klemenčič and Sonja Lukanovič, eds, *Manjšine v prostoru Alpe-Jadran/Minderheiten im Alpen Adria-Raum/Manjine na području Alpe-Jadrana, Le minoranze nell' area di Alpe-Adria/ Kisebbségek az Alpok-Adria Térségeben* (Ljubljana: Delovna skupnost za manjšine Alpe Jadran, 1994), p. 206.
66. Rezolucija o zaštiti ustavnog demokratskog poretka i nacionalnim pravima u Hrvatskoj [Resolution on Protection of Constitutional Democratic Development and National Minority Rights in Croatia], *Narodne novine 34/90*, Zagreb, 1990.
67. Ustav Republike Hrvatske [Constitution of Republic of Croatia], *Narodne novine 56/90* and *Narodne novine 135/97*, Zagreb, 1990 and 1997.

68. Deklaracija o uspostavi suverene i samostalne Republike Hrvatske [Declaration on Establishment of Sovereign and Independent Republic of Croatia], *Narodne novine 31/91*, Zagreb, 1991.
69. Povelja o pravima Srba i drugih nacionalnosti u Republici Hrvatskoj [Decree on the Rights of Serbs and Other Nationalities in Republic of Croatia], *Narodne novine 31/91*, Zagreb, 1991.
70. Zakon o ljudskim pravima i slobodama i o pravima ethničkih i nacionalnih zajednica ili manjina u Republiki Hrvatskoj [Law on Human Rights and Freedoms and on Rights on Ethnic and National Communities or Minorities in Republic of Croatia], *Narodne novine 65/91* and *Narodne novine 105/00*, Zagreb, 1991 and 2000.
71. Zakon o upotrebi jezika i pisma etničkih i nacionalnih zajednica ili manjina u Republiki Hrvatskoj [Law on Language and Alphabet Usage of Ethnic and National Communities or Minorities in Republic of Croatia], *Narodne novine 51/00* and *Narodne Novine 56/00*, Zagreb, 1991 and 2000.
72. Branko Milinković and Sanja Milinković, eds, *Nacionalne manjine—u medjunarodnom i jugoslovenskom pravnom poretku* [National Minorities—in International and Yugoslav Legal Order] (Belgrade: Medjunarodna politika, NIU "Službeni list SFRJ," Pravni fakultet, Fakultet političkih nauka, Institut ekonomskih nauka, and Institut za medjunarodnu politiku i privredu, 1997), pp. 312–313.
73. Komac, *Protection of ethnic communities*, p. 53.
74. Flavio Dessardo, "Unija Italijanov—kaprica ali potreba?" [Union of Italians—Caprice or Need?], *Primorska srečanja*, No. 212, 1998, p. 887.
75. Boris Šuligoj, "Unija tudi v Sloveniji, a le kot zveza društev" [Union Also in Slovenia, but Only as the Union of Societies], *Delo* (Ljubljana), Vol. 40, No. 75, 1998, p. 2; Boris Šuligoj, "Le še eno društvo manjšine ali kaj več? Italijanska unija registrirana tudi v Sloveniji" [Only One Society of Minority or Something More? Italian Union Registered Also in Slovenia], *Delo* (Ljubljana), Vol. 40, No. 196, 1998, p. 2.
76. Andrew Ludanyi, "Titoist Integration of Yugoslavia: The Partisan Myth and the Hungarians of Vojvodina, 1945–1975," *Polity*, Vol. 12, No. 2, 1979, pp. 245–248.
77. Perica Vučinić, "Vlast i manjine" [Authority and Minorities], *Vreme International* (Belgrade), Vol. 6, No. 238, 1995, pp. 23–24.
78. Milinković and Milinković, *Nacionalne manjine*, pp. 288–290.
79. Zoltan Bujnik, "Moguči model obrazovanja na jezicima manjina u Vojvodini" [Possible Model of Education in Languages of Minorities in Vojvodina], in *Aspekti obrazovanja na jezicima etničkih manjina* [Aspects of Education in Languages of Ethnic Minorities] (Novi Sad: Centar za multikulturnost, 2001), pp. 3–7.
80. *Ljudska prava u tranziciji—Srbija 2001* [Human Rights in Transition—Serbia 2001] (Belgrade: Helsinški odbor za ljudska prava u Srbiji, 2002), pp. 166–167.
81. S. V. Popovic, "Predsednik GO Saveza vojvodinskih Madjara o rušenju madjarskih spomenika na gradskom groblju" [President of City Council of Federation of Vojvodina Hungarians on Demolition of Hungarian Monuments on the City Cemetery], *Dnevnik*, 6 February 2003, < http://www.vmsz.org.yu/sh/onama/0129.htm >, 11 July 2004.
82. *Blic* (Belgrade), 12 January 2001.
83. *Gradjanski list* (Belgrade), 8–9 November 2001.
84. *Gradjanski list* (Belgrade), 26 November 2001.
85. *Gradjanski list* (Belgrade), 25 September 2001; *Ljudska prava u tranziciji*, pp. 183–186.
86. P. Potočnik, "Šovinistična farsa v srbski različici" [Chauvinist Farce the Serb Variant], *Delo* (Ljubljana), 26 June 2004, < http://arhiv.delo.si/article.jsp >.
87. M. Laketić, "Mladića nabili na bejzbol palicu" [Youngster Impaled on Baseball Stick], *Politika*, 29 June 2004, p. 4).

88. M. Laketić, "Nejasni motivi gnusnog zlodela" [Unclear Motives of Disgusting Criminal Act], *Politika*, 1 July 2004, p. 12).

89. P. Potočnik, "Nova različica primera Martinović" [New Variant of the Case of Martinović], *Delo* (Ljubljana), 2 July 2004, < http://arhiv.delo.si/article.jsp >.

90. M. Lakctić, "Izvršioci imaju kriminalnu prošlost" [Those Who Did It Have Criminal Past], *Politika*, 30 July 2004, p. 20).

91. Alfred A. Reisch, "Hungarian Foreign Policy and the Magyar Minorities: New Foreign Policy Priorities," *Nationalities Papers*, Vol. 24, No. 3, 1996, p. 459.

92. Székely, "The Hungarian Minority in Croatia and Slovenia," p. 453.

93. Reisch, "Hungarian Foreign Policy and the Magyar Minorities," p. 460.

94. Sporazum o zagotavljanju posebnih pravic slovenske narodne manjšine v republiki Madžarski in madžarske narodne skupnosti v Republiki Sloveniji [Agreement on Assurances of Special Rights of Slovene National Minority in Republic of Hungary and Hungarian National Minority in Republic of Slovenia], *Uradni list republike Slovenije– Mednarodne pogodbe*, No. 6/93, Ljubljana, 1993.

95. Pogodba o prijateljstvu in sodelovanju med Republiko Slovenijo in Republiko Madžarsko [Agreement on Friendship and Cooperation Between Republic of Slovenia and Republic of Hungary], *Uradni list Republike Slovenije–Mednarodne pogodbe*, No. 6/93, Ljubljana, 1993.

96. Adopted by the Hungarian parliament on 19 June 2001. Available from < http:// www.htmh.hu/law.htm >.

97. Zoltán Kántor, "Hungarian National Politics and the Status Law," *Studia Historica Slovenica*, Vol. 3, No. 1, 2003, pp. 121–138.

98. For details, see the government program "For a Civic Hungary on the Eve of a New Millenium from 1998," < http://www.htmh.hu/govprog.htm >, 15 August 2001—quoted after Kántor, "Hungarian National Politics and the Status Law," p. 125.

99. George Schöpflin, "The Hungarian Status Law: Political, Cultural and Sociological Contexts," paper presented at Szabad Identitásválasztás conference, Budapest, 21 November 2001—quoted after Kántor, "Hungarian National Politics and the Status Law," pp. 125–126.

100. Information on the Law on Hungarians Living in Neighboring Countries (Act T/4070)— quoted after Kántor, "Hungarian National Politics and the Status Law," p. 126.

101. Jozsef Szabo, "Pozitivna diskriminacija" [Positive Discrimination], *Delo* (Ljubljana), Vol. 43, No. 103, 2001, p. 5.

102. "OVSE kritizira zakon o zaščiti Madžarov" [OSCE Is Criticizing Law on Protection of Hungarians], *Večer* (Maribor, Slovenia), Vol. 57, No. 251, 2001, p. 6.

103. "OVSE kritizira madžarski zakon o Madžarih v sosednjih državah" [OSCE Is Criticizing Hungarian Law on Hungarians in Neighboring Countries], *Primorski dnevnik* (Trieste), Vol. 57, No. 264, 2001, p. 18.

104. "EU: Zakon je diskriminatoren" [EU: Law Is Discriminatory], *Večer* (Maribor, Slovenia), Vol. 57, No. 277, 2001, p. 39.

105. Jozsef Szabo, "Kako ohladiti jezo sosed" [How to Cool down Anger of Neighbors], *Delo* (Ljubljana), Vol. 43, No. 176, 2001, p. 4.

106. Memorandum of Understanding between the Government of the Republic of Hungary and the Government of Romania concerning the Law of Hungarians Living in Neighbouring Countries and Issues of Bilateral Co-operation, Budapest, 22 December 2001.

107. *Ljudska prava u tranziciji*, pp. 177–178.

108. Kántor, "Hungarian National Politics and the Status Law," pp. 121–138.

169

109. "Madžarski parlament sprejel dopolnila k statusnemu zakonu" [Hungarian Parliament Passed Amendments to the Status Law], *Primorski dnevnik* (Trieste), Vol. 59, No. 152, 2003, p. 22.

110. D. Kolundžija, "Od matice tražimo štap, a ribu cemo sami upecati. Potpredsednik skupštine Vojvodine Šandor Egereši o izmenama Statusnog zakona koje je usvojio parlament Madjarske" [From the Homeland We Demand Stick, We Are Going to Fish Alone. Vice-President of Assembly of Vojvodina Szandor Egereszi on Changes on Status Law Passed by Hungarian Parliament], *Dnevnik*, 24 June 2003, <http://www.vmsz.org.yu/sh/onama/0129.htm>, 11 July 2004.

111. "Schengen regime" represents a system of border controls at the outer borders of states that were admitted into the Schengen Agreement Regime that was signed in Schengen, Luxembourg, in 1992. The signatories accepted the abolition of persons and customs controls at the borders among signatories. At the same time they decided on increased level of controls at so-called outer borders. Slovenia and Hungary have not become members yet. They shall become members by 2007.

112. Mariša Zagradnik, "Slovenija–Jugoslavija–Italija po letu 1945, 1. del: Terjatve in dolgovi ob zahodni meji" [Slovenia–Yugoslavia–Italy after 1945, Part 1: Demands and Debts along the Western Border], *Delo* (Ljubljana), Vol. 37, No. 233, 1995, Sobotna priloga pp. 32–33.

113. Italian Peace Treaty, *United Nations, Treaty Series: Treaties and International Agreements Registered or Field and Recorded with the Secretariat of the United Nations*, Vol. 49, No. 747, Paris, 10 February 1947.

114. Memorandum of Understanding between the Governments of Italy, the United Kingdom, the United States and Yugoslavia Regarding the Free Territory of Trieste, *United Nations, Treaty Series: Treaties and International Agreements Registered or Field and Recorded with the Secretariat of the United Nations*, Vol. 235, London, 5 October 1954.

115. Based on explanation of the Decree of Constitutional Court of Republic of Slovenia, No. U-I-283/94, *Uradni list Republike Slovenije*, No. 20/98, Ljubljana, 1998.

116. Lojze Kante, "Osimo in slovenska manjšina" [Osimo and Slovene Minority], *Delo* (Ljubljana), Vol. 37, No. 260, 1995, p. 7.

117. Akt o nostrifikaciji nasledstva sporazumov nekdanje Jugoslavije z Republiko Italijo [Act on Nostrification of Succession of Agreements of Former Yugoslavia with Republic of Italy], *Uradni list Republike Slovenije*, No. 40/92, Ljubljana, 1992, pp. 127–128.

118. Mojca Drčar-Murko, "Aktualnost zgodovine" [Actuality of History], *Delo* (Ljubljana), Vol. 37, No. 260, 1995, p. 7.

119. Kante, "Osimo in slovenska manjšina," p. 7.

120. *Gazzetta Ufficiale* (Rome), No. 56, 2001.

121. Ferenc Mák, "A Horvátországi Magyarok Szövetségének szerepe müvelödési életünk fejlesztésében," in *Horvátországi Magyarok Szövetségé évkönyv 1* (Osijek Eszék: HMSZ, 1979), pp. 149–151.

122. Székely, "The Hungarian Minority in Croatia and Slovenia," pp. 484–486.

123. *Ethnic Hungarians in Ex-Yugoslavia* (Ottawa: SOS Transylvania, 1993), pp. 3, 8–9, 10–13.

124. Arday, "Hungarians in Serb-Yugoslav Vojvodina since 1944," pp. 478–480.

125. Vučinić, "Vlast i manjine," pp. 23–24.

126. Andrej Ivanji, "Dogovor, a ne konflikt" [Agreement and Not Conflict], *Vreme International* (Belgrade), Vol. 6, No. 238, p. 24.

The Milošević Trial: Purpose and Performance

James Gow and Ivan Zveržhanovski

The trial of former Yugoslav President Slobodan Milošević before the International Criminal Tribunal for the Former Yugoslavia (ICTY) in The Hague is a vehicle both for achieving justice and for pursuing historical truth. At this first-ever trial of a former head of state before an international tribunal, the same evidence serves two purposes: the quests for '"truth" by those involved in the judicial process, on one side, and those engaged in academic historical interpretation, on the other. In each sphere, there are expectations to be satisfied. Those of the peoples of Serbia and the other former Yugoslav lands, international governmental and non-governmental actors, and observers are all different from each other; and they are all distinct from the viewpoint of future students of history. The two frameworks for truth are neither necessarily competitive nor complementary, and the tests of their validity may differ. But the raw material they use may be identical and the outcome of each may be parallel and consistent. And the two varieties of truth may reinforce one another in the quest to restore peace and security, to establish justice, and to compile a broadly accepted account of contentious, awful events.[1]

The present article assesses the performance of those at the Tribunal, particularly that of the Office of the Prosecutor (OTP), in the contexts of judicial process, on the one hand, and historical record, on the other. On the basis of the evidence presented so far, is the Milošević trial more useful as a judicial process that might foster peace and security, or as a gathering of material that can lead to a more or less undisputable account of events? Our response is that the balance, at the end of the prosecution case, lay with the historical record rather than the quest for justice. We begin by considering the purposes for the establishment of the ICTY. Then we examine the problems faced by the prosecution in carrying out the Tribunal's entwined missions of criminal justice and peace and security and the limited achievements of the Prosecutor. We continue by examining the value of empirical evidence, mainly resulting from witnesses appearing in the Trial Chamber. In doing so, we follow the view both of the Prosecutor, as accepted by the Trial Chamber, and of our own earlier work, that we are dealing with one war.[2] We seek, therefore, to avoid the somewhat incomplete and casual understanding of many observers that there was a series of discrete wars because armed conflict occurred in different theatres and at different times. Following the chronology of the Prosecutor's case, rather than that of events, we consider the Kosovo phase first, then Croatia and Bosnia. In the end, we augment our conclusion that, at the end of the prosecution case, the historical record is a greater benefactor than justice, inferring further that the contribution to history is less regarding the war in the southern theatre in Kosovo than in the western theatre embracing Croatia and Bosnia.

The ICTY, Peace, Justice, and History

The International Criminal Tribunal for the Former Yugoslavia may be said to have a number of purposes. Its primary purpose is to contribute to the maintenance and restoration of international peace and security. This is a political purpose, established by the political authority of the U.N. Security Council. But the Tribunal was also given a purely judicial mission to employ due process in the investigation and trial of individuals suspected of committing war crimes and crimes against humanity during the war that accompanied the break-up of the Yugoslav federation. In the western theatre, many of these crimes had already been committed by the time the Tribunal's statute was adopted by the U.N. Security Council in May 1993. The notion of adopting a war crimes tribunal rested in part on immediate needs to address a war that was underway and that prominently featured atrocities.

There were two core issues in the war. One set constituted statehood and borders—preserving the borders of states in the west against Serbian attempts to change those borders and consolidating Serbia's borders in the south against separatist sentiment. The other comprised the manner in which the war was fought, with apparent war crimes and crimes against humanity being essential features of the war.[3] While there was fighting in Slovenia and Croatia, beginning with the declarations of independence by those two states on 25 June 1991, and subsequently in Bosnia-Hercegovina from the following spring, as well as eventually in Kosovo after 1997, the separate geographies and political specifics should be seen as one whole event. That war ran over a decade and was not a series of discrete events. Only the fighting in Slovenia might be seen as separable, since Belgrade had no ambitions concerning either borders or ethnic cleansing there; and the period of armed conflict there was limited to ten days in June and July 1991. However, because the armed conflict in Slovenia was intimately linked to the onset of war in Croatia, it cannot wholly be separated. For the remainder, Belgrade's strategy provides a unifying factor that cannot be overlooked. Croatia and Bosnia were both fighting for their independence and territorial integrity while Serbia sought to create a new set of borders to its west that would incorporate ethnic Serb populations and the resources and communications regarded as necessary to that project.

To ensure the security of territory under Serbian control, the infamous strategy of "ethnic cleansing" was introduced to remove any other potentially hostile ethnic groups from the territory under control. By the time this Serbian strategy reached the south and threatened the majority ethnic Albanian population in the province of Kosovo, various manifestations of what was called the "internationally community" had also become involved in a multitude of different ways in seeking to combat the

Serbian project. At the same time, given the complexity of the old Yugoslav federation's dissolution and war, "ethnic cleansing" was used to some extent or another by other "Yugoslav" belligerents. It was the prominence of atrocity as an integral part of the war that prompted calls to create an international war crimes tribunal.

Discussions to create the Tribunal were informed by two related but discrete ideas of how such a process could contribute to a post-conflict peace.[4] The first of these was the idea that genuine peace, especially following a conflict so extensively characterised by atrocities, could only be established through justice. Only by ensuring accountability and rendering both restorative and retributive justice could the conditions for future armed hostilities be removed and reconciliation made possible.[5] This idea in part stemmed from an understanding of the "Nuremberg legacy"—the idea that the International Military Tribunal (IMT) that dealt with Nazi war crimes at the end of the Second World War played a significant role in the later transformation of Germany into a liberal democracy.[6] A second interpretation of the Nuremberg legacy, which folds into the first, is the idea that the trial established an undisputable record of the crimes committed by the Nazi regime, a record that could not then genuinely be questioned by pro-Nazi revisionists. No one could have any doubt about the Nazi regime of industrial mass murder. In a sense, the trial did the work of justice in producing evidence by which to hold some of those involved responsible for their crimes and so paving a path to peace and renewal. But that same evidence base, in a way, also did the work of historians, creating a record of detail and interpretation which was judged to be beyond dispute.

Nuremberg sets a standard for any similar enterprise. It does not matter that most people have no real idea of the Nuremberg process and its outcome, including many who have faith in its outcome and virtues, as well as those who promote similar judicial action in other cases. Even less understood are the crucial distinctions between Nuremberg and later innovations, such as the International Criminal Tribunal for the Former Yugoslavia.[7] The crucial test, in a sense, is for the outcome and the evidence generally to be accepted. With the work of the Yugoslavia tribunal only partly completed and with the Milošević trial only one part of that overall process, a definitive direct comparison cannot be made. Furthermore, in many ways, the two processes are not wholly comparable. Nuremberg was an international military tribunal, created by the victors in a war to try the losers, with deficiencies in defence and no right of appeal. By contrast, the ICTY is a civilian criminal court, created within the United Nations system to address suspected crimes committed by all sides in a continuing armed conflict, where due process and observance of the rights of the defendant and defence, as well as extensive possibilities of appeal, make the tests applied quite different. Evidence allowed at Nuremberg would not be admitted in The Hague.[8] Despite the problems and the differences, Nuremberg remains the standard. And despite the large number of other cases handled by The Hague, it is the Milošević trial that will define the Tribunal's success or failure in the eyes of the world and of history.

By the standard of general acceptance, the ICTY and particularly the Milošević trial have some way to go. The present article is written at a point when the prosecution case has closed, but the defence case and the adjudication, to say nothing of any appeals that might be made, have still to happen. Thus, there could yet be an outcome to parallel that of Nuremberg. Certainly, the uncertain performance of the Prosecutor does not mean that nothing worthwhile has emerged to date in the Milošević trial. Indeed, in terms of both criminal evidence and the historical record, material of great value has been introduced. This can be said without either second-guessing the judges' final opinions, or anything that might yet emerge to add to the historical record.

Indeed, it should be clearly stated that, although the trial is incomplete, it has already generated an enormous amount of evidence, for both criminal justice and historical purposes. The uses of evidence are different for justice and history. In terms of criminal justice, the full picture is not there yet. But, there is sufficient evidence to be able to test some of the big questions confronted in the trial and to assess the quality of the prosecution case and the prospects for conviction. In terms of history, the failure to secure conviction because of missing material evidence on crimes to secure a verdict beyond reasonable doubt, or a legal technicality, such as failing to establish subject matter jurisdiction,[9] does not mean that evidence of actions by Milošević and others is invalid for the historian or strategic analyst. Indeed, where legal technicalities might see the Serbian leader acquitted to the bemusement of some and satisfaction of others, the empirical base on which the case is made can help determine judgements of responsibility in the eyes of history. And, should it need to be stated, the historian does not need to wait for the judges' verdict to be able to evaluate evidence, whether introduced in indictments, or at trial. The indictments and material introduced at trial are evidence themselves, for making judgements regarding both criminal culpability and history. The extent to which they are reliable is a matter of the quality of the evidence itself and the discrimination of the analyst. It is with this understanding that we proceed to investigate the problems of the prosecution. We look first at the prosecution's efforts to secure a successful conviction. We then turn to the degree to which the prosecution case has produced evidence that significantly adds to the historical record, first in terms of the war in the south, in Kosovo, and then in terms of the war in the west, which embraced both Croatia and Bosnia-Hercegovina.[10]

Problems of Prosecution

On 25 February 2004, the ICTY Prosecution in The Hague abruptly concluded its case against ex-Serbian leader Slobodan Milošević, who is charged with a variety of alleged crimes committed during a decade of war in Croatia, Bosnia, and Kosovo. At that stage, the Prosecutor still had two days of hearings left, scheduled for March, after the defendant had been unable to complete the final two days of the Prosecutor's case in February, due to the latest of a series of health problems. The Prosecutor's decision to close the case came only days after the President of the Trial Chamber dealing with it had announced his resignation, indicating that he would leave the Tribunal in three months because of health concerns.[11] The early closure of the prosecution case added to the sense that overall the Milošević trial was damaging the cause of international justice more than it was serving it. This could be seen in relation to three broad areas: the prosecution case, the impact on the U.S., and the impact on Serbia.

In terms of the first of these areas—the difficulties with the prosecution case—the abrupt manner in which Chief Prosecutor Carla del Ponte closed the case without completing the final two days of evidence was wholly unexpected. But it was typical of the uncertain manner in which the prosecution case has often been conducted. There are three aspects to this: friction with the judges, the adding of charges, and weaknesses in the case.

Regarding the first of these aspects of prosecutorial weakness—friction with the judges—the Prosecutor complicated the Milošević trial by adding additional charges involving Croatia and Bosnia to the original Kosovo indictment. This was a source of friction with the Trial Chamber dealing with the case and, in particular, its President, Judge Richard May. The prosecution was seeking to put the Kosovo case, which was ostensibly ready, together with those for Croatia and Bosnia, which still required time—thus requiring a delay to the start of proceedings. Eventually, the Trial Chamber agreed that the cases could be heard together, but that the Prosecutor would have no delay in starting on Kosovo and would have the duration of the Kosovo presentation to prepare the other cases. This was a rod for her own back that del Ponte had made in the attempt to buy preparation time from the Trial Chamber.

Adding to the charges themselves made the picture particularly dispiriting in some regards. The former Serbian leader was originally indicted under two articles of the ICTY statute: ((3) law and customs of war and (5) crimes against humanity) on 24 May 1999, during the Kosovo campaign. Milošević was indicted at that stage, against the wishes of the NATO countries, because it was the first time that the Prosecutor's office had been in a position to make a clear case against him. This was because he had formally become leader of all Serbian forces the previous March when Belgrade declared a state of war in the face of NATO's intervention to end Belgrade's ethnic-cleansing campaign in Kosovo. The Prosecutor (at that time Louise Arbour) had gathered sufficient evidence of crimes in Kosovo to charge Milošević with command responsibility, breaches of the laws and customs of war, and alleged participation in a joint and common plan to commit crimes against humanity. However, once Milošević was already in custody (he was transferred to The Hague on 28 June 2001), rather than concentrating on the case that had been prepared, the new Chief Prosecutor, del Ponte, added indictments for Croatia[12] and Bosnia,[13] which made the case more difficult.

Finally, the weaknesses of the case should be noted. For example, the Croatian indictment added to the difficulties by including a new class of charge—grave breaches of the Geneva Conventions of 1949. It required the Prosecutor to demonstrate that the alleged crimes were committed as part of an international armed conflict; yet during the relevant period, the old Yugoslav federation was breaking up and the states were not yet generally recognised as possessing independent personality in international law. The Bosnian indictment also included the additional burden of grave breaches charges, but added yet another hurdle—genocide. This charge of genocide had already been shown to be a major test in the ICTY context, with three cases having been made of which only one had gained a conviction—and that was for aiding and abetting the massacre at Srebrenica. This meant that the Prosecutor had made the case as a whole much harder by adding Croatia and Bosnia and by adding charges that were unlikely to be proved beyond reasonable doubt. Along the way, the Prosecutor introduced many witnesses whose evidence seemed largely political and of limited material relevance to the case. When it was relevant, it often did much to confirm Milošević's position during cross-examination. In the end, as the prosecution case closed, del Ponte acknowledged in press interviews that a conviction for genocide was almost impossible. She stopped short of making comment on the other difficult issues, but her admission concerning the charge of genocide is perhaps the greatest testimony to the weakness of the case that the prosecution has made.

The second broad difficulty with the prosecution case was its impact on the U.S. administration and the latter's support for the Prosecutor's work. This was more significant to the work of the Prosecutor than it might immediately seem. This was not an issue of general hostility to the United Nations and its bodies by some in the U.S. administration of George W. Bush, although those attitudes compounded the question and, indeed, were compounded by it. Despite the reservations of some of its adherents, the Bush administration had to maintain support for a key plank of U.S. policy. The damage caused by del Ponte's approach related to the crucial role of U.S. support to the Tribunal as a whole in terms of funding, and to the Office of the Prosecutor, in particular, given the need for cooperation in various areas, such as information, obtaining witnesses, and getting cooperation from Belgrade and other Southeast European capitals. The weakness of the Prosecutor's case had an especially damaging impact in terms of the U.S. administration. This has two dimensions. The first concerns the general U.S. perspective on support for international judicial institutions, where weakened general support also meant a weakening of support for the ICTY—and even incipient hostility. In this respect, del Ponte's performance validated U.S. suspicions about the problems of an independent prosecutor without diplomatic sensitivity.[14] The U.S. was never very positive about the International Criminal Court. The fear of an unreliable and politicised independent prosecutor was a major factor in persuading the U.S. not to support a body that it had largely been responsible for creating. The U.S. was prepared to monitor the performance of the Chief Prosecutor at the ICC over a number of years to see if at some point it would be able to become a party to the ICC treaty. Del Ponte's behaviour at the ICTY helped to confirm all U.S. fears in this regard.

Secondly, del Ponte's behaviour has also deeply affected U.S. support for the Yugoslavia tribunal itself and the Office of the Prosecutor in particular. Cooperation has been significantly drawn down, particularly in the field of intelligence and evidence assistance, given the ICTY Chief Prosecutor's propensity to be undiplomatic in criticizing the U.S. and NATO regarding the detention of war crimes suspects and for revealing sensitive information in public— often making it that much harder for the U.S. and NATO to pursue war crimes suspects. Nevertheless, the U.S. continues to support the Tribunal in principle and to insist that Belgrade cooperate with The Hague.

The third broad area of difficulty in the prosecution's performance concerns the impact of the case on Serbia. As with the impact on the U.S., it is important to be clear that the Tribunal did not create nationalist sentiment in Serbia. However, one of the roles assigned to it is that of transitional justice. In this context, put simply, the role of the Tribunal should not be to reinforce conditions and attitudes that led to war and atrocities, but should be to contribute to transforming those conditions. For Serbia the outcome of the Tribunal's work in general and the Milošević trial in particular has been the opposite of that which was desirable. The impact of the Milošević trial in Serbia has been significant in three ways. The first concerns Serbian elections at the end of 2003, which saw rising support for the extreme nationalist Serbian Radical Party (SRS) and to a lesser extent for the Serbian Socialist Party (SPS) of Slobodan Milošević. Both charged the government, headed by the Democratic Party, with betrayal in cooperating at all with the Tribunal and, in particular, in arranging the transfer of Milošević to The Hague. While other factors clearly played a role in the election, there can be little doubt that the most striking position these parties took was in opposition to the The Hague. It, therefore, seems likely that a good part of the electoral support they gained owes to their position on cooperation with The Hague— an issue that a recent poll put as a priority for only 0.1% of the Serbian population. With all parties refusing to countenance cooperation with the SRS, the single largest party in parliament, and refusing to cooperate with each other in some cases, the SPS saw an opportunity to regain prominence. It was involved in some discussion about taking the Speaker's role in parliament, but in the end it did not join the government which was formed after more than two months of very difficult negotiations. It was vital to the formation of that government, however.

Secondly, the trial was a factor in the formation of the Serbian minority government that took office on 2 March, headed by the new prime minister Vojislav Koštunica. That government was formed on the basis of minority support, with nine places going to Koštunica's Democratic Party of Serbia, five to the G-17 party, and four ministerial posts shared by the New Serbia coalition and the Serbian Movement for Renewal (SPO) headed by Vuk Drašković. (Drašković opposed joining the government, which means that this was the first time the party he created at the end of the 1980s ever voted against his position.) The minority government was made possible by support from the Serbian Socialist Party, which Milošević still technically leads from his cell. Despite some first signs of renewal and reform within its ranks, the SPS vowed to keep the minority government afloat in parliament on two conditions: that there is no further cooperation with The Hague and that domestically those involved in what the party regards as the illegal "kidnapping" of Milošević are arrested and prosecuted. Thus, a sword of Damocles was hanging over the government.

Cooperation with The Hague has also been a factor in Serbian political life. For example, Koštunica, the minority government prime minister, was very reluctant to work with the ICTY. He addressed parliament stating that cooperation with The Hague would not be a priority. More important, perhaps, he set tough terms for cooperation with the Tribunal, such as arranging to hold trials in Serbia and insisting that Serbian prisoners serve their sentences in Serbia and Montenegro. These terms were wholly unacceptable to the Tribunal for security reasons and to the international community more broadly. This means that Koštunica set terms that only encourage confrontation. The issue of cooperation has been a major source of difficulty between the Belgrade authorities and the international community. Cooperation with The Hague continues to be a condition for the renewal of U.S. financial assistance to Belgrade. The absence of that assistance has serious implications for the Serbian government and economy. Without that aid the government finds it difficult to sustain public sector programmes, which depend on outside assistance; and confidence in the private sector is damaged, particularly by the lack of support from foreign investors, who are concerned about political instability and financial insecurity.

Perhaps the most decisive influence of all on Serbian politics was the murder of the political leader who had done most to ensure Milošević's appearance in The Hague and who probably offered the best prospects for his country's future. Serbian Prime Minister Zoran Djindjić was shot in March 2003 because he had transferred Milošević to the ICTY and was preparing to transfer other war crimes suspects to The Hague before the end of that month. This was perhaps the most significant setback for Serbia and was a result of Serbian attitudes to the Milošević trial. Given the failure of the prosecution in The Hague to complete its case convincingly, there is little prospect that the image of the Tribunal in Serbia will improve.[15] Continuing reluctance to cooperate with The Hague along with persistent pressure from the international community suggests that a difficult period lies ahead for any new Serbian government.

Given the lack of success of the Tribunal's mission to restore peace and security, especially in Serbia, the onus on the trial has to be on the contribution it can make to the emerging historical record. Following the chronology of indictment by the Tribunal and subsequent prosecution, we will first assess the prosecution's contribution regarding the war in the south—in Kosovo—and then regarding the war in the west—in Croatia and Bosnia.

The War in the South: Kosovo

For most of the Kosovo part of the trial, the prosecution team appeared confused concerning the direction of the case, although some order was later put into the second and longer part of the trial which involved Croatia and Bosnia. To begin with, the list of witnesses was a subject of controversy. It was curtailed first by the Trial Chamber, in order to speed up the proceedings, and later subject to a large number of changes as the trial went on. Those following the trial had to wait until Lord Ashdown's appearance in court on 14–15 March 2002 for the first truly good witness—and, even then, Ashdown's contribution was to stand up to Milošević politically rather than to contribute significantly either to the case or to the historical record.[16] Before this, there had been a succession of generally poorly performing witnesses. This cast a shadow of doubt over the competence of the prosecutorial team.

The beginning of the "trial of the century" was a fiasco. The prosecution presented a former senior Communist official in Kosovo, Mahmut Bakalli, as first witness. Bakalli was a poor choice. First of all, he was a politician and his appearance could be interpreted as proving the defendant's point that the trial was politically motivated. Secondly, the prosecution's purpose in calling him was unclear, since he did not bring any substantial evidence to the case. At best, calling him might have been intended to confirm Milošević's *de facto* authority, but other witnesses were better placed to do this and did so more successfully. Thirdly, Bakalli was ill-prepared and was an easy prey for Milošević, who managed to discredit his testimony.[17] For example, Bakalli claimed that the notorious speech that Milošević made in Gazimestan on the 600th anniversary of the Battle of Kosovo brought about the constitutional changes that denied Kosovo its autonomy. Milošević only had to point out that those changes were made three months prior to the speech. Milošević also successfully discredited the witness by pointing out his role in the 1981 demonstrations in Kosovo. The traps set by Milošević proved too much for Bakalli.[18]

The second defeat for the prosecution came soon afterwards. The judges decided to deny them the second witness, since it was considered that his statement would be "second-hand" evidence.[19] This was followed by a number of Kosovo Albanian witnesses testifying about the conduct of operations in Kosovo and the crimes committed by Belgrade forces against them. Milošević cross-examined each one and tried hard to discredit their testimony. In some cases he was helped by the witnesses themselves, as they sometimes changed their testimony and often seemed insecure and confused. The witness of a massacre in Izbica described how he survived an execution from only a few metres and showed his shirt with bullet holes in the back. Asked whether he was wounded, he answered negatively, explaining that God saved him.[20] Much of this testimony tended to have a negative effect upon the public perception of the trial and on the material evidence that could contribute either to successful prosecution or to the historical record.

The prosecution wasted a lot of time and energy in demonstrating that the alleged crimes had happened.[21] It was widely assumed that the Prosecutor would gain an easy success in the Kosovo part of the case. After all, the original indictment over Kosovo had come in 1999 (rather than years earlier regarding Croatia and Bosnia) because a strong case seemed possible with Kosovo. However, in the words of Dušan Pavlović, otherwise a strong supporter of the ICTY, "if the Prosecutor is hoping to prove anybody's guilt on the basis of most of the testimonies that have been heard so far, the [Serbs] should better start preparing for Milošević's return."[22] Even the few Serbian witnesses who appeared proved to be of little value to the case, since Milošević was able to compromise almost all of their statements. The first "insider" witness, Ratomir Tanić, was received with great scepticism in Serbia. He testified on his role as an infiltrator in Serbia's opposition parties and described how he participated in many political meetings. His most valuable testimony concerned the parallel command structure created within the regime which went from Milošević through Deputy Prime Minister Šainović to General Nebojša Pavković, who at the time was Commander of the Third Army responsible for Kosovo. This was hailed as a great breakthrough. It was a useful confirmation of something that was "common knowledge" in Serbia; in fact, it had been confirmed by General Momčilo Perišić after his dismissal. Thus, it validated Milošević's authority for trial purposes and added weight to the historical record, but it was neither a dramatic nor a significant contribution to the trial itself.

Dragan Karleuša, the high-ranking police officer in charge of investigating trucks with Albanian corpses found in the Danube, proved to be of very little help. Although he could testify on the investigation, the judges were surprised that the investigation had not yet managed to locate all of the bodies from the trucks in question. Karleuša then testified on a statement written by Radomir Marković, former head of the Security Service, in which Marković described a meeting about the operations in Kosovo to clear out dead bodies. Milošević pounced on this immediately. He claimed that the statement was probably made under duress, since it was clearly not true.[23] Marković confirmed this a few days later when he testified that the statement was only an interpretation of what he said during the interrogation. In clarification he said that what was discussed was the usual process of clearing dead bodies from a battlefield. He denied that his statement concerned the concealing of the bodies of executed Albanians.[24] Marković's testimony remained subject to controversy in the cases brought against him in Serbia.

In the Kosovo part of the trial, the most impressive witnesses were politicians (with the exception of Bakalli). Most of these were Albanians and representatives of the international community; none of them was Serbian. Milošević's unsuccessful sparring with Paddy Ashdown had questionable value for the case, but showed Milošević in a different light. He lost his nerve in the robust exchanges with Ashdown and seemed to be a less skilful debater than many had originally thought. Addressing Milošević directly, Ashdown accepted the challenge to debate what the accused called "NATO aggression" and the "legitimacy" of the struggle against terrorism. Even when he agreed with the accused that the Kosovo Liberation Army (UÇK) was a terrorist organisation, Ashdown missed no opportunity of denouncing what he saw as an unacceptable level of the use of force on the part of Belgrade. The exchanges between the two had a curious resemblance to a televised debate, with the two politicians as central figures, overshadowing the Prosecutor and judges. For a time, the courtroom looked more like a talk show studio than a tribunal, much to the despair of the three-judge panel.

Although no one during the Kosovo part of the trial was as successful as Ashdown, other politicians, such as Ibrahim Rugova, long-time leader of the Kosovo Albanians and president of the U.N.-administered province, did not allow Milošević to walk over them. Rugova's testimony brought no apparent benefit to the case, but did serve as a clear example of a further politicization of the courtroom. Just as Milošević used the courtroom primarily to address an audience back in Serbia, Rugova was addressing an audience in Kosovo that might be expected to vote for him. He calmly answered questions and refused to look at Milošević during cross-examination, carefully evading the few traps set by the accused.[25]

One success for the Prosecutor, although not an expected one, came from the last two witnesses before the summer recess on 26 July 2002. The cross-examination of Radomir Marković was not the silver bullet the Prosecutor might have expected, given this witness's key position, but it was not a self-defeating shot in the foot either. Although he did not provide evidence to back the allegations concerning Milošević's personal criminal responsibility, Marković was helpful in identifying more potential insider witnesses. So impressed was the Office of the Prosecutor that it used the summer recess to track down former (and present) high-ranking MUP (Serbian Interior Ministry forces) and regular army officers, but it was unsuccessful in persuading them to testify (for example, MUP General Dragan Ilić).

Marković also showed, unwillingly, that Milošević was well informed and that he received daily briefings from the head of the MUP, Vlajko Stojiljković, one of four original Kosovo indictees who subsequently committed suicide. With the testimonies of Markovic, Ratomir Tanić, and the police technician in charge of disposing of the trucks mentioned above, the prosecution managed to portray a strong picture of the way Serbia and the Federal Republic of Yugoslavia (FRY) functioned. Hallmarks of this regime were the infiltration of political parties and an atmosphere of fear, wherein any discovered bodies, such as those mentioned above, were destroyed before any investigation could establish where they were from.[26] These were significant, but limited, contributions to the Prosecutor's case.

By the end of the Kosovo phase of the trial, the overall impression was mixed. The judges had expressed their frustration at the large number of witnesses. Judge May even ventured to say that most of the witnesses had not spoken about the most important and most difficult part of the indictment: the participation in a joint criminal enterprise.[27] In contrast, to the observer—and it might be presumed, to the judges—there was credible testimony that confirmed the former Serbian leader's responsibility and seemed to point to the prospect of a conviction on at least one of the charges. There were also limited but useful contributions to the historical record, but only to the degree that evidence confirmed much that was already widely understood to be true. This was significant, but it amounted to far less than the rich evidentiary base that had been widely and reasonably anticipated.

The War in the West: Croatia and Bosnia

Marković's testimony was reinforced throughout the part of the trial that focused on Croatia and Bosnia-Hercegovina, as was the sense that Milošević had both knowledge of and control over events there. This is where the Prosecutor, after a poor initial showing, began to produce more interesting material. While this might not have been as useful for judicial purposes as might be supposed, it certainly added something in terms of history. The prosecution produced a large number of witnesses to show that Serbian Interior Ministry troops and special units were involved in the war in the west and that Milošević as president of Serbia had knowledge of and command responsibility for their actions. The evidence pointed towards the existence of a "Serbian Project"[28] that was led by Milošević with the able assistance of his security chiefs and their deputies, and in which regular and irregular armed groups played a vital part.

This part of the prosecution case saw an effort by the Prosecutor to prove a number of complicated points. First, it was argued that Serbia was directly involved in the war in Croatia and Bosnia-Hercegovina throughout the 1991–1995 period. This was alleged to have been through the role of its security forces, paramilitary units, and army units, or through the financing and overall support of local Serb forces in the two regions. Secondly, the Prosecutor continued to argue that the war was part of an overall "Serbian Project" planned and instigated by Milošević. Finally, the prosecution case tried to establish that crimes mentioned in the indictment had actually occurred by producing witnesses to such crimes.

A notable difference in these later phases of the trial was the smaller number of victims who testified. Two-thirds of the witnesses in the Kosovo part of the trial were witnesses to crimes and victims eager to tell their story. By contrast, the Prosecutor's strategy in the second part of the trial centred on proving a link between Milošević and the crimes that occurred in Croatia and Bosnia-Hercegovina by producing witnesses who knew the accused. These can be classified in six broad categories. The first involved high-ranking insiders, such as Milan Babić, president of the Croatian

Serb proto-state, Republika Srpska Krajina (RSK). The second group included low-ranking soldiers and others who participated on the Serbian side, most of whom testified as protected witnesses. The third set of witnesses comprised international actors such as General Rupert Smith, commander of U.N. forces in Bosnia-Hercegovina during 1995, and General Wesley Clark, Supreme Allied Commander in NATO during the Kosovo campaign. The fourth category comprised "experts," such as analysts in the Prosecutor's office and military intelligence officers from NATO countries. The fifth group included prominent political actors from the Yugoslav lands, who had material evidence to offer on the Serbian leader's role and its impact, such as Ante Marković, the last prime minister of the Socialist Federative Republic of Yugoslavia (SFRY), and Stipe Mesić, former president of the SFRY and president of Croatia. Finally, the Prosecutor called a number of victim-witnesses, but, as indicated above, significantly fewer than in the Kosovo phase of the prosecution.

The change in the prosecution's strategy meant that fewer victims had the opportunity to talk about their experiences. The Prosecutor judged that the victims would not be able to make the crucial link for which she was looking. In practice, testimony from individuals such as witness B-1115, who spent 18 months in a Bosnian Serb prison where he suffered constant abuse, did little to advance the case.[29] However, they did help to confirm that the crimes set out in the indictment actually happened; and they ensured that victims had a voice, which was an important aspect of the "peace through justice" mission of the Tribunal.[30] Hence the trial chamber heard witnesses in this category, many of them people who had to use a pseudonym and give evidence under protective measures. These testimonies often concentrated on the role of paramilitary units or reports of atrocities committed by Belgrade forces—the JNA (Yugoslav People's Army), the JSO (Jedinica za Specijalne Operacije), and other units with a link to Serbia.[31] Witness B-1058 described how her son was murdered by Arkan's Tigers in Zvornik, Bosnia, [32] while witness B-1701 told the story of how he escaped two executions. Perhaps Sulejman Tihić, a member of the tripartite Bosnian presidency, gave the most compelling testimony. Testifying on 2 December 2003, he told of the takeover of the town of Bosanski Šamac by what he described as "Arkan's forces" in April 1992.[33] Tihić was taken prisoner and severely beaten. He was transported between various prisons in Bosnia, finally ending up in Sremska Mitrovica, in Serbia, from where he was released in August 1992. His testimony gave important insight into the cooperation between the JNA and the paramilitary units and, if assumed to be truthful and credible, to Serbia's direct involvement.[34]

The most widely publicized witnesses were those whom the prosecution presented as insiders, capable of revealing the inner workings of the Milošević regime and its involvement in the Yugoslav war. The willingness of such witnesses to testify concerning Croatia and Bosnia-Hercegovina contrasts with their absence at the Kosovo stage. Despite the apparent success of the Prosecutor in bringing insiders to The Hague, it should be noted that the most important witnesses never appeared.

These included Biljana Plavšić, Momčilo Perišić, Jovica Stanišić, and Franko Simatović 'Frenki', and their absence left an important gap in the story.

The prosecution case gained momentum when, on 18 November 2002, Milan Babić, president of the RSK from 1991 to 1995, began his 12-day-long testimony as protected witness C-061.[35] He testified on Milošević's role in instigating and supporting the rebellion of Serbs in Croatia, as well as in arming and controlling Croatian Serb forces through his security service chief, Jovica Stanišić (also an ICTY indictee). Babić's testimony exposed the extent to which Milošević had actively sparked the rebellion of Croatia's Serbian minority in the summer of 1990, using the security service and his control of the media in the process. According to Babić, it was Milošević-controlled propaganda that caused the radicalization of the Serbian position from seeking autonomy to demanding outright independence. Babić also outlined an aspect of Milošević's strategy that was confirmed by a number of other witnesses, namely his reliance on two chains of command: the first going through the JNA and territorial defence units; the second going through the Serbian security services and involving paramilitary units. The second chain of command was used to establish parallel structures that would undermine the Croatian Serb leadership. Babić claimed that Milošević never had any interest in the maintenance of the SFRY—the old Yugoslav federation—and that he wanted instead to establish a "Greater Serbia," incorporating all territories inhabited by Serbs.[36]

The next high-ranking witness to provide important insight into the workings of the Milošević regime and its strategy in Croatia and later Kosovo was General Aleksandar Vasiljević, head of the counter-intelligence arm of the JNA in 1991 and later deputy head of the same department during the war in Kosovo. Vasiljević confirmed that Milošević exerted influence over the rump presidency of the SFRY in 1991, giving him *de facto* control over the JNA (he also had, as president of Serbia, *de jure* control over Territorial Defence Units from Serbia, which found their way to Croatia and Bosnia). Vasiljević confirmed that despite the appearance of three armies (the VJ (Army of Yugoslavia), the VRS (Bosnian Serb Army), and the VSK (Croatian Serb Army)), the FRY (the "new Yugoslavia" proclaimed by Serbia and Montenegro in April 1992, following the shattering of the SFRY) treated them as one. Belgrade provided commanding officers for all three, with as many as 13,000 VJ officers serving in the armies of the other two "Serbian states" between 1992 and 1995. However, the most interesting part of the testimony was Vasiljević's insight into the training, equipping, and use of paramilitary forces throughout the war. He testified, for example, that the notorious Željko Ražnatović Arkan's Tigers were under the direct control of the Ministry of the Interior of the Republic of Serbia and had special status. He also claimed that the army's General Staff had warned the President of Serbia of the crimes being committed by paramilitary units in Croatia—an important contribution potentially in terms of securing a war crimes conviction. He also claimed that the same was true during the war in Kosovo.[37]

After failing a number of times during the Kosovo phase of the prosecution, the Prosecutor finally managed to introduce Zoran Lilić, former president of the FRY and a long-time a member of Milošević's inner circle. Lilić confirmed the link already identified between the three Serbian armed forces by explaining that the wages for some 4,000 VRS officers were paid out of the Belgrade budget. According to his account, those on the payroll included General Ratko Mladić, infamous commander of the VRS and perhaps the single most important war crimes suspect after Milošević (still at large at the time of this writing), who remained on the payroll even after the Srebrenica massacre in 1995. In Lilić's words, the financing of the VRS was only terminated in 2001. Lilić also provided an account of the rising importance of the Ministry of the Interior of Serbia and the army's loss of influence as a result. Lilić confirmed other earlier evidence regarding the parallel command structures maintained by Milošević in order to circumvent and undermine the army. Lastly, in a crucial contribution, Lilić testified that Milošević had nothing to do with the Srebrenica massacre.[38] This, if taken as credible evidence, would run contrary to the belief of many observers, but confirm the judgement of some others.[39] Most important, it could help to make a genocide conviction against the former Serbian leader very difficult.

In October 2003, the prosecution produced another witness whose testimony it hoped would rival Babić's. Milan Milanović was a deputy defence minister in the Republika Sprska Krajina and testified that the majority of the officer corps in the Croatian Serb military came from the JNA and later the VJ, and that all RSK military personnel were formally members of the VJ and on its payroll.[40] However, the prosecution then called Borisav Jović, another Milošević insider and key ally in the break-up of the SFRY. Jović did not produce the smoking gun that the prosecution had sought throughout the trial. Nevertheless, he shed further light on the workings of the Milošević regime. His testimony centred on his published diaries,[41] cited on a number of occasions in the prosecution case, and large parts of which the Trial Chamber agreed to admit as evidence. Jović's crucial claims were that Milošević had absolute authority in Serbia, that he was not a nationalist but simply loved power, and that he manipulated the news media. Jović was also able to give first-hand accounts of key negotiations in the final days of the SFRY. However, during cross-examination, Jović mostly agreed with Milošević. He claimed that neither he nor the defendant had any knowledge of the Vukovar massacres, and he argued that the only plan they had was the preservation of the SFRY. Even that plan is open to interpretation, given that others, such as General Veljko Kadijević,[42] have stressed that their aim was the preservation of Yugoslavia for those who wanted it—a subtle but important difference. Moreover, there were clearly preparations for a set of linked Serbian "statelets." The April 1992 Federal Republic of Yugoslavia Constitution made that clear in Article 2, which indicates that other states might join Serbia and Montenegro in the future.[43]

The evidence produced by insiders was matched by that of scores of protected and unprotected witnesses who were in one way or another implicated in the Serbian effort during the war. Despite the lack of media attention, these witness statements and the transcripts from the trial provide a valuable source of information on the Yugoslav war for the historical record. Important evidence was presented by a number of witnesses who decided to testify under their own identity. Early in the Croatia and Bosnia-Hercogvina phase of the trial, two former JNA counter-intelligence officers testified to the extent of Belgrade's control of Croatian Serb and Bosnian Serb militaries. Mustafa Kandić and Slobodan Lazarević each gave accounts of the arming of the Serbs in Croatia and Bosnia. Lazarević testified that all the major decisions were made by Belgrade, and he connected Milošević with those decisions.[44] A year later, Dobrila Gajić-Glišić, who worked in the cabinet of the former Serbian defence minister Genral Tomislav Simović in 1991, testified on Milošević's plans for a Serbian army (which were later abandoned) and on the close links Arkan had with the Serbian president. She also testified that Milošević had to be aware of the crimes committed by Arkan's forces as well as other paramilitary units because Arkan was openly boasting about it to General Simović.[45]

However, most of the evidence linking Serbian security forces and the VJ to the Bosnian Serb and Croatian Serb militaries came from witnesses who testified under protection. A number of former "Red Berets" (members of the JSO) came forward with accounts of involvement in Bosnia and Croatia and the crimes they committed.[46] Other protected witnesses testified about arms-smuggling operations from Serbia under the auspices of the Ministry of the Interior and the VJ.[47] The prosecution also produced witnesses who confirmed that, as officers of the former JNA, they continued to be paid by and answer to a personnel section in Belgrade's Ministry of Defence.[48]

Links between the Ministry of the Interior and paramilitary forces were confirmed by most of the above witnesses. However, it was a former secretary in Arkan's headquarters (witness B-129) who provided the most vivid account of the direct link and financing that existed between Arkan's SDG (the Tigers) and MUP officials[49]. Her testimony outlined a special link that Arkan had to the office of "Frenki" Simatović of the JSO, as well as the inter-operability of the two units. B-129 testified that Arkan would not lead the unit into battle for fear of being recognised and implicating Serbia in the war in Bosnia. Instead she claimed that a JSO commander, Milorad Luković 'Legija', led mixed units of Tigers and JSO personnel without insignia on numerous operations throughout Bosnia. Her testimony confirmed that of Vasiljević, witness B-24 (who gave evidence on 19 May 2003), and a number of others.

As in the Kosovo part of the case, the prosecution decided to devote important space to high-ranking (and some less so) outsiders who had dealings with Milošević throughout the years of the war. General Wesley Clark, former Supreme Commander Allied Forces Europe, and Lord David Owen, former EU negotiator, gave evidence aimed at proving Milošević's knowledge of events. These witnesses had arguable value for the process itself, but their testimony certainly provided additional material for the historical record. To their testimonies were added those of U.N. officials, negotiators, and other outsiders whose views the prosecution insisted on presenting.

British General Sir Rupert Smith testified in October 2003 that from his experience as commander of the UN peace force in Bosnia, it was clear that Milošević was superior to Mladić.[50] Smith also claimed that Milošević was aware of the killings in Srebrenica as they were happening (although this did not necessarily mean that he was behind them). Lord David Owen gave a somewhat different account and one much less friendly to the prosecution's case by claiming that Milošević wanted peace from April 1993.[51] General Wesley Clark testified on the central role played by Milošević in any negotiations for the Serbian side and how the former Serbian leader regularly exercised authority over the Bosnian Serb negotiators. This suggested to General Clark that Milošević was in charge.[52] Clark also expressed his belief that Milošević had prior knowledge of the Srebrenica massacre, although this did not mean that he was necessarily responsible for it, and certainly not that he was behind it.

The prosecution called on a number of expert witnesses to support their claim that Milošević had ultimate control in Serbia and that Belgrade forces were directly involved in the war in Croatia and Bosnia-Hercegovina. On 10 April 2003, a financial expert working for the OTP, Morten Torkildsen, gave evidence relating to the cash flow from Serbia into Republika Srpska and Republika Srpska Krajina between 1992 and 1994. His evidence was based on tens of thousands of pages of documents concerning financial transactions. Torkildsen, confirming Lilic's statement, testified that there was a single financial plan from which all three armies—the VJ, VRS, and VSK—were financed.[53]

In support of this view, the prosecution introduced a report prepared by a Belgian military intelligence officer who studied the Balkans from 1992. Reynaud Theunens focused on what the Prosecutor described as the "issues of military command and control, as well as the Yugoslav army's relations with the various armed groups that operated in Bosnia and Croatia." He concluded that the Serbian authorities not only created the Croatian Serb and Bosnian Serb militaries and supported them in material and financial ways, but also supplied them with officers and closely coordinated operations with them. Theunens said that evidence shows that JNA units operated in close cohesion with paramilitary and Territorial Defence forces in the Vukovar area in 1991. Additionally, Milošević and VJ Chief of Staff Momčilo Perišić had received all daily combat reports of RSK activity at least from 1993, and VJ troops assisted VRS forces in a number of operations in eastern Bosnia. Theunens also confirmed previous testimony by others regarding tight links between Serbian paramilitaries and MUP forces.[54]

Finally, in an attempt to provide more historical context and to show Milošević's role in the break-up of Yugoslavia, the prosecutor called a number of witnesses who had close dealings with Milošević in the last days of the SFRY. Stipe Mesić, former president of the Presidency of the SFRY; Ante Marković, its last prime minister; and

Hrvoje Šarinić, one of Franjo Tudjman's most trusted advisors, each gave testimony to show that Milošević was instrumental in the break-up and had remained in control of Serbian forces throughout the former Yugoslavia. Marković's testimony provided an interesting account of the final days of the SFRY, and is all the more valuable because it was the first time he had spoken publicly about the dissolution of the state since 1991. It also served to confirm the validity of evidence that the Prosecutor had only been partly successful at introducing at the very first trial that opened the Tribunal.[55] This was evidence on Milošević's direct links with the Bosnian Serb leadership in the early days of dissolution and war, including his specific instructions to work with particular JNA officers.[56]

Apart from being the first instance of a serving head of state testifying at an international trial, President of Croatia Mesić's appearance in the witness box and his cross-examination offered an insight into the content of the political debate in the SFRY in the early 1990s. In a moment of sincerity, Mesić admitted that "they all took part in the destruction of Yugoslavia" (reminiscent of the original title of his book on the subject, which has subsequently changed[57]), but blamed Milošević for instigating it with his "Greater Serbia" policy. Mesić claimed that in May 1991 Milošević had acquired control over the Yugoslav presidency, which was the supreme commander of the JNA. He accused Milošević of "Serbianizing" the JNA and using it to achieve his own political goals. Mesić also provided a vivid account of relations between the key actors in the SFRY, as well as a portrait of Milošević's methods, accusing him of double-crossing everyone, from his enemies to his closest associates, including the Croatian Serbs.[58]

Among the last witnesses, the prosecution produced Hrvoje Šarinić, who was Tudjman's envoy to Milošević from 1993. Šarinić's testimony was an interesting insight into the Machiavellian world of Balkan politics and nefarious deals. He confirmed the agreement that existed between Milošević and Tudjman on dividing Bosnia, but shed more light on the thinking behind it. According to Šarinić, Tudjman viewed Bosnia as a historical anomaly while Milošević viewed Muslims as a demographic threat to both Serbs and Croats. Šarinić also admitted that Milošević always denied having control over the Croatian Serb leadership, and that he was plotting against the Bosnian Serb leaders from at least 1995. The court heard that Milošević reportedly admitted that Arkan was working for him, something denied by the accused during cross-examination.[59] Overall, Šarinić's testimony provided important corroboration for much of what had been heard in the courtroom during the trial.

Significant question marks remained against the prosecution case concerning Croatia and Bosnia-Hercegovina when it closed on 25 February 2004. The issue of internationality regarding the period of armed conflict in Croatia was still an open question. It seemed likely that a number of charges would fall if it could not be agreed that this was a clear "international" conflict. There was a chance that responsibility for crimes against humanity in Croatia might be established and a greater chance that the same might be true for Bosnia-Hercegovina. On the other hand, it appeared most probable that the genocide charges would fail. Thus, in terms of law and justice the prospects were mixed. However, much of the evidence introduced clearly demonstrated the former Serbian leader's central role in much of what happened. Even if this would not eventually meet the test of truth at trial, it added significantly to the evidence base for establishing truth in the historical record.

Conclusion

An important part of the legacy of the Milošević trial in terms of historical record is the vast array of evidence presented by the prosecution. This goes a long way towards establishing a historical narrative of the events and includes military and political documents, forensic evidence (including pictures and videos), and tapes of phone conversations.

Among the official documents presented as evidence, the prosecution case introduced several aimed at showing the extent of Serbia's involvement in the war in Croatia and Bosnia-Hercegovina. Prosecutors presented the Trial Chamber with evidence of financing from Belgrade including pay orders, wages, and letters requesting money for the purposes of paying the armed forces. Other items documented the role of the VJ in the recruitment and training of RSK troops. Many of the documents that were presented as evidence had been previously classified and were obtained with great difficulty by the ICTY. But the documents presented by Reynaud Theunens go a long way towards establishing links among the three armed forces—links that were first sketched in evidence at the Kosovo section of the trial. Nevertheless, there are a number of problems with some of the evidence. The trial's evidentiary value is somewhat tempered by the large number of closed sessions, leaving observers and the public unable to gauge the merit of some of the material being considered and so limiting any judgements, at least *ad interim*. Moreover, the limitations required by the need to protect certain witnesses, the absence of some important witnesses altogether, and the absence of some documents all set further boundaries on the inferences to be drawn at the end of the prosecution case.

When the prosecution case ended on 25 February 2004, it was possible to draw clear conclusions on several aspects of both the judicial and historical quests for truth. In terms of the judicial measure of truth, there were significant problems regarding the need to demonstrate a joint and common plan regarding Serbian action in Kosovo, as well as important difficulties in establishing evidence of the defendant's responsibility for genocide. Moreover, while evidence was produced for Milošević's pivotal role in making the war in the west, it was not at all clear that it would meet the test of subject matter jurisdiction. Failure to do so would mean that some material evidence would not be admitted into evidence for judgement; thus there could be no prospect of conviction regarding the relevant charges. Clearly the poor performance of the Prosecutor, reinforced by other problems such as the

189

defendant's continuing ill health, have produced very uneven judicial proceedings. At the same time, some of the most important and vital evidence introduced to demonstrate the former Serbian leader's role could help obtain conviction on other charges. Such evidence includes the tapes, written and oral evidence of the last SFRY prime minister, Ante Marković; the testimony of the Serbian interior minister, Radomir Marković; and the testimony of the leader of the RSK, Milan Babić.

All this evidence can serve the quest for historical truth. While the prosecution case regarding Kosovo was weak, it was not without some benefit to the record—confirming many events and showing that Milošević had extensive knowledge of and was at the heart of developments. However, it was the evidence clearly linking him to the organization and operation of Serbian forces in the war in the west that emerged as the major achievement of the prosecution case. By producing an array of witnesses from different backgrounds and with knowledge at different levels, the Prosecutor added significantly to the body of evidence available—albeit for the most part confirming existing knowledge and understanding. The problem in the relationship between the two quests for truth might well be that failure to establish an incontestable outcome judicially might undermine the degree to which a clear historical record is accepted as being beyond dispute by non-specialists. The twin quests for truth could each produce a worthy outcome, but the evidence seems stronger for history than for judicial process. In the final analysis, however, perhaps the most significant contribution of all was the ICTY's instrumental role in removing Milošević from the political scene in Serbia—another dimension altogether in the interaction of history, justice, and peace.

NOTES

1. We wish to express our thanks to those who have assisted by reading, commenting, and indeed editing drafts of this article, which at one stage was on the way to being a short book. The most prominent of these are Tom Emmert, Charles Ingrao, Bob Donia, and Rachel Kerr. But we are also grateful for comments from members of the War Crimes Research Group at King's College London, Mark Davison, and Sasa Fatić.

2. James Gow, *The Serbian Project and Its Adversaries: A Strategy of War Crimes* (London: Hurst, 2003); James Gow and Ivan Zveržhanovski "Legitimacy and the Military Revisited: Civil–Military Relations and the Future of Yugoslavia," in Anthony Forster, Tim Edmunds, and Andrew Cottey, eds, *Soldiers and Societies in Post-Communist Europe: Legitimacy and Change* (London: Palgrave, 2003), pp. 203–218. As noted below, the Prosecutor argued that the cases against Milošević regarding Kosovo, on the one hand, and Croatia and Bosnia, on the other, should be treated together because they constituted one armed conflict, albeit with geographical and temporal differences. This is a sensible view, given that no one would regard the war in different theatres of the Second World War at different stages as being separate wars.

3. In addition to our own work, cited already, those seeking further understanding of the war, might consult any of the following instances of what has become a voluminous literature. Sabrina Ramet, *Balkan Babel*, 4th edn (Boulder: Westview, 2002); Laura Silber and Allan Little, *The Death of Yugoslavia* (aka *Yugoslavia: Death of a Nation*),

2nd edn (London: Penguin, 1997); Christopher Bennett, *Yugoslavia's Bloody Collapse* (London: Hurst, 1992); Gow, *Triumph of the Lack of Will: International Diplomacy and the Yugoslav Crisis* (New York: Columbia University Press, 1997); Jan Willem Honig and Norbert Both, *Srebrenica: Record of a War Crime* (London: Penguin, 1996); Louis Sell, *Milošević and the Destruction of Yugoslavia* (Durham, NC: Duke University Press, 2002).

4. On the creation of the Tribunal and discussion of its purposes at the legal–political boundary, see the excellent volume by Rachel Kerr, *The International Criminal Tribunal for the Former Yugoslavia: A Study in Law, Politics and Diplomacy* (Oxford: Oxford University Press, 2004).

5. On the peace through justice argument see Aurélien J. Colson, "The Logic of Peace and the Logic of Justice," *International Relations*, Vol. 15, No. 1, 2000, pp. 51–62.

6. The same is implicitly understood to apply to the equivalent IMT at Tokyo for war crimes in the Far East, although the latter is often overlooked in discourse on the benefits of international trials for transitional justice. However, there are significant differences in the records of the IMTs. Although both entail questions of "victors' justice" generally, as well as weaknesses of process, the criticisms that can be raised are more significant regarding Tokyo than Nuremberg. The Nuremberg legacy as transformative certainly does not apply in the Far Eastern context, where the trials were almost entirely ignored by Japanese society, including scholars, for the first forty years after the end of that war.

7. See Kerr, *International Criminal Tribunal*.

8. The International Military Tribunal statutes allowed for what would be deemed "hearsay" at criminal hearings, such as that in The Hague, which aspires to operate at the highest standards of criminal justice. This meant that allegations or assertions by those claiming to know would be accepted at Nuremberg but would be rejected by the ICTY.

9. On the problems of establishing subject matter jurisdiction, see Gow, *Serbian Project*, Chapter 1. Among the issues that could affect the Milošević trial is that of international-ity, given grey areas regarding both the internal or international status of the conflict and also the Serbian leader's formal status regarding the parties to the conflict.

10. As already indicated, in note 1, our understanding is that there was one continuous war with different theatres, with Belgrade at the core of that war.

11. Judge Richard May died on 1 July 2004.

12. *Prosecutor* v. *Slobodan Milošević*, IT-01-50-I

13. *Prosecutor* v. *Slobodan Milošević*, IT-01-51-I

14. Members of the U.S. negotiating team to the ICC negotiations in Rome have confirmed to Gow that when the U.S. found itself in a position where it was unable to sign the Rome Treaty creating the International Criminal Court, the approach was then one of "wait and see," regarding prosecutorial performance. This meant that future decisions were to be gauged against U.S. judgements regarding the "reliability" of international prosecutors.

15. Our assumption here is that a competent prosecution case, producing clear evidence to support the allegations against Milošević and others, could have a positive influence on Serbia—that is, a recognition of and coming to terms with the past. We do not presume that the population of Serbia, including its political and media elite, are incapable of recognising clear empirical evidence and of dealing with that evidence over time. While strong resistance to international initiatives is all that could be expected following years of externally imposed economic sanctions and the 1999 NATO bombing campaign, this does not necessarily equate to a reluctance to recognise the wrongs of the Serbian authorities and of some Serbian citizens. The indictment of the Prosecutor's performance is to have had a retrograde impact in this context. A convincing case, in contrast, would

have fostered balanced awareness of war crimes issues and might have assisted in reform. Of course, we recognise that the Tribunal is one factor among many that affect the political scene in Serbia. However, it is a salient factor, with an identifiable impact.

16. *IWPR Tribunal Update*, No. 258, 2002.
17. *The Independent*, 20 February 2002.
18. *Vreme*, 21 February 2002; *NIN*, 21 February 2002.
19. *The Independent*, 21 February 2002.
20. *Vreme*, 1 August 2004.
21. While there can be no doubt that establishing that the alleged crimes had occurred was essential to the prosecution case, the more important demand on the Prosecutor was to demonstrate the connection of the accused to the crimes. Thus, taking time to confirm repeatedly that which had already been established, seemingly because witnesses were available, did not appear to be the best use of the court time available for making the prosecution case.
22. *Reporter*, 9 April 2002.
23. *New York Times*, 24 July 2002.
24. *New York Times*, 27 July 2002.
25. *Vreme*, 9 May 2002.
26. *New York Times*, 26 August 2002.
27. *Vreme*, 13 June 2002.
28. See Gow, *Serbian Project*.
29. *IWPR Tribunal Update*, No. 39, 2003.
30. Kerr, *International Criminal Tribunal for the Former Yugoslavia*.
31. For explanation concerning these and other armed forces contributing to the Serbian project, see Gow, *Serbian Project*, Chapter 3.
32. *Prosecutor* v. *Slobodan Milošević*, IT-02-54 case transcripts (9 September 2003), < http://www.un.org/icty/transe54/030909ED.htm >.
33. "Arkan" was the *nom de guerre* of Željko Ražnatović, founder and leader of the Serbian Volunteer Guard (SDG), also know as "the Tigers," a paramilitary force established with the cooperation of the Serbian Security Service and elements in the Belgrade military. See Gow, *Serbian Project*.
34. *Prosecutor* v. *Slobodan Milošević*, IT-02-54 case transcripts (2 December 2003), < http://www.un.org/icty/transe54/031203ED.htm >; *IWPR Tribunal Update*, No. 337, 2003.
35. Babić first appeared as witness C-036, but as many observers at the trial guessed his identity, the court gave him a new witness number, C-061. As protected identity meant that most of his testimony was in closed session, Babić subsequently decided to reveal his identity to be able to respond to Miloševic's cross-examination in a public session.
36. *IWPR Tribunal Update*, No. 290, 2002; *IWPR Tribunal Update*, No. 292, 2002; *Prosecutor* v. *Slobodan Milošević*, IT-02-54 case transcripts (18 November 2002 to 3 December 2002), < http://www.un.org/icty/cases/indictindex-e.htm >.
37. *Prosecutor* v. *Slobodan Milošević*, IT-02-54 case transcripts (5–13 February 2003), < http://www.un.org/icty/cases/indictindex-e.htm >; *IWPR Tribunal Update*, No. 300, 2003.
38. *Prosecutor* v. *Slobodan Milošević*, IT-02-54 case transcripts (17 June 2003), < http://www.un.org/icty/cases/indictindex-e.htm >; *IWPR Tribunal Update*, No. 317, 2003.
39. Gow, *Serbian Project*, p. 188.
40. See *Prosecutor* v. *Slobodan Milošević*, IT-02-54 case transcripts (8 October 2003), < http://www.un.org/icty/transe54/031008ED.htm >.
41. Borisav Jović, *Poslednji Dani SFRJ: Izvodi iz Dnevnika* (Belgrade: Politika, 1994).

42. Veljko Kadijević, *Moje Vidjenje Raspada* (Belgrade: Politika, 1993).
43. See *Prosecutor* v. *Slobodan Milošević*, IT-02-54 case transcripts (18–20 November 2003), < http://www.un.org/icty/cases/indictindex-e.htm >.
44. *IWPR Tribunal Update*, No. 287, 2002.
45. *IWPR Tribunal Update*, No. 330, 2003.
46. For example, witness K-2 (9 January 2003); witness C-17 (11 June 2003); *Prosecutor* v. *Slobodan Milošević*, IT-02-54 case transcripts, < http://www.un.org/icty/cases/indictindex-e.htm >.
47. For example, witness B-1709 gave an account of an elaborate operation involving the army, the security service, and an organisation formed to provide humanitarian aid, and aimed at transferring army weapons to Bosnian Serbs. Witness C-013 (27 January 2003) testified on the delivery of weapons from Serbia to Croatian Serbs with the help of state institutions. *Prosecutor* v. *Slobodan Milošević*, IT-02-54 case transcripts (27 January 2003), < http://www.un.org/icty/transe54/030127ED.htm >.
48. For example, witness B-127 (22 July 2003); *Prosecutor* v. *Slobodan Milošević*, IT-02-54 case transcripts, < http://www.un.org/icty/transe54/030722ED.htm >.
49. *IWPR Tribunal Update*, No. 309, 2003.
50. *IWPR Tribunal Update*, No. 328, 2003.
51. See Lord David Owen's testimony; *Prosecutor* v. *Slobodan Milošević*, IT-02-54 case transcripts (3–4 November 2003), < http://www.un.org/icty/transe54/031104ED.htm >.
52. See *Prosecutor* v. *Slobodan Milošević*, IT-02-54 case transcripts (15–16 December 2003), < http://www.un.org/icty/transe54/031215ED.htm >.
53. See *Prosecutor* v. *Slobodan Milošević*, IT-02-54 case transcripts (10–11 April 2003), < http://www.un.org/icty/cases/indictindex-e.htm >.
54. See *Prosecutor* v. *Slobodan Milošević*, IT-02-54 case transcripts (28 January 2004), < http://www.un.org/icty/transe54/040128ED.htm >.
55. *Prosecutor* v. *Duško Tadić*, IT-94-1.
56. *Prosecutor* v. *Slobodan Milošević*, IT-02-54 case transcripts (23 October 2003), < http://www.un.org/icty/transe54/031023ED.htm >.
57. Stipe Mesić, *Kako Je Srušena Jugoslavija* (Zagreb: Globus, 1994) was originally published as *Kako Smo Srušili Jugoslaviju* (Zagreb: Globus, 1993)—the original title meaning "How We Destroyed Yugoslavia" and the later title more passively meaning "How Yugoslavia Was Destroyed."
58. See *Prosecutor* v. *Slobodan Milošević*, IT-02-54, case transcripts (1–2 October 2004), < http://www.un.org/icty/transe54/021001IT.htm >,
59. See *Prosecutor* v. *Slobodan Milošević*, IT-02-54 case transcripts (21–22 January 2004), < http://www.un.org/icty/cases/indictindex-e.htm >.

Facing the Violent Past: Discussions with Serbia's Youth

Maryanne Yerkes

As nations emerge from repressive regimes and societies begin to rebuild following violent intranational conflict, the notion of "facing the past" has become an increasingly important and pressing issue. How should new regimes address the crimes of their predecessors? How should societies deal with individuals who committed grave crimes against humanity? Who should be held responsible for what happened during the dark periods of violence and war?

While there has been an explosion of literature and debate on the topic of facing the past, most of the focus has been on transitional justice and, more specifically, on the theoretical, legalistic, and procedural aspects of transitional justice. Very little attention has been given to how local people, those most affected by the transitional processes, feel about the sensitive issue of confronting the past. How do they perceive initiatives purportedly aimed at assisting the society in addressing this difficult topic? What does "facing the past" mean to them?

I explored these questions in a study conducted in Serbia from October 2001 until December 2002. The study examined how young people in Serbia view the discourse on facing the past and, more specifically, how they perceive the local, national, and international initiatives purportedly aimed at confronting the past. In the present article I will submit the research findings on the youths' perceptions of local and national initiatives, homing in on the variables that increased or decreased their trust in these initiatives. In presenting a detailed analysis of each of these variables, I will also make suggestions on how the initiators of facing processes may address the concerns manifested in the variables and potentially improve the public's perceptions of their programs on facing the past. It is important to keep in mind that this article is focused on data collected in 2001 and 2002; therefore, more recent developments on the topic are not addressed.

Relevance of the Study for the Initiators of Facing Processes

During a recent round-table discussion at the American Bar Association, the venerable Justice Richard J. Goldstone, former Chief Prosecutor of the United Nations International Criminal Tribunals for the former Yugoslavia and Rwanda, advised the roomful of international lawyers, human rights activists, and transitional justice experts not to forget who the "clients" of transitional justice processes are: the local people. They are, after all, the people who will be most affected by the facing processes, be they victims, perpetrators, or bystanders. Unfortunately, this advice is rarely incorporated into current literature and debate on transitional justice, particularly at the international level. By seeing the facing process only through a transitional justice lens, many scholars and practitioners focus primarily on state-level and other top-down processes that rarely consider and involve the people. Lower-level processes, such as grassroots and civil society initiatives, escape the view of analysts, as do the opinions of the "clients" of the processes.

Should the views of local people matter simply because they are the ones most affected by the initiatives? Is it merely an act of kind consideration to hear their views? I argue that it is in the best interest of the initiators of facing processes to inquire into the opinions and concerns of the local people, since they will ultimately play an important role in confirming or denying the legitimacy of the processes. As noted by Carla Hesse and Robert Post in their book on human rights and transitional processes, successful legal institutions—and, one can argue, general facing pro-cesses—depend on widespread legitimacy.[1] In this context, legitimacy is not deter-mined solely by what is considered right according to the law—as is the case in the current discourse on transitional justice and facing processes—but also according to the people. Do the people affected by these processes consider them legitimate and trustworthy? Why or why not? How can processes be improved to become more legitimate and trustworthy in the eyes of the people without compromising their goals of confronting the past?

These should be areas of interest for all proponents of transitional justice and facing processes. While strict adherents to theories of retributivism may only be concerned with the punishment of crimes and the prosecution of the guilty, most advocates of facing processes emphasize the societal benefits of confronting the past. For them, it is not simply a question of punishing abusers; one must also establish or re-establish the rule of law and pave a path for the democratization of the society. They frequently argue that the future of the society depends on a thorough con-fronting of the past.

With this interest in the societal benefits of facing processes, issues of trust and legitimacy cannot be ignored. If transitional justice initiatives and facing processes are to have a profound impact on the society at large, more research is needed on the factors that increase or decrease the level of trust local people have in these processes. It is precisely these factors that the present article explores.

Explanation of the Study

The study referred to in this article took place in Serbia between October 2001 and December 2002. During that time period, I lived and worked in Belgrade, and traveled frequently throughout the country and to other parts of the Balkans. Using documentation reviews, observations, and structured and unstructured qualitative interviews, I explored the dynamics of the facing process in Serbia, concentrating primarily on people's reactions to initiatives purportedly aimed at assisting the society in facing its violent past. In order to narrow the scope of the study, I ultimately focused my analysis on interviews conducted in Belgrade. A comparative study between people in rural and urban areas, or between Belgrade and the periphery, would have been extremely informative; however, while I did conduct numerous interviews outside of the capital, I did not have enough information for a comparative study.

The interviews, which lasted from 30 minutes to four hours, were divided into two sets: one focused on the target population, which was composed of "reform-minded," educated youth aged 25 to 35 and residing in Belgrade, and one focused on members of the Serbian elite who were engaged in or knowledgeable about the facing process (*e.g.*, political analysts, NGO representatives, academics, and journalists). A total of 78 qualitative interviews were conducted, 37 with the target population, and 41 with the Serbian elite.[2] This breakout of the interviews is represented in Table 1.

TABLE 1 Categorization of the interviewees

Category	Interviewees
Target population	37
Serbian elite (NGO representatives, political analysts, journalists, *etc.*)	41
Total	78

Concerning the target group, the term "reform-minded" referred to youth who either supported the DOS coalition (Democratic Opposition of Serbia) or OTPOR (the social movement "Resistance"), both of which played a significant role in ousting the Milošević regime from power in October 2000. "Educated" youth were youth who had attended courses at the university, though it was not required that they had actually completed their studies. The vast majority of the interviewees were not directly affiliated with a particular political party and they represented a wide variety of professional backgrounds, ranging from medical doctors to philosophy professors.

The broad categorization of "reform-minded" youth was a way to focus on youth who were interested in political change and supported or participated in democratization efforts, but were not unequivocally "pro-Western." I chose to focus on this target group because many analysts consider "reform-minded" youth to be the future of a "democratic Serbia," having supposedly opposed the Milošević regime and having played a role in his ousting from power, yet they rarely ask their opinions on topics such as facing the past.

The interviews with the Serbian elite shed light on the dynamics of the facing process in Serbia: Who are the actors? What is taking place at the different levels of society? How do the facing processes fit into the larger political, social, and economic context of post-war Serbia? They helped familiarize me with the current discourse on facing the past and the various reactions members of the Serbian elite

197

have to this discourse. The interviews also illustrated some of the major fissures within the NGO community specifically related to the sensitive topic of facing the past.

Understanding "Facing Processes" in Serbia

In this study, the term "facing processes" refers to initiatives purportedly aimed at shedding light on crimes committed during the recent Balkan wars and on events that led up to the wars. In addition to shedding light, these processes may also seek accountability for what happened and acknowledgment from the wider society. They may be organized at the international and national levels, such as prosecutions and truth commissions, or at the local level, such as civil society initiatives intended to encourage discussion and reflection on issues of guilt and responsibility.

Through an analysis of the facing processes taking place within Serbia, I discovered that the organizations and societal actors that were most vocal on the topic and were shaping the discourse on facing the past were local NGOs and independent media. Virtually nothing was happening at the state level. No significant reforms had been made in terms of education; and the Serbian Truth Commission, which had initially been supported by members of civil society and the international community, lost much of that support when the then Federal President Vojislav Koštunica became an advocate for the Commission. According to many civil society actors, Koštunica attempted to use the Truth Commission in order to avoid cooperation with the International Criminal Tribunal for the Former Yugoslavia (ICTY) and had too great an influence over the Commission. Whether or not this was the case, at the time the study was conducted, the Commission was not very productive and many Serbs were not even aware it existed.

It is also important to note that during the interviews the only local and national initiatives mentioned by the interviewees were those of the NGOs and the independent media. According to interviewees, this group of actors formed the discourse on facing the past, at least at the local and national levels. As this was the case, the research findings presented in this article refer to the "facing processes" of NGOs and the independent media. While the role of ICTY was also frequently mentioned, reactions to the Court are not specifically covered in this article. However, many of the factors that increased or decreased trust in local and national initiatives are also relevant for the Hague Tribunal.

Serbian Civil Society and "Facing the Past"

While Serbian NGOs and independent media were the most vociferous societal actors on facing the past, the work of several organizations is of particular relevance: the Humanitarian Law Fund, the Helsinki Committee for Human Rights in Serbia, and Radio/Television B92. These three organizations were the most outspoken on this difficult issue and were the most frequently cited by interviewees. Other organizations that address or have addressed the topic of facing the past include, but are not limited to the following: the Center for Cultural Decontamination, Women in Black, the Belgrade Center for Human Rights, the Center for Nonviolent Action, the Committee for Civic Initiative, and B92's Documentation Center for the Wars of 1991–1999.

Of all the work done on this topic, with the exception of the ICTY, the work of the Helsinki Committee and the Humanitarian Law Fund is the most controversial. This is not only the case for the general populace, but also for many members of the NGO community. The mildest critics of these organizations accuse them of having an aggressive agenda on facing the past, of focusing primarily on crimes committed by Serbs, and of "rushing" the facing process. They are also accused of making Serbs collectively responsible for what happened during the recent wars. The response of these organizations, which I will henceforth refer to as the "human rights organizations," has been that many of their critics are finally revealing their "true, nationalistic colors." They argue that behind the criticism is an unwillingness to truly confront the crimes committed by Serbs and accept responsibility for what was done in the name of the Serbian nation.

The fissures within this community were most pronounced during and following the Kosovo war in 1999. Members and supporters of the Helsinki Committee and the Humanitarian Law Fund were heavily criticized by other NGO and civil society actors for supporting NATO's decision to intervene militarily in Kosovo. These organizations were accused of being traitors, despite their argument that in the long run the intervention would be in the country's best interest.

The arguments among the NGO community again came to a head in the summer of 2002 with a series of caustic debates on facing the past and other related issues in the news magazine *Vreme*. Though I will not elaborate on the *Vreme* debate in the present article, it illustrates how divisive and politicized the process of facing the past had become in Serbia at the time of the research, particularly among the Serbian elite.

Despite the vicious debates among this small circle of organizations, many of the interviewees in this study still tended to group the NGOs together, seeing them as all members of one family. The exceptions were people who were either extremely critical or supportive of the human rights organizations.

Among media organizations, the independent news outlet Radio/Television B92 has been the most active on the topic of facing the past and was mentioned frequently by interviewees during the research process. In addition to providing live broadcasts of Slobodan Milošević's trial at The Hague, B92 also has a weekly television program entitled *Truth, Responsibility, and Reconciliation* and a radio program, *Catharsis*, which deals with confronting the past. While other independent media such as the daily newspaper *Danas* also contribute to the facing process, their contribution is minimal compared with that of B92.

This brief summary of facing processes in Serbia is important background for understanding the research findings. As mentioned earlier, many interviewees feel that the facing process in Serbia is defined by the NGOs and independent media and group their initiatives together into one discourse on facing the past. As that is the case, when I mention "the facing process" I am referring to the collection of efforts by this small group of actors on confronting the past or to the general concept of facing the past. On other occasions, I will clearly separate the initiatives, speaking about one organization's activities versus another. However, it is important to re-emphasize that, with only a few exceptions, the vast majority of the interviewees saw the NGOs as being a homogeneous group. There was more of a tendency to make distinctions between the independent media and the NGOs than between the NGOs.

Research Findings and Analysis

The most important finding of this study was that though nationalism often played a role in determining interviewees' reactions to the facing process, it was not the only variable affecting people's attitudes. An in-depth analysis of the target group's views on confronting the past revealed a number of other variables that affect the extent to which people consider facing processes trustworthy and legitimate. While closely related, the variables are distinct enough to be separated for analysis. They are listed as follows, though not in order of importance:

1. Contextual factors, such as Serbia's post-war environment and the phenomenon of civil society building.
2. The extent to which people believe the facing process is benefiting them. (*e.g.*, For whom is the process or initiative designed? How does it help them? Is it perceived as being deleterious to them in any way?)
3. The extent to which people feel involved in the process. (*e.g.*, Is the process participatory? Do people feel they have a voice? Does the method used for facing the past help to engage them in the process?)
4. Whether or not people perceive the process as being indigenous.
5. Degree of trust people have in the leaders of the initiatives. (How do they view their previous activities? Are they viewed as doing positive things for the public?).
6. Personal and group psychological factors connected to interviewees' views on facing the past. (*e.g.*, Do people feel that their identities are being threatened? Do they have personal interests that conflict with the facing process?).
7. Extent to which facing processes are supported by the media and those in power.

In the pages that follow, I will expound upon each of the variables listed above, drawing from the interviews, documentation reviews, and observations used in the study. In addition to presenting the findings, I will also suggest ways in which initiators of facing processes, if so inclined, may draw lessons from each variable to potentially improve their work and the impact it may have on the public. These findings may be useful to people working on transitional processes not only in Serbia but also in other post-conflict societies.

Contextual Factors (*i.e.*, Serbia's Post-war Environment and the Phenomenon of Civil Society building)

As previously noted, one of the primary initiators of facing processes in Serbia are local non-governmental organizations. Unfortunately, however, the study found that despite the political changes in 2000 that allowed these organizations to operate more openly in society and with fewer repercussions from the state, most Serbs still do not understand or fully trust these organizations, whether they are controversial human rights organizations or traditional humanitarian organizations. Interviewees' narratives on NGOs reflected the following themes: (1) people simply do not understand what NGOs are and what they do; the NGOs are not transparent enough; (2) NGOs are inaccessible to the public and are elitist; and (3) NGOs are too connected to the West and are primarily interested in and motivated by the funding they receive from external donors. In other words, NGOs are seen as being a closed business.

While the themes mentioned above may be connected to the Milošević regime's propaganda against non-governmental organizations, the post-war realities of Serbia and the phenomenon of civil society building also contribute to and even strengthen these negative views.

First, it is important to note that this lack of understanding of NGOs may be due to the fact that they are a relatively new phenomenon in Serbia. It was only during the crises of the past decade that NGOs as they are understood today materialized. Similar organizations had existed prior to the 1990s; however, they were not independent, non-state actors. They were under the control of either the Tito regime or the royal family and the Serbian Orthodox Church.[3]

The way Serbian NGOs came into existence during the 1990s also contributes to their being little known and understood by the public. Many of the organizations were formed by friends and colleagues who gathered together around kitchen tables and in living rooms to address crises arising from the political realities of the 1990s. As many of these organizations were in opposition to Milošević's policies, they necessarily maintained a low profile in order to stay off the regime's radar screen. Unfortunately, this also resulted in the public's ignorance about them.

To further aggravate the situation, NGOs themselves do very little to increase the public's understanding of their work. Serbian NGOs, just like NGOs worldwide, are not very strong on public relations. They tend to focus their attention on administering their programs at the expense of advertising and explaining their work to the public. A poll of NGOs administered by the NGO Policy Group in 2001 revealed that only 26% of 821 NGOs surveyed communicate directly with the public.[4] The poll also found that the majority of the organizations publicize their work via their websites, NGO journals and printed material, and, purportedly, the media.[5] Despite the fact that a large number of the polled organizations stated that they use the media, 32 out of the 37 target group interviewees indicated that the public knows very little about NGOs and that the organizations need to better publicize their work.

While there may be some organizations that prefer that the public be uninformed about their work, perhaps because they are in fact inactive or they are not making a substantial contribution to society, it is likely that most NGOs simply lack public relations skills and expertise. The poll cited above revealed numerous organizational and managerial problems affecting NGOs, ranging from having weak boards of directors to not engaging in strategic planning. The latter weakness may be related to constraints placed on NGOs by external donors, who primarily fund short-term projects. While many NGOs in other countries have similar problems, particularly those that are just getting off their feet, weaknesses in Serbian NGOs contribute to the general lack of trust the public has in this sector.

Another post-war reality that shapes public narratives on NGOs is that many of them, especially the larger organizations based in Belgrade, do indeed rely on Western funding. This, however, is a post-war reality in that resources are limited. It is also true that Western governments and organizations funneled an enormous amount of money into the country, supporting organizations that opposed Milošević. Additionally, as in many post-war and transitional societies in which there is a large international interest, foreign non-governmental organizations provide considerable salaries to local staff, especially compared with salaries earned by people in other sectors. Considering this influx of funds into economically depressed societies such as Serbia, it is not surprising that there would be individuals interested in this sector solely due to the monetary benefits. While this is unlikely to be the case for all NGOs and NGO staff, these post-war realities strengthen the negative narratives on the non-governmental sector.

The study revealed that this general skepticism of NGOs contributed to a lack of trust in initiatives on facing the past. However, if NGOs are concerned about improving their relationships with the public, there is much that can be done. For example, NGOs can attempt to be more transparent and to improve their public relations activities. Increased communication between NGOs and the public would also help inform the latter about the real difficulties facing NGOs, such as the lack of funding sources. The interviews with the target group revealed that while there is a great deal of misunderstanding regarding NGOs, many people are interested and willing to learn more about them.

Extent to Which People Believe the Facing Process Is Benefiting Them

Another very important factor that impacts on the level of trust interviewees have in facing processes is the extent to which they believe that the processes are benefiting them. While abstract arguments such as "facing processes benefit the whole of society" are accepted in international discourse on transitional justice and facing the past, they are seldom believable to people on the ground. People need to be able to clearly determine that the process is benefiting or can benefit *them*. It must certainly not be perceived as being detrimental to them. This is best illustrated by a juxtaposition of the research findings on interviewees' reactions to the independent media outlet B92 with the findings on their reactions to the initiatives of the NGO sector.

While NGOs were heavily criticized by interviewees for supposedly being too connected to the West and for being motivated by money, B92 was generally excused. Interviewees were aware that B92 received and still receives considerable funding from the West; however, all but one of the members of the target group expressed respect for B92 and its work. This was despite the fact that the news outlet has programs aimed at facing the past.

One of the most common themes in the narratives concerning B92 was the positive role it played in keeping the public informed about what was happening during the fall of 2000, when Milošević was eventually ousted from power. Interviewees explained how the station had operated against the odds in order to inform the public about protests and street demonstrations. For the vast majority of the interviewees, B92 is considered as being on their side, and on the side of the people. Obviously, this does not mean that all Serbs view B92 in this way; however, it is a stark contrast with how the target group perceives the NGO initiatives.

While most of the interviewees grouped all the NGOs together, a minority made a clear distinction between the human rights organizations (e.g., the Helsinki Committee and the Humanitarian Law Fund) and the other NGOs. Six interviewees were extremely critical of the human rights organizations, and particularly of their directors, insisting that they were traitors and were against Serbs. They also blamed them for tarnishing the image of Serbs internationally. An equal number of interviewees were extremely supportive of the work of these organizations, arguing that the directors were very brave and therefore provoked the jealousy of other NGO actors. The vast majority of the interviewees were relatively neutral about these organizations, either stating that they were skeptical of them but didn't know enough about their work (12 interviewees) or that they were supportive of NGOs generally, but were critical of the methods used by the human rights organizations in facing the past (13 interviewees). Overall, however, interviewees did not consider the facing processes initiated by NGOs as being beneficial to Serbia. They felt that the initiatives were too confrontational and were propelled by external actors. The interviewees felt uncomfortable with the facing processes and were fearful that they would keep Serbia in the past.

Though B92 also has programs on facing the past, the interviewees pinpointed specific instances of how the news outlet had done something *for Serbs*. Additionally, as a news agency, B92 is able to easily get its message out to the public, whereas, as mentioned earlier, NGOs are very weak on public relations. This is particularly the case for the human rights NGOs, at least regarding their work that directly benefits Serbs. While these organizations have programs that provide specific assistance to their fellow compatriots, or to Serbs from other parts of the former Yugoslavia—such as the Helsinki Committee's program for Serbian refugees from Croatia, Bosnia, and Kosovo, and the Humanitarian Law Fund's documentation of human rights abuses committed against Serbs—they do not do a sufficient job of advertising these programs. While it is possible that the news media are also responsible for not readily sharing such information, the NGOs themselves could work on improving their public relations. If more people were aware of their programs, it would be difficult for them to accuse the organizations of not doing anything beneficial for Serbs.

It is human nature for people to be more open to things that have a clear benefit for them. Taking this into consideration, interested NGOs could attempt to diversify their programming to include more projects that have tangible benefits for the people. If their programming is already diversified and has concrete benefits, they may want to work at better publicizing their activities. Once again, improving communication with the public may help in increasing people's trust in their work.

Extent to Which People Feel Involved in the Process

Another variable that played a major role in affecting the attitudes of interviewees towards facing processes is the degree to which the processes are participatory. Not only did interviewees complain about initiatives that they perceived as being exclusive and closed to the public, but they also expressed their frustration about being voiceless. This feeling of voicelessness and disempowerment was present throughout the entire research process, from interviewees insisting that the discourse on facing the past is dominated by a select group of organizations to interviewees lamenting that they do not have the opportunity to express their 'truths," not only to people within their own country, but also to people from other countries. Some interviewees expressed a fear that their voices would be silenced by the larger metanarrative on the past which they perceive as being created by the local human rights organizations and by the Hague Tribunal. Several interviewees insisted that the facing process must be more open to the public and that ordinary people should be involved. Participation would ensure a sense of ownership of the process.

Ownership—which involves investment—is definitely an essential element in a societal discourse on facing the past.

Organizations that take this variable seriously may choose to explore ways in which they can increase public participation in their work. While not all initiatives must include direct public participation, people's trust in the respective organization may increase if it at least has some highly participatory projects.

Extent to Which the Interviewees Consider the Process Indigenous

This variable is particularly relevant for the Serbian context. Anything perceived as being "external" (*i.e.*, foreign) was considered suspect by many interviewees. Even if the initiative *is* indigenous, as are many of the programs of the local NGOs working on the issue of facing the past, the less amount of contact it has with anything or anyone foreign, the better. This perception of the "external" being negative is due to many years of the former regime's propaganda, and to such experiences as the numerous external invasions of the territory over the years, and most recently the NATO bombing. Interviewees also said that they feel "misunderstood" by people in the West. All of this combined has made many people skeptical of foreigners and foreign initiatives, while at the same time desirous to reach out and tell their story. This schizophrenic relationship with the West will be further explored in the section on "Personal and Group Psychological Factors."

The argument for indigenous programs is relevant for any cultural context, even when there is not a strong aversion to that which is "foreign," as is the case in Serbia. Scholars in the fields of international development and peace and conflict resolution often support this claim, noting that indigenous programs are more likely to be culturally relevant and participatory—which encourages a sense of ownership of the process—and may increase the likelihood that the program will be sustainable.

The concerns manifested in this variable are more difficult to address, since the organizations *are* indigenous. They are mistrusted due to their connection, or what is perceived to be their connection, with other countries and governments. Non-governmental organizations may attempt to prove their independence to the public; however, this does not address the deeper problem, which is the fear that many Serbs have of the outside world. Numerous interviewees noted that one of the most important things for Serbia is having more contact with the outside world. A relevant anecdote is my personal experience in the research process reveals the relevance of this point. While many people were leery or suspicious of me, they were also very eager to approach me and talk with me. They were curious about me, but they were most interested in knowing what I thought about Serbia and its people.

The fears connected to this variable will clearly take a long time to assuage; however, addressing some of the variables, such as that of participation, may help the process.

Degree of Trust People Have in the Leaders of the Initiatives

It is logical that the impressions people have of the leaders of the initiatives will affect their views of the initiatives themselves. This is especially true for sensitive topics such as confronting the past. For many NGOs in Serbia, the directors of the organizations make the organizations. Interviewees who admire the human rights organizations spearheading the facing processes were very complimentary of the directors of these organizations, citing their consistency over the years in their responses to human rights abuses as examples of respectable behavior. Those interviewees who were critical of these organizations frequently referenced the directors' pasts—connections to Tito's Communist Party, for example—as reasons to distrust them. While the majority of the interviewees did not react strongly to the directors—either positively or negatively—they were critical of the approaches they used. They often argued that the leaders of the human rights organizations were too aggressive on this sensitive issue of confronting the past.

Ideally, societal processes on confronting the violent past would be spearheaded by individuals with moral authority who enjoy widespread respect in the society. Unfortunately, at the moment, Serbia lacks people who meet both of these criteria and who are interested in leading the country in a sincere facing of its past. The current initiators of the process are, in my view, very moral and admirable, but at this point in time they do not have enough respect in the society to have a major impact on the public. Being criticized by other members of the Serbian elite and by the media has tainted their public image, making it difficult for them to be able to reach many people. Their work, however, is still necessary. They serve as catalysts for the facing process, and as watchdogs for and documenters of human rights abuses.

What is desperately needed are organizations and leaders who are viewed by the society as being sympathetic to them—though not compromising—and who can lead the public through the extremely difficult process of facing the past. Such a role may be hard for organizations that have already been branded as being biased. It is difficult to play the roles of both watchdog and compassionate leader. While the public image of these organizations may eventually change if there is a real system change in Serbia, in the meantime they are limited to their roles of catalyst and watchdog.

Personal and Group Psychological Factors

An analysis of personal and group psychological factors is critical for understanding people's attitudes towards facing the past. Unfortunately, rarely does the current scholarship on transitional justice and facing processes address these issues. This may be due to the fact that most contributors to the international discourse—lawyers, human rights activists, and democracy theorists—concentrate on the legalistic and procedural aspects of facing processes. Despite this oversight on the part of the primary contributors to the debate, the role of psychological factors was definitely revealed throughout this study.

First, it is important to note that many of the interviewees expressed and exhibited an enormous amount of fatigue in discussing the topic of facing the past. After more than ten years of "politics being imposed on people's everyday lives," interviewees stated that they simply wanted to live a normal life. This feeling of fatigue and heaviness was manifested in the interview process itself. Prior to our meeting, many interviewees insisted that the interview should be short and that they did not have much to share. A number of them only agreed to be interviewed at the request of a mutual acquaintance. However, as the interview progressed, they became more engaged in the topic and eventually wanted to extend the interview. Many of interviewees stated that, although difficult, the process of discussing these issues was helpful for them.

One of the reasons why people may have reacted this way is that the interview process gave them an opportunity to release tension and to share their views with a foreigner. They were given a voice and the opportunity to participate, at least to a certain extent, in a discourse in which they normally do not participate.

Role of Identity

Identity, a social psychological phenomenon, is clearly another prominent factor in the facing process. A number of interviewees reacted negatively to efforts to face the past, out of a fear that their identity was being threatened, that the image of Serbs would be further tainted. These fears indicate a clear link between their personal and national identities. Though interviewees were frequently opposed to notions of the "collective," and particularly to assigning responsibility to the "Serbian collective," their narratives were often contradictory. Many criticized the human rights organizations for being "against Serbs," for "not being on their side," and for trying to force them to look at the past. This aversion, or fear, of facing the past may be due to the fact that over the past decade their personal and national identities became intricately enmeshed. Facing the past would be a challenge to what had become their "conflict identities."

Conflict resolution theorists explain that conflict identities are created during intractable conflicts and are necessary to both fuel the conflict (*e.g.*, creating exclusive categories of "us" and "them" and solidifying these categories through the dehumanizing of the "Other")[6] and protect members of the collective from cognitive dissonance (*e.g.*, psychological processes are used, such as the dehumanization process, to allow certain actions to be considered acceptable that under normal conditions would be unacceptable).[7] Rather than acknowledging the creation of these identities, and looking honestly at their role in contributing to an atmosphere in which Milošević and his regime were able to flourish, people prefer to ignore this "negative past" and allow Milošević to be the scapegoat. After all, *he* was responsible for what happened. Several interviewees made the observation that their fellow compatriots do not want to look at their own personal responsibility, arguing that this tendency to not want to take responsibility for one's actions is inherent in Serbian culture, a byproduct of the country's socialist past. While this may be a valid point, it is also likely that psychological mechanisms are involved. Ignoring what happened or placing the blame on someone else is a way to protect the individual from cognitive dissonance and from a negative self-image.

Despite attempts to make Milošević the scapegoat, the collective mentality is not so easily shirked. Interviews revealed that during the Milošević trial people who "hated" him were beginning to empathize with him, seeing him as a "Serb being attacked by the rest of the world." Some interviewees who had long fought against Milošević admitted this, expressing a great deal of cognitive dissonance. On the one hand, they were glad he was no longer in Serbia— though they would have preferred for him to have been tried in the country—and they were not disappointed when he was indicted by ICTY and ultimately extradited; on the other hand, they now sympathize with him and view ICTY as being biased against Serbs. However, they could not provide clear examples of this bias. The ICTY, which was frequently described as being the extended hand of NATO or of being too connected to the West, had become the larger and more threatening "Other."

This confusion, or cognitive dissonance, is very unsettling for people. Many interviewees want simply to live normally and surround themselves with positive things. Of utmost importance is feeling positive about oneself and having a positive identity. However, if people have not untangled their conflict identities, facing processes may not provide them with this positive identity, or at least that is what they fear.

This search for a positive identity, particularly in a national sense, was obvious when Serbia won the world basketball championship in 2002. Several interviewees noted that this was the first time in a long time they were able to actually be proud of something. The streets of Belgrade were filled with people for two days. People were ecstatic. While on the surface this anecdote may seem trivial, it highlights the need people have to feel positive about something, to be proud of their national identity.

Is it possible to create a positive image of oneself and one's nation while at the same time addressing its uncomfortable past? This dilemma may be explored through current scholarship on "positive approaches to peace."[8] Theorists claim that being able to have a positive image of one's self and the future is essential for people to move forward and make positive change. This is particularly relevant for post-conflict societies that are weighted down by the violence and the crimes of the past, yet need to move forward. Proponents of facing processes argue that in order to have a positive future, one must first face the past. It is only through this facing of the past that one will be able to create a positive identity. The public, on the other hand, seems to need hope *now*, prior to delving into the uncomfortable past.

Theories on dehumanization and rehumanization may provide insight into this dilemma. For example, many perpetrators or members of groups that are considered to be perpetrators (*e.g.*, bystanders) may also need to be rehumanized in order to be able to truly accept and acknowledge that atrocities were committed in their name. As noted by psychologist Raphael Moses, a group dehumanizes itself in the process of dehumanizing others.[9] As explained earlier, dehumanization processes are commonly used during and in the build-up to war. In an effort to convince their people to go to war, or to support war, leaders will frequently portray the other side as being less than human, as possessing characteristics that are less than human, or as behaving in an inhumane manner. Such absolute categories as "human and inhuman" or "good and evil" are often used to justify violence against the other side.

Dehumanization processes clearly took place in the former Yugoslavia, as evidenced through the enormous amount of propaganda produced during the wars of the 1990s. In the case of Serbia, they were strengthened by a prevailing sense of victimhood. The fact that many Serbs felt demonized by the rest of the world further increased this feeling of victimhood.[10] The NATO bombing and the trials of Serbs in The Hague, and notably that of Slobodan Milošević, seemed to confirm this sense of victimhood.

As revealed by psychological research, it is very difficult for victims—or for people who perceive themselves as victims—to acknowledge that they can also be victimizers.[11] It is also difficult to admit that one or one's group has done harm to the dehumanized "Other." If harm were done, it was done in self-defense and the enemy deserved it. Some psychologists and social psychologists have theorized that groups will project their own negative characteristics or behaviors onto "the Other" in order to maintain a clear self-image, an unfragmented self-identity.[12]

It is not easy for facing processes to counter such complex psychological processes. Initiatives that are based on rationality and that present 'facts' with the expectation that the receiver must believe them are unlikely to be effective. This is not simply a question of "getting the facts straight." As noted by analysts of the recent Balkan wars, the problem is not in a lack of knowledge about atrocities committed during the wars. Many people have heard about Srebrenica and about the siege of Sarajevo; however, they are not willing or able to fully digest the information and acknowledge what happened without responding, "Well, they did X to us."

Considering the complexity of the facing process and its irrational nature, one may need a variety of methods in order to truly reach people. For example, initiatives that bring the public in direct contact with average people from the "other side" or that give people the opportunity to visit other parts of the Balkans where crimes were committed, may be able to help in the rehumanization component of the process. Other initiatives, such as artistic and creative programs, may also be able to touch people's emotive, irrational side.

So far, the initiatives that have been mentioned focus on the rehumanization of the "Other." However, as noted earlier, this rehumanization process may depend on the rehumanization of one's own side. This argument is rooted in Raphael Moses' assertion that people who dehumanize others dehumanize themselves in the process. Yet, what can be done to rehumanize one's own group? One possibility may be in re-establishing or reconfirming the society's value system. This is very important for post-conflict societies; however, as seen in the case of Serbia, it is also extremely difficult. Numerous interviewees noted that the country's system of values had been destroyed or at least severely weakened during the past decade of war and that many people have lost their basic points of reference for making value judgments. According to them, people are lost and confused. Unfortunately, with the exception of a handful of NGOs, which tend to be focused primarily on facing the wartime past, there is no major societal actor addressing this "value void" in a way that can lead to the rehumanization of Serbs and their various groups of "Others." While the Serbian Orthodox Church (SOC) is attempting to define the value system, this is not necessarily a positive development, since the SOC leadership has not faced the role it played in fomenting nationalism and militarism during the recent wars.

Considering the difficult state in which Serbia finds itself, what can be done? One possibility is for concerned individuals and organizations to examine the country's repertoire of previous experiences for honorable deeds and evidence of shared societal values that are not exclusive. The key would be finding examples that would not be overly politicized and pinpointing ethical leaders or people in society who could guide discussions on these issues. These discussions may be able to lay a foundation for the more difficult questions raised in the discourse on facing the wartime past.

In summary, it is obvious that more creative thinking is needed on this topic and on the role of identity in the facing process. The study revealed that many youth are still struggling with their identities, and that these struggles definitely have an impact on the way they approach initiatives aimed at facing the past. Being able to feel positive about one's self and one's group, and rediscovering a shared sense of humanity and system of values, definitely contributes to the rehumanizing of others. This rehumanization process and a restored positive sense of self could assist in creating an open and sincere facing process and in lowering people's defensive reactions to the organizations initiating the process.

Extent to which Facing Processes Are Supported by the Media and Those in Power

Following such an in-depth exploration into the psychological factors involved in the facing process, it is important to close with the clear-cut variable concerning the support of the media and people in power. This variable is extremely important and must be kept in mind when evaluating any facing process. It is common knowledge and there is empirical evidence that the media and people in power have enormous influence over the public. They have even more of an impact in conflict-ridden societies, as was seen in the former Yugoslavia with the intense bombardment of regime propaganda throughout the 1990s.

Despite overwhelming evidence supporting this variable, it was difficult to measure its relevance for interviewees in this study. However, it is logical that most people's trust in initiatives focused on the past would increase with the support of the media and government. While interviewees did not admit this for themselves, they frequently made the point that it would make a difference for the public at large. The only obvious example of the impact of this variable on interviewees was that the influence of the media was frequently noted in discussions on the ICTY. For example, in expressing their impressions of the Tribunal, a number of the interviewees repeated verbatim phrases used by journalists, such as "ICTY is a circus" and "ICTY is like a sports match."

There has been no support from the state and the state media for the facing process. In fact, they have played a negative role through their persistent criticism of and inflammatory comments about the Hague Tribunal and its supporters. Governmental cooperation with ICTY has been reluctant, if not forced, and portrayed as merely a means to obtain international funding.

While direct criticisms of the NGO sector have diminished since the fall of Milošević, the new government has not been very supportive. This is unfortunate considering how important it is to have strong leadership and governmental support in addressing such a difficult subject. Unfortunately, while the support of the government and media is one of the most important variables affecting facing processes, it is the one most absent in Serbia.

Conclusion

In concluding, it is important to note that, despite the numerous challenges and impediments to the facing process, there are some positive points that can be extracted from the findings of this study. Isolating the factors that affected interviewees' feelings about initiatives aimed at facing the past revealed that not all of the reactions were motivated solely by blind nationalism. While it was present in many cases, with signs of it peppered throughout the other variables, there were other factors that impacted on interviewees' attitudes toward facing the past. These factors are fortunately more malleable than nationalism. By understanding them and developing ways to address them, one may be able to improve initiatives aimed at facing the past and increase the public's trust in them. While this may not fully solve the problem, it may be able to help.

An examination of these factors may also reveal the need for more initiatives, or for different types of initiatives. For example, subtle or creative programs that affect people's emotive sides may be able to address impediments inherent in the variable on personal and group psychological dimensions. More direct initiatives, such as those of the Humanitarian Law Fund and the Helsinki Committee, may be needed in lobbying the government or in impacting the media and other members of the Serbian elite. It is evident that in order to address the complexities of the facing process, a combination of actors and methods are needed, and the facing process must take place at all levels of society.

Clearly, this study only touches the tip of the iceberg of the dynamics and complexities of the facing process in Serbia. It is my hope that it will inspire further scholarship on the human elements of the facing process, and that it will make a positive contribution to the numerous efforts to confront the past in Serbia and in other transitional societies. I also hope that it will ultimately benefit the local people who are most affected by these processes.

NOTES

1. Carla Hesse and Robert Post, eds, *Human Rights in Political Transitions: Gettysburg to Bosnia* (New York: Zone Books, 1999), p. 20.
2. This number does not represent the total number of interviews conducted. I also interviewed people outside of Belgrade and in other parts of the former Yugoslavia; however, I did not include these interviews in the analysis presented in the present article.
3. NGO Policy Group, *Third Sector in Serbia: Status and Prospects* (Belgrade: Center for the Development of the Non-profit Sector and the NGO Policy Group, 2001), p. 16.
4. *Ibid.*, 29.
5. *Ibid.*
6. See John E. Mack, "The Enemy System," in Vamik D. Volkan, Demetrios A. Julius and Joseph V. Montville, eds, *Psychodynamics of International Relationships, Volume I: Concepts and Theories* (Lexington, MA: Lexington Books, 1990), pp. 57–69. See also Ervin Staub, *The Roots of Evil: The Origins of Genocide and Other Group Violence* (New York: Cambridge University Press, 1989).
7. Rafael Moses, "Self, Self-View, and Identity," in Vamik D. Volkan, Demetrios A. Julius and Joseph V. Montville, eds, *Psychodynamics of International Relationships, Volume I: Concepts and Theories* (Lexington, MA: Lexington Books, 1990), pp. 47–55.
8. See Cynthia Sampson, Mohammed Abu-Nimer, Claudia Liebler and Diana Whitney, eds, *Positive Approaches to Peacebuilding: A Resource for Innovators* (Washington, DC: PACT, 2003).
9. Moses, "Self, Self-View, and Identity," 53.
10. These points are backed by numerous interviews in which people either identified themselves as victims of larger processes and powers (not in the sense of being a direct victim of a particular incident) or spoke about the prevailing sense of victimhood in Serbian society.
11. Vamik Volkan's concept of "chosen traumas" is relevant here. According to him, "[chosen traumas] are powerful experiences of loss and feelings of humiliation, vengeance, and hatred that trigger a variety of unconscious defense mechanisms that attempt to reverse these experiences and feelings" (Vamik Volkan, *Bloodlines: From Ethnic Pride to Ethnic Terrorism.* (New York: Farrar, Straus & Giroux, 1997), pp. 82–84).
12. Vamik D. Volkan, *The Need to Have Enemies and Allies: From Clinical Practice to International Relationships* (Northvale, NJ: Jason Aronson, 1988).

INDEX

For Product Safety Concerns and Information please contact our EU
representative GPSR@taylorandfrancis.com Taylor & Francis Verlag GmbH,
Kaufingerstraße 24, 80331 München, Germany

Batch number: 08151566

Printed by Printforce, the Netherlands